WORKING CLASS HERO:

Memoirs of a Providence Fireman

Tom Kenney

PublishAmerica
Baltimore

First printing

ISBN: 1-4137-3107-4
PUBLISHED BY PUBLISHAMERICA, LLLP
www.publishamerica.com
Baltimore

Printed in the United States of America

This book is dedicated to my friends,
the Firefighters of Providence.
Without your support and inspiration,
none of these stories would have happened.
You guys are truly my heroes.

To firefighters everywhere, both past and present.
I'm proud to belong to this very special brotherhood.

And to Nancy.
My love, my inspiration, and my editor.
You believe in me so much, it scares me sometimes.
Your love and confidence
inspired me to begin this endeavor,
and never allowed me to give up.
I love you.

Contents

Glossary of Terms 11

Providence Fire Department 18

Chapter 1: Working Class Hero 19

Chapter 2: Living the Dream 22

Chapter 3: Sometimes You Laugh… 27

Chapter 4: …Sometimes You Cry! 44

Chapter 5: Lieutenant Gloom & Doom 54

Chapter 6: Kids, Kids, Kids 61

Chapter 7: Is this a Fire Truck or a Rescue 73

Chapter 8: Hayward Street 85

Chapter 9: The Unknown 96

Chapter 10: Chiefs (The Good, the Bad & the Ugly) 127

Chapter 11: Stealing the Fire 136

Chapter 12: Some Funny Little Thingies 142

Chapter 13: Nagging Little Injuries (It Hurts So Good) . 155

Chapter 14: First-In 163

Chapter 15: Cow Snots 173

Chapter 16: 911/Ground Zero 178

Chapter 17: The Worcester Six 187

Chapter 18: Odd Jobs 191

Chapter 19: My Driving Adventures
(Get Ready 'Cause Here I Come) 200

Chapter 20: Meals on Wheels 206

Chapter 21: Odds and Ends (The Pros, The Cons, & The
Routine) 211

Chapter 22: My Heroes – My Teachers (Past and Present)
219

End Notes 224

Creation of the Firefighter

When the Lord was creating firefighters, He was into His sixth
day of overtime when an Angel appeared and said,
"You're doing a lot of work on this one."
And the Lord said,
"Have you read the specifications on this person?
Firefighters have to be able to go for hours fighting fire
or tending to a person that needs their help,
while putting in the back of their mind the circumstances.
They have to be able to move at a second's notice
and not think twice of what they are about to do,
no matter what the danger.
They have to be in top physical condition,
running on half-eaten meals,
and they must have six pairs of hands."
The angel shook her head slowly and said,
"Six pairs of hands…no way."
"It's not the hands that concern me," said the Lord,
"it's the three sets of eyes a firefighter has to have."
"That's on the standard model?" asked the angel.
The Lord nodded
"One set that sees through the fire and where they
and their fellow firefighters should fight the fire next.
Another set to see their fellow firefighters and keep them safe.
And another set of eyes so that they can look for
the victims caught in the fire that need their help."
"Lord," said the angel, touching His sleeve,
"rest now and work on this firefighter tomorrow."
"I can't." said the Lord.

"This firefighter can carry a 250 pound man down a flight of stairs
and to safety from a burning building,
and can feed a family on a civil service paycheck."
The angel circled the model of the firefighter very slowly.
"Can it think?"
"Yes," said the Lord,
"a firefighter can tell you the elements of a hundred fires,
and can recite in their sleep the procedures
that are needed to care for a person
until they reach the hospital.
And all the while they have to keep their wits about themselves.
This firefighter also has phenomenal personal control.
They can deal with a scene full of pain and hurt,
coaxing a child's mother into letting go of the child
so that they can care for the child in need.
And they rarely get the recognition for a job well done,
other than from fellow firefighters."
Finally, the angel bent over and ran her fingers across the
cheek of the firefighter.
"There's a leak," she pronounced.
The Lord, "It's a tear."
"What's the tear for?" asked the angel.
"It's a tear from bottled-up emotions for fallen comrades.
A tear for commitment for that piece of cloth
called the American flag.
It's a tear for all the pain and suffering they have encountered.
And it's a tear for their commitment to caring for
and saving lives of their fellow man!"
"What a wonderful feature, Lord," said the angel.
The Lord looked somber and said, "I didn't put it there."

– Author Unknown

Introduction and Glossary

My purpose in writing this book is to share these experiences with average everyday people, one person at a time. I've tried to write in such a way as to allow the reader to experience these events through the eyes of a fireman – see what he sees and feel what he feels. In my awkward attempt to do so, I've tried to use the terminology that firefighters use in order to give the reader a 'feel' for what it's actually like to be riding along with us. I've also tried to explain the reasons behind some of our actions. Whenever possible I have explained the terms during the course of the story. This, however, is not always possible. It makes for awkward reading when there are too many definitions scattered throughout a paragraph or story, so I'm including a glossary to give the reader a chance to fully understand the meaning of fire department terms commonly used throughout this book. These terms are mostly ones that will be familiar to those brothers in the fire service, but some might be specific to the Providence Fire Department.

This book is a collection of stories, with only a couple of exceptions, of my personal experiences in a twenty-three plus year career on the Providence Fire Department. It is in no way meant to be a documentary of the events described. It is my perspective on what happened at these events from my own subjective recollection, and as such are not always the entire picture. In large fires and emergencies I was only a small part of a much larger effort and can only give reliable first hand information on my actions. It is my hope that by using this method the reader can ride to the scene of one of these events through the perspective of an individual firefighter. The descriptions of actions taken by the other firefighters and the victims are related through information I've received second or third hand – either by talking to the firefighters after the fact or by reading accounts of the victims. There are many more stories relating to these incidents that are not included in this book.

This began as a therapeutic endeavor. Putting some of the more disturbing experiences I've had on paper was a way of purging these demons from my subconscious. I had been diagnosed with PTSD (Post Traumatic Stress Disorder) and began talking to a counselor about some of these things. This brought them back into my conscious thoughts, but talking about them seemed to have a soothing effect on me. I had the idea of taking this one step further and writing them down so I could put them in a drawer and lock them away. When my fiancée read what I had put on paper, she encouraged me to write about more of my experience – both good and bad – to give my kids an understanding of what I was going through when I went off to work. From that point it just snowballed.

Thank you, Nancy, for encouraging me along the way. Your love and support have made this possible…make all things possible! Thank you to all the firefighters of the Providence Fire Department for being who you are – the best and bravest group of guys I've ever been associated with! You've always had my back, and I'll always have yours!

Glossary of Terms

Aerial Ladder – The aluminum ladders mounted on Ladder trucks. These are usually between 75 & 110 feet long. They are hydraulically run and are usually in 4 equal sections that can extend to the ladder's maximum length.

Air Pak – The equipment firefighters carry strapped to their backs enabling us to breathe fresh air in hazardous atmospheres. The air pak consists of the harness (which straps to our backs), the facepiece (or mask), a regulator (which controls the flow of air), and the air cylinder (a fiberglass reinforced bottle filled with fresh air).

Battalion – A geographical area within a city or town with a certain number of fire companies. Much the same as a fire district.

Battalion Chief – A Chief Officer who is in charge of a Battalion and the fire companies within. Usually the first Chief Officer on the scene of any working fire.

Bell – A bell in a firehouse which signals a response call for one of the companies housed in that station. Most firehouses use an electronic tone system now but a bell was the normal signal in the fire service for many years. In Providence, we switched to the tones in the late 90's.

Box Alarm – An emergency signaling device used by the public to transmit a request for fire department response. These are usually mounted on telephone poles or pedestals mounted on street corners. They transmit a numbered code which corresponds to that particular location to the fire dispatchers, who will dispatch the closest fire apparatus to the scene.

Break Numbers – Building numbers on a street at the point which it intersects with another street. Memorizing these allow you to instantly know whether to turn left or right for a particular address.

Bucket – The bucket-like platform mounted on the tip of the aerial ladder on a Tower Ladder. These platforms allow the firefighters to more easily work while being lifted up to 8-stories above the ground. They are also ideal for rescuing trapped victims from windows.

Bunker Pants – A firefighter's fire-resistant protective pants worn over station uniform and connected to his boots. Firefighters just step into the boots and pull up the pants.

Call – An emergency response by a fire or EMS company. We also refer to them as runs.

Callback – An overtime shift.

Captain – In most fire departments, the second level of advancement beyond firefighter. He commands a fire company and is responsible for everything that has to do with this company (whether he is on or off duty).

Chauffeur – The driver of any fire apparatus.

Code Blue – A code word in the Providence Fire Department meaning a malicious false alarm. (Most fire departments have their own particular set of codes.)

Code Red – A code word in the Providence Fire Department meaning a working building fire.

Code Yellow – A code word in the Providence Fire Department meaning that a single fire company can handle the situation. (Such as a trash fire or an auto fire)

Code 99 – A code word in the Providence Fire Department meaning an EMS patient is showing no signs of life – no pulse or respirations. In a Code 99 patient we begin CPR, defibrillation, artificial respiration, and other life saving efforts and transport the patient to the nearest hospital.

Command Post – An area somewhat remote from the scene of an emergency, designated by the first arriving Chief (Incident Commander) that allows the IC to coordinate the running of the scene without being in the midst of the chaos.

Detail – A temporary (usually a single shift) deployment of a member of a fire company to another fire company.

Division Chief – A Chief Officer in charge of multiple Battalions. (In the Providence Fire Department we have one Division Chief and two Battalion Chiefs on duty at all times).

Dress the Hydrant – The act in which a firefighter removes the caps and connects hoselines and gated valves to all ports of the fire hydrant. This allows us to insure a water supply to the Engine Truck that is pumping water to the attack hoselines.

EMS – Emergency Medical Services. In the Providence Fire Department this consists of 5 Rescue Trucks (each manned with 2 EMS personnel). All fire companies are trained to be support units to the Rescue Trucks.

Engine Truck – A fire truck equipped with a fire pump, hoselines and a water tank. Supplies water to the hoselines used by firefighters to extinguish the fire.

Feeders – Hoselines connected from a hydrant to an Engine Truck to supply water.

Fire Alarm – In the Providence Fire Department this is our dispatch center where calls and alarms are received and then transmitted to the fire and EMS companies for response.

Firefighter (rank) – The basic rank of the fire service. All members under the command of a Company Officer.

First-called – The fire company that is listed first in the order of dispatch.

First-in – The fire company that actually arrives first at a fire scene. This could be different from the first-called company due to traffic problems or response from a location other than the firehouse.

Flashover – The point in a fire when all the combustibles in a room reach their ignition temperature and ignite at once, filling the entire room with flame.

Floor Watch – Used during the old bell system of dispatch in the Providence Fire Department. One member would sit at the 'Watch Desk' on the apparatus floor and monitor the dispatches of the entire department. When a call for one of the companies in the firehouse came over the vocalarm, he would 'tip the bell' in the station alerting members of a call.

Haligan Tool – A hardened steel hand tool carried by fire officers with a pry bar on one end and a claw and adz on the other. It is about three feet long and considered by most firefighters as on of the most versatile and valuable tools we carry.

Handline – The hoseline (usually 1 ¾" in diameter) connected to an Engine Truck and having a nozzle at the tip. Used by firefighters to carry into the fire building and attack the fire.

Hose Bed – The area on top and in the rear of an Engine Truck that carries the hose.

Ladder Truck – A fire truck that carries ladders to the scene of a fire. Most Ladder Trucks carry ground ladders (ladders that are place on the ground and leaned onto the building) in lengths from 12' to 55.' Most Ladder Trucks also have an aluminum aerial ladder mounted to the apparatus.

Lieutenant – In most fire departments, the first level of advancement beyond firefighter. He is in command of a fire company and is responsible for everything that applies to his company, while he is on duty. The basic Company Officer.

Master Box – A Box Alarm (see above) connected to the fire alarm system of a building or complex.

Mutual Aid – An agreement between neighboring cities and towns where fire companies will cover calls in the neighboring towns when requested.

Nozzleman – The firefighter on an Engine Company that is assigned to the nozzle of the attack hoseline. He controls the application of the water on the fire.

Pipeman – Same as the nozzleman (see above).

Plaster Pole – A long tool carried primarily by Laddermen. It is a pole of 4' to 12' with a point and a hook on the tip, used to punch through ceilings and pull down the plaster and lads to search for hidden fire. Also known as a 'pike pole.'

Primary Search – A quick search at the earliest possible stage of any fire. The purpose is to locate any obvious victims trapped or unconscious in the fire building.

Rescue Truck – In the Providence Fire Department these vehicles are EMS trucks. They are staffed with 2 EMS personnel and equipped with medical equipment The primary purpose of these vehicles is to treat and transport medical patients.

Run – An emergency response by a fire or EMS company. We also refer to these as calls.

SCBA – Self Contained Breathing Apparatus. Same as air pak (see above)

Secondary Search – A more complete search of the areas in a fire building. This is done after we gain control of the fire to insure there are no victims who may have been hiding from the smoke and missed on the Primary Search.

Size-up – The initial assessment of the first-in officer at a fire scene. He tries to gather as much information as possible in a very few seconds – fire location, occupancy, what type of building, the presence of exposures (buildings close to the fire building in danger of catching fire), etc.

Sliding the Pole – Using the fire pole in the firehouse to slide to the apparatus floor.

Special Hazards Unit – Providence Fire Department's equivalent of a Heavy Rescue. This unit carries many specialized tools such as the 'Jaws of Life', air bags, gas meters, Thermal Imaging Cameras, extrication tools, and computers for contacting agencies regarding Hazardous Materials, etc. This unit responds to all working fires in the city and any other emergency at which any specialized tools are needed.

Special Signal – Any company which responds to an incident at the request of another company already on the scene.

Staging Area – An area remote from the emergency scene where units will respond so that they are available to quickly respond to the emergency upon being requested. Like an on-deck area.

Standpipe – Fixed piping on each floor in a building (usually in the stairwells) used for fire hoses. These can be supplied water via a water tank from above, a fire pump located in the building, or an FDC (Fire Department Connection) on the outside of the building being fed by an Engine Company.

Still Alarm – A response by one or two fire department vehicles at the request of a call to Fire Alarm (see above).

Still Box – A response by a full compliment of fire department vehicles, as a result of a phone call to Fire Alarm, to a reported building fire. The dispatchers send the companies assigned to the nearest street box.

3-decker – A 3-story apartment building common in the Northeastern portion of the country. Usually one apartment per floor. Usually wood-framed. Often built very close to the next building (within 6' to 10').

Tiller Truck – An Aerial Ladder Truck in which the aerial ladder is mounted on a trailer (tiller) which is towed by the front cab. These trailers have wheels which can be steered by a firefighter (the tillerman) riding in a small cab mounted at the rear of the trailer.

Tip the Bell – The act of striking the alarm at a firehouse. This can be done manually by a firefighter at the station or remotely by Fire Alarm.

Tower Ladder – An Aerial Ladder mounted with a platform, or bucket, at the tip of the aerial.

Trainee – A candidate to become a firefighter assigned to the Training Academy.

Turnout Gear – A firefighter's protective clothing – coat, bunker pants, boots and helmet.

Vocalarm – The intercom system connecting all stations with Fire Alarm. Any transmission of alarms or departmental notifications can be immediately sent to all stations via this system.

Watch Desk – The desk on the apparatus floor of each firehouse which is manned by a single firefighter assigned to monitor transmissions of alarms and 'tip the bell' when needed.

Providence Fire Department

The Providence Fire Department is the second oldest continually operating paid fire department in the country. It was established March 1st, 1854. We have approximately 500 active members and work with a 4-platoon system. Each platoon (or Group) works two day shifts (8:00AM-5:00PM), then two night shifts (5:00PM-8:00AM), and then has four days off. We have 14 Fire Stations and cover approximately 20 square miles of typical Northeastern urban area. Providence has approximately 175,000 residents and about another 50,000 people who commute to and work in the city every day.

The Providence Fire Department has 15 Engine Companies, 8 Ladder Trucks, 1 Special Hazards Unit, 5 Rescue Companies, 2 Battalion Chiefs, and 1 Division Chief per shift. We typically respond to around 50,000 calls per year. Each Engine and Ladder is manned with either 3 or 4 people per shift. Special Hazards has 4 people, and 2 people per shift man the Rescues.

Our Engine Companies vary between 1,000 and 4,500 runs per year. Our Ladder Trucks have between 750 and 1,500 runs per year. The Rescue Trucks each run about 5,000 times per year.

The Providence Fire Department also has a Fire Prevention Bureau, an Arson Unit, a Division of Training, a Dive Team, a HazMat Team, a Decon Unit, an Air Supply Station, and a Repair Division.

Tom Kenney

22Sep80	Appointed to 37th Training Academy of the Providence Fire Department
20Mar81	Sworn in as Firefighter
	Assigned to Engine 2 - Branch Ave. Fire Station
	Assigned to Engine 8 - Messer Street Fire Station
	Assigned to Ladder 2 - Messer Street Fire Station
17Dec92	Promoted to rank of Fire Lieutenant
	Assigned to Ladder 7 - Branch Ave. Fire Station
12Sep93	Assigned to Engine 15 — Mt. Pleasant Ave. Fire Station

Chapter 1
Working Class Hero

I grew up with The Beatles being a major influence on my life. My taste in music, my taste in fashion, my entire way of seeing the world was influenced in some way by rock and roll in general and The Beatles in particular. From "All You Need Is Love" to "Revolution," their music ran the gamut of what was happening in the world at that time. Their lyrics, particularly those of John Lennon, helped shape my way of looking at the world. When John released "Working Class Hero" on his first solo album, I immediately related to the words:

As soon as you're born, they make you feel small
By giving you no time, instead of it all
Till the pain is so big, you feel nothing at all
A working class hero is something to be
A working class hero is something to be

They hurt you at home and they hit you at school
They hate you if you're clever and they despise a fool
Till you're so fucking crazy, you can't follow their rules
A working class hero is something to be
A working class hero is something to be

When they've tortured and scared you for 20 odd years
Then they expect you to pick a career
When you can't really function, you're so full of fear
A working class hero is something to be
A working class hero is something to be

Keep you doped with religion and sex and TV

And you think you're so clever and classless and free
But you're still fucking peasants as far as I can see
A working class hero is something to be
A working class hero is something to be

There's room at the top they are telling you still
But first you must learn how to smile as you kill
If you want to be like the folks on the hill
A working class hero is something to be
Yes, a working class hero is something to be
If you want to be a hero, well just follow me

The struggle to raise yourself above your social standing only to realize that deep down you're the same as your parents and ancestors seems universal. Most of us want to be like "the folks on the hill"– the ones with all the money and power and the higher social standing. It often comes down to what you're willing to compromise to achieve that goal. It seems that most of what teenagers resent and rebel against – the rules and the morals of parents and society – are too deeply rooted to shake totally in a single generation. Most of us grow to embrace these ideals with only minor modifications. We grow to learn that there is no shame in working for a living, as long as you are true to yourself and your beliefs. I believe that working class, blue-collar people are the backbone of our society in much the same way as firefighters are the backbone of the fire department. Solid and dependable.

I first heard this song almost exactly 10 years prior to beginning my career as one of "America's Heroes." This is a nickname dubbed to firefighters long before I began my journey in the fire service and long before John Lennon penned these lyrics. It is a label given to firefighters by the public. Firefighters seldom look at themselves as heroes. Heroes are born of opportunity and circumstance. Firefighters are simply working class people toiling in a noble profession. We're not afraid of getting our hands dirty or even risking our safety to do our job – saving life and property. I believe firefighting is the most rewarding career to which I could have ever hoped to aspire. Firefighting has an incredibly rich tradition and history that lives on in every firehouse, in every part of the world, each and every day. The rewards far outweigh the risks. Someone much more eloquent than I once said, "You can't choose how you will die, but you *can* choose how you will live." I believe this with all of my heart.

I'm proud to be living my life as a firefighter – much the same way my father did before me. The fire service has a way of drawing generation after generation into its midst. In firefighting families, little boys still grow up rebelling against their parents – just like in most families. However, they're regularly exposed to, and surrounded by, men who love their work. They seem to have a special bond that is apparent, even to outsiders. This makes a strong, favorable impression on these boys as they grow into young men. It often makes them realize that they want, more than anything, to become a part of this brotherhood.

Firefighting *is* a true 'brotherhood', in every sense of the word. It's difficult to explain to someone who's not a member of our society just how strong this bond really is. When a group of firefighters pay the ultimate price for doing what we do, firefighters from all over the world share in their loss. As witnessed at the memorials in Worcester and NYC, firefighters from numerous different countries, as well as all over the U.S. made the trip to honor their comrades.

I feel special, I feel grateful, I feel proud…all because I can count myself as a member of this brotherhood. We don't always see eye to eye. We don't always get along. Hell, I don't like *every* fireman I know, but as a whole, there's not a man I trust more than a Providence fireman. There's not a man I love more than a Providence fireman. Since I've been traveling to NYC for the many funerals and memorials, my respect for firemen has grown. The firefighters I met from FDNY were as loyal and dedicated as any men I've ever met. They made all the firefighters who attended from other places feel welcome and appreciated. The same holds true for firemen from other departments whom I've met – Worcester, Boston, Ottawa…

Chapter 2
Living the Dream

It just occurred to me tonight, while riding around my district in the officer's seat of Engine 15, that I'm living my dream. This may seem strange to anyone who knows me. I always wanted to be a fireman, as far back as I can remember. Now, here I am, 48 years old, and I've been a fireman in the City of Providence for the last 23 years. My father was a fireman for the 22 years prior to that – so I've been around fire stations and fire trucks all my life. And firemen. I guess that's why it just struck me all of a sudden tonight – I've just taken it for granted.

Firemen seem to take their jobs, and each other, for granted. I don't mean this in a derogatory way. What I mean is that most firemen assume this identity on a full time basis – 24/7 – we are always "on duty" in our minds. We always describe ourselves as firemen, first and foremost, above anything else we may be. As for taking each other for granted, we always assume that our comrades are right behind us – covering our backs – whether on duty or off. This kind of camaraderie, it seems to me, is only found in groups of people who stand united against a common enemy; people such as firemen, police officers or combat veterans.

I love being a fireman. Every fireman I know loves being a fireman. The fact that each workday holds the potential to change someone's life for the better is an incredibly stimulating work environment. We continually try to prepare ourselves for the unexpected challenges some fireman will most certainly face in the future. We relish the challenge of being prepared for anything. We don't know when our next call will come. We don't know what type of assistance we will be called upon to provide. We do know, however, that it won't be exactly the same as any other call to which we've responded in the past.

Every emergency call has its own set of circumstances which make it unique. Tactics that successfully mitigate a situation today could have disastrous consequences tomorrow because one element of the equation is different. We regularly respond to many different types of emergencies: house fires, high-rise fires, auto fires, brush fires, hazardous material emergencies, medical emergencies, explosions, lock-ins, lock-outs, people trapped in elevators, water emergencies, electrical problems, gas leaks, cave-ins, people trapped in autos. Every type of emergency you could envision. At every disaster, natural or otherwise, almost without exception, the first people to respond, to lend assistance, are firemen. If someone is committing a robbery or threatening someone with violence, people call the police. When a person faces any other type of emergency and needs immediate assistance, the fire department is called.

It's just this type of diversity in tasks and the unpredictability of a daily routine that makes this job so attractive to most of us. Most firemen are, to a certain degree, adrenaline junkies. We thrive on being in the middle of chaotic situations, taking charge and restoring some semblance of order. As such, we encounter many people at the very worst moments of their lives. Some people treat us with a great deal of respect and look up to us. Some people do not. They look down at us as merely public servants. In any case, it is the respect of another fireman that means the most to us. No one else fully understands the rewards and the sacrifices of this job but another fireman. No one else truly knows whether a fireman is good or bad at his job but another fireman.

At a working fire, the firemen the public see on the news are sometime not the firemen who are best at doing their job. Firemen sarcastically refer to these individuals as "outstanding firemen." You can always find them *out standing* around, instead of being in the fire building. Another small group of individuals enter the building and quickly find a reason to stay near the door as other firemen rush past. We call these people "ticket takers." The real work at a fire is inside the building, and no one sees this but firemen. The news cameras never see what's going on inside. It is a sense of pride in himself and his company and a determination not to let the team down that drives most firemen. A pat on the back or a muttered "good job" from a respected colleague means more to most firemen than a medal for heroism. These medals usually have more to do with the particular incident than they have to do with the fireman himself. They are mostly awarded for the more high profile jobs, or in a case when a fireman is lucky enough to locate a victim and pull him out of harm's way. The efforts put out and the risks taken by these firefighters are the same put out and taken by every other fireman searching the rest of that building. They are the same that most firemen exert at every fire in which someone could possibly be trapped. Therefore every fireman realizes that the real heroism is that which is displayed on a day-to-day basis, at every fire to which we respond, not just those where we happen to be lucky enough to "make a save."

My friends outside the department and my family have always thought it strange when I would refer to a fire as a "good fire." In a fireman's vocabulary a "good fire" is actually what most civilians would refer to as a bad fire. A "really good fire" would be a terrible fire. Firemen just seem to have a different perspective on disasters than most people. We don't wish them to occur, but we know they are inevitable. When they do occur, we just want to be there. That's our job. That's our purpose. That's what we get paid for. Most firemen feel we have the best job in the entire world. Most of the general public probably couldn't understand that when a reporter interviewed one of the FDNY firemen on September 11th he said, "this is the greatest job in the world." When the reporter asked him, "Even on a day like this?" Fewer still understood when he answered, "especially on a day like this!" Firemen understood.

Firemen tend to be people who seek the bottom line. This is a direct result of the necessity of beginning to minimize the emergency immediately upon our arrival. In order to be successful in this goal we need to gather as many of the pertinent facts as quickly as possible, in order to prioritize our actions. Time is one of the most critical factors in whether an incident is brought under control with minimal negative effects or escalates beyond our resources. Therefore, tact is one quality we don't have the luxury of cultivating in much abundance. At least not until the situation is under control.

When we respond to a house filled with smoke, we don't want to hear that your landlord never bothers to fix things in the house and is only interested in collecting rents. What we want to hear is that the boiler malfunctioned and that's what is causing the smoke. When we respond to an auto accident, we don't want to know who was at fault. We do want to know whether you are injured or not. We are not there to determine who's right and who's wrong. That's the job of the police. We are there to aid whoever may be in need of assistance. The best way to accomplish this is to stay objective and not get involved in who may be at fault. This 'apparent' lack of tact or compassion serves a fireman well in an emergency situation, but can cause problems on the personal side. I know my family tends to think that I have very little patience or compassion at times. I believe that I have more compassion than they realize – I just can't allow myself to have a bleeding heart. No fireman can. We see too much of the tragic side of life. A bleeding heart would certainly destroy us.

This is not to say that we don't get involved or allow ourselves to feel compassion for those unfortunate victims we too often encounter. We just don't allow these emotions rise to the surface while on the scene. In my experience, I've witnessed the extraordinary lengths my fellow firemen have gone to help these victims after the fact. Firemen, as a whole, are among the most compassionate and caring people you will ever encounter. We just don't wear it on our sleeves for the whole world to see. In many situations, the toughest two minutes of the entire ordeal are the two minutes we spend responding to the incident. These are the moments that a fireman may feel anxious about what he is about to face. Thinking about the child lying in the street after being struck by an auto, or about the family trapped in a fire building. Once we arrive on the scene, however, we begin to take action to help insure the incident has the most favorable outcome possible. There is no place or time for emotions here, and it is usually not that difficult to separate ourselves from the human side of the situation while performing our duties.

Usually.

Sometimes it is impossible to stay detached, especially when children are involved. I remember – riding in a Rescue truck while a 16-year-old boy who had just been stabbed squeezed my hand and asked me over and over if he was going to die. I lied and told him no. I remember – pulling up to the scene of an accident where a 2-year-old girl was run over by a car. The girl's Big Wheel was lying broken in the middle of the street and all we could see was the girl's feet sticking out from under the car. I couldn't keep my voice from cracking (ever so slightly) while I gave a report over the radio to the incoming Rescue. I remember – trying to push open a door to the front stairway of a building completely engulfed in fire and not being able to budge it before being forced back by the heat and flames. Later, seeing the lifeless bodies of a mother and her five children stacked against it on the inside, I couldn't help but think about my kids sleeping safely in their beds. The same way this family was about ten minutes before I tried forcing my way through their front door. I remember – a young mother grabbing me when I pulled up to a house fire with flames so intense that the cars in the driveway and the power lines in front of the house were ablaze. She pleaded with me to save her 3-month-old baby who was still inside. We crawled through the house but couldn't locate the baby due to the smoke and the clutter in the apartment – not until it was too late. I can still hear her screams when we carried out her baby's charred body. I remember – pulling up to a reported drive-by shooting and finding a 4-year-old girl lying in a pool of blood on the sidewalk outside a candy store. Although she survived the shooting, she still carries the bullet in her little body – too close to her spinal cord to safely remove. I remember – being awakened one morning to respond to a report of a baby not breathing. When I walked into the apartment the mother was screaming and the father was kneeling over the baby. When he moved I could see that the baby's face had been mauled by the family's pit bull. Although the baby was not breathing and her nose and part of her face was missing, we just couldn't accept this gruesome outcome. We transported her to the hospital, trying in vain to resuscitate her on the way. I went home later that morning, crouched down in the corner and wept like a baby. Some memories will never stop haunting me.

Not all the emotional moments firemen encounter on the job have such tragic outcomes. I remember – climbing the stairs to a second floor apartment to find a 9-month-old child who was not breathing and had no pulse. He had choked on a piece of solid food given to him by his aunt. We started CPR on the infant while trying to dislodge the obstruction to his airway and rushed him outside to the arriving Rescue. By the time we arrived at the hospital, we had successfully resuscitated him. I stood outside the Emergency Room and cried tears of joy at the thought of my grandchild who would be born later that month. There are probably as many pleasant memories as there are haunting ones. I'm sure there must be, because it seems like such a rewarding 23 years. I guess the traumatic experiences just seem to conjure up the more vivid memories.

Regardless – I'm living the dream!

Chapter 3
Sometimes You Laugh...

It's true; sometimes you just have to laugh. Over the years I've seen some pretty horrific sights and been involved in many tragic situations. I've also had my share of some fairly comical and downright laughable moments as well. We really never know what to expect when we roll out that door. No matter what type of call it is.

We were sitting in the station one morning listening to my Lieutenant reading the latest S.O.P. (Standard Operating Procedure) that had just been released by our Division of Training. These are written guides to the handling of different types of incidents to which we might be required to respond. When S.O.P.'s are released, they become our 'bible' on the particular type of incident covered. The Department expects every fire company to follow the procedures as written. The idea is to assign a responsibility to each company according to function (Engine – Ladder – Rescue) and position (first-due, second-due, etc.). This insures that all vital functions are taken care of, and that no company or member will 'freelance' at an incident. 'Freelancing' is the act of working on your own, whether as an individual or as a company, outside the coordinated team effort of all the firefighters on the scene. Firefighters always have the desire to be 'where the action is.' This trait is part of what makes us good at our jobs. This trait has also led to problems in the past, as companies all try to attack the largest areas of fire, leaving other areas uncovered.

There was a fire in the City of Providence a number of years ago, which perfectly illustrated this point. Companies arrived to find a three-story, wood-framed, vacant building with fire on all three floors. The heaviest amount of fire was on the third floor. When deciding where to place the first hoseline we have a rule of thumb that says, "you never pass fire to get to fire." In other words, if there is fire on the first floor and the second floor, the first hoseline must go to the first floor. Otherwise a company can be 'cut off' from the exit by the advancing fire below. At this particular fire, the first engine company took their line to the first floor – the second engine company to the second floor – and the third engine company to the third floor. When the fire was knocked down on the first floor, that company took its line to the third floor, 'chasing' the heavy fire. The company on the second floor extinguished its visible fire and took its line to the third floor also. The fire, however, was still burning in the walls on the lower floors. It eventually broke out and engulfed the lower floors, trapping the companies on the third floor with no way out! Firefighters outside the building had to scramble to hurriedly put up ladders to third floor windows to provide the trapped firemen a way out. The bucket of one ladder truck and the aerial ladder of another were also used. Thankfully, all the members were rescued – some just in the nick of time! This generation of Providence Firefighters learned a valuable lesson that day. I haven't seen this mistake repeated since.

If an officer leads his men to the 'action' without regard to the full picture, he may be passing over some other extremely vital, but possibly boring, tasks. Tasks such as providing a backup hoseline for the first engine company, or securing the utilities (shutting down the gas and electric) in the building. If these jobs are 'skipped', the next company assumes they have been taken care of and deploys elsewhere. This often results in chaos. An individual member leaving his company to 'chase' the action can put himself in danger, with no one to 'watch his back' or report any problem. This can also jeopardize the objective, as an attack on the fire quickly becomes a rescue mission.

When the Battalion Chief delivers new S.O.P.'s, each company officer goes over them with his crew to make sure everyone fully understands his role. On this morning, as we were talking over the S.O.P on 'Code C Response', the alarm came in for a possible dwelling fire in our first-in district. I was riding the side of Engine 2, so I would 'have the pipe.' This means that if we had a fire, it would be my job to grab the hoseline from the truck and put 'first water' on the fire. To most Engine men this is the best job in the whole world. I was psyched.

As we neared the house, I could see a column of smoke coming from the direction of the reported address, so I knew we had a "Red" (a building fire). I pulled up my fire boots, strapped on the air pak harness, and put on my gloves – all set! We put on our air paks while still on the truck or in the street, before entering the building, but not our masks. Before we enter a smoky building we'll usually 'turn in' the air bottle so that it's ready. We'll then enter with our masks hanging by our side. If the smoke gets too thick, we'll stop and don our facepiece. We don't want to put them on too early, as we only have about a 12-minute supply of fresh air strapped to our backs. We don't want to use up all of our air while trying to locate the fire. Another reason for not donning the mask too early is that it severely limits your visibility. Firefighters have fallen into holes in the floor (and even down elevator shafts) because of poor visibility. As we were pulling past the building, a pet store on the first floor with two apartments above, I saw flames licking out a window and beginning to ignite the outside shingles. I made a mental note of the location – second floor, second room on the right.

As soon as we came to a stop, I jumped off the truck, grabbed the hoseline and headed for the front stairs. I could hear my officer radio Fire Alarm, "Code Red, 3 story, occupied dwelling, fire on the second floor." I also heard the manager of the pet store tell him that everyone was out of the house, and that the people who live on the second floor were not home. This meant we'd have to use forcible entry. When I reached the second floor landing, I kicked the door open and crouched down low. There wasn't much smoke in the apartment, so I assumed the door to the fire room must be shut. As I entered the apartment I saw movement out of the corner of my eye, and quickly turned in that direction. I was shocked at what I saw before me. A man and a woman, both naked as the day they were born, going at it like two rabbits on the sofa! They were completely oblivious to the fire in the next room. I was speechless, and stood there in silence for a moment as I tried to make sense of this picture. They both turned to look at me and just stared. I must have looked as out of place to them as they did to me. Our silence was broken when my Lieutenant came in and said, "Get the fuck outta here. Your fuckin' apartment's on fire." They both jumped up and ran past us to the door. I'll never forget that image as long as I live. "Let's go," my Lieutenant said to me while crawling toward the bedroom, "it's over here."

I learned a lot from my first Lieutenant, Joe. He was a great fireman – and a great teacher! He also had a lot of patience. He needed it, because he had two kids (Pete and I) who were about as green as you can be. We made a lot of mistakes that first year or so. Most of these mistakes were the result of being a little too aggressive, or too anxious. He liked us, though, so he took us under his wing. He told me, years later, that he liked us because being aggressive was a good trait for a new fireman, and he knew he could always rein us in when needed. He said that if a fireman is too timid, an officer can't make him go where he's too afraid to go. I tell the guys who now work for me: "It's *your job* to be as aggressive as possible. Get as close to the fire as you can, and just keep pushing forward until it's out. Don't worry about getting too close or about not being able to get out. That's *my job*. I'll lead you in, and I'll lead you out!

If it gets too dangerous, *I'll* tell you to back out." I've come to learn that this is the great balance of the fire service. When you're young and strong you're able to knock down walls single-handedly, but you don't have the experience to recognize when to push, and when to back down. When you've been doing this work for 15 or 20 years, you tend to lose a little of your strength and stamina from the beating your body takes day after day and fire after fire. You gain the knowledge and experience, however, to lead these young bulls into battle…and safely home!

Joe also taught us to slow ourselves down, just a notch, and be observant when we first arrived at a fire. For one thing, we want to save our energy for the battle inside the building, not waste it running around outside. For another, the 10 or 15 seconds taken to observe the conditions from the outside, trying to locate the fire prior to entering the building, will give us a huge advantage once we're *inside* – trying to locate the fire in the heat and smoke. This is part of what we call 'size-up.' In the fire above, knowing that the fire was on the second floor, *and* in the second room on the right, saved us valuable time in getting the "wet stuff on the red stuff." If it weren't for the 'love birds' we encountered, everything would have gone just fine.

Joe also taught us about the ball busting that is such a big part of life on the fire department. Firemen can be merciless in this area. The last thing any firefighter wants to do is reveal his weaknesses or fears to another fireman. For instance, I got into a serious accident with the fire truck about 12 years ago. I was driving, and we hit a patch of 'black ice.' We skidded over a hundred feet before knocking over a huge tree, sending all three firefighters on board to the hospital. When I returned to the station a few days later, on crutches, to pick up my paycheck there was a large branch hanging on my locker. I took it down and threw it out of the window. I didn't say anything to anyone at the firehouse. I knew that complaining would only make matters worse. When I returned the following week to visit, I found that someone had replaced the branch with the bent airhorn from the truck. This time I left it on my locker. It stayed there until I made Lieutenant a couple of years later and had to leave that station. It's now on my desk at home. If I had made too big a fuss, it would have never stopped. You have to be able to take it if you want to dish it out. Sometimes, however, practical jokes have a way of being turned around on the person who starts them.

One night Pete and I were riding the side of Engine 2 together. This was unusual because it meant that we had four men on the truck that evening. We would normally ride with three men. Sometimes the department would 'beef up' the manpower by giving all the companies in the city an extra man. This was done on extremely cold or stormy winter nights. This particular night it was snowing and about zero degrees. The coldest night of the year!

At about midnight, we were called to a report of a house fire at the far end of our district. We were the third Engine Company called, so we stayed out in the street, and the cold, while the first-in companies investigated the problem. When it turned out to be a boiler problem, the first-in officer called it a "Code Yellow." This meant that his company could handle the situation, and that the other companies were 'back in service', and free to return to their stations. We began the long ride home. Back in those days, we didn't have enclosed jumpseats on the side of the trucks. The guys who 'rode the side' were exposed to the elements. Pete and I were already freezing from the ride to the scene and the wait outside. He then made a fatal mistake – he complained to me that he was cold. I just couldn't let that go. I said, "Oh, you're nothing but a pussy. The cold doesn't bother a real man." I then proceeded to take off my turnout coat and stand up in the wind and snow. He couldn't resist a challenge, so he stood up and took off his coat – and then his shirt. I took off my shirt – then my boots. He took of his boots – then his T-shirt. We went back and forth until we were both down to our socks, undershorts, and helmet! As cars were passing us, they would honk their horns. When Joe looked back, he saw the two of us standing there half-naked! He just shook his head. We were freezing to death, but neither one of us would back down. When we pulled up to the traffic light in front of the station, Pete and I were thankful that this long ride was finally over! When the light turned green, however, Joe told the driver, George, to drive past the firehouse and continue up the street! We were dying by this time, but neither of us would be the first to back down. George drove to a Dunkin' Donuts shop about a mile away. Joe casually got off the truck, went inside, and ordered coffees for himself and George. All the while, Pete and I were standing on the truck in our underwear while people in the parking lot whistled at us! We then slowly returned to the station. When we finally got inside, Joe went upstairs and right to his room. He never even mentioned our little striptease. Needless to say, we never tried this again. Not in the winter!

Practical jokes around the firehouse are a part of life on the fire department. They are an ongoing tradition, and they serve the purpose of cutting the tension that can build up while waiting for your next call. Most are pretty simple, involving only a couple of guys at a time. Some, however, can be quite elaborate, involving the entire group at the station. One such elaborate joke happened just prior to my joining the department. I relate it here because I consider this the mother of all practical jokes, which I've heard played in the department. Even though it's a bit cruel.

There was a new firefighter assigned to one of our stations right out of the Academy. He had a reputation for being a bit of a know-it-all. He was also very gullible. After he had been with the company for about a year, the other guys thought it would be funny to see if they could pull one over on him. They 'doctored' a General Order, which is a document that sends official Departmental information to the members, to state that this firefighter was the winner of the 'Rookie of the Year Award' for 1976. These documents usually come from Headquarters. The boys at the station showed him the G.O. late on Friday afternoon, when they knew Headquarters would be closed until Monday morning. The firefighter couldn't call and confirm his award. The G.O. further said that the recipient should report to the office of the Commissioner of Public Safety at 0800 Hrs. (8:00 AM) on Monday morning in Dress Blues. It said that he could bring his family with him.

He was skeptical at first, having been the brunt of a few practical jokes in the past, but was finally convinced when one of the firemen in the station produced a prior 'Rookie of the Year' award from his locker. This 'previous winner' said it was a huge honor, which the Department only bestowed on special occasions. They had him! At 8:00 Monday morning he brought his family down to the Commissioner's Office and sat outside on the bench waiting to be called in for his award. When the Commissioner's secretary came to work and saw the firefighter and his family waiting she asked him why he was there. When he proudly stated the reason, she told him she'd check with the Commissioner. She came back out and told him that there was a mix-up on the time and date and that they'd let him know when to come back. This allowed him to save face in front of his family, but didn't let him off the hook with his station buddies. When he returned to work the following day, it was quite evident by their reaction that he had been set-up. He took the ribbing like a man, and even pulled off a few practical jokes of his own before transferring to another station a couple of years later. Until the time he retired many of his old station mates still referred to him as "The Rookie."

Another classic from the Providence Fire Department's 'Hall of Shame' happened when I was fairly new on the job. I learned pretty quickly that when you're a new guy, you don't act too cocky around the firehouse. Especially when you're working at a different station with guys you don't know that well yet. Some guys never learn to keep their mouth's shut!

One night a fireman was working a Callback (an overtime shift) on Ladder

1. He had been on the department for about two years and had never worked with this group of guys before. In those days, Ladder 1 was a 100' Aerial 'tiller' truck. A 'tiller' truck is a ladder truck which has a cab followed by a trailer – similar to a tractor-trailer. The difference is that the trailer (tiller) is independently steered by a person sitting in the rear – the 'tillerman.' He sits in a box nestled at the tip of the aerial ladder and 'tillers.' There is no brake or gas pedal, only a steering wheel. The driver of the cab pulls the trailer and the tillerman guides the rear. This gives these trucks a great deal of maneuverability, but it takes a cooperative effort between the driver and the tillerman. If an officer or driver of one of these trucks sees that there is someone new in the tiller seat he will usually take him out for a ride to get in some practice before having to respond under the pressure of an emergency run.

On this night, when he relieved the tillerman from the day shift, the Lieutenant asked him if he could tiller. His response was, "Any asshole can tiller!" The Lieutenant just laughed and said, "O.K." As fate would have it, about an hour later the station alarm bell tipped, and all three trucks from the station were being sent to a report of a building fire. The firefighter climbed into his boots, put on his coat and climbed up into the tiller seat. The driver in the cab waited for the signal (a buzzer) from the tillerman that signified he was ready. When it came the driver started out of the door. As the cab pulled out and started to the right, the trailer proceeded to drift to the left and crash into the side wall of the station, causing major damage to the trailer. After that night, any time any firefighter in Providence was asked if he could tiller, the answer was always, "*Any* asshole can tiller!!"

People are always stopping at fire stations asking for directions. They figure the firemen know their city and its roads better than anyone. They're right, most firemen know the streets in their district like the back of their hand, and know the quickest route to any other street or area in the city. We spend many hours studying maps and quizzing each other on streets. It's a matter of pride to know all the streets in your district. It's also a matter of shame to miss a street when the call comes in. The general public seems to know this and flocks to us when they're lost.

As I stated earlier, *most* firemen know the streets well. There was a young guy years ago, who was detailed to drive Rescue 3 at my station for the day. He had only been a firefighter for about a year and this assignment was in a different part of the city than where he usually worked. He arrived at work and met the Lieutenant for the first time. He proceeded to get a cup of coffee and went downstairs to check out the rescue truck. As he was on the apparatus floor checking the truck, a man stopped by to ask for directions. He asked how to get to Livingston Street. The firefighter had never heard of this street and tried to look it up in the street directory found in the cab of the rescue. For whatever reason, he was unable to find it in the directory. He then walked the man to the side of the apparatus floor where there was a map on the wall. They both scoured the map – with no luck. He then decided to call his Lieutenant.

The Lieutenant had worked the previous night on a Callback and had been out most of the night. He had decided to take a shower to help him wake up for the day shift. He had been in the shower for about five minutes when he heard the "call bell" ring 1 – 2. This was the code for the Rescue Officer. This signal meant that he was to report to the apparatus floor immediately. He hopped out of the shower without rinsing off, wiped off with a single swipe of the towel, and put his clothes over his still wet body. He slid the pole and was met by the firefighter and the man looking for directions. They told him what they were looking for and the Lieutenant scowled at the firefighter. He didn't say a word. He just walked to the front door and motioned for them to follow. When they got to the street in front of the station he pointed to a street sign on the corner, about 40 feet away – Livingston Street. He turned and walked past the red-faced firefighter and back into the station. The fireman explained to the civilian that he didn't normally work in this district and returned inside to wash the truck. He stayed downstairs almost all day to avoid having to see his Lieutenant. I understand that this firefighter had to ask for the Lieutenant to look up a few streets that day on runs. I can only imagine how difficult it was to ask. About a month later he was transferred to work in our station permanently. When we quizzed each other on streets, whenever it was his turn, the person asking the street would always ask – "Livingston Street?"

Some stations are known for having to give directions – the stations located just off the highway and the station in the downtown area. Most of the time we try to oblige the person who is lost. Sometimes we just can't help ourselves from having a little fun. One night a car full of pretty young girls stopped in front of the downtown station looking for directions to one of the local clubs. It was a hot summer night and most of the guys were standing in front of the station. One of the single guys approached the car and started talking to the girls. He eventually gave them directions: "Go down to the second light and take a right. Go straight down that street until you come to the first light and take a right. Stay on that road until you come to the second light – take another right. When you're on this street, go about a block and then bear to the right." He asked if they understood. When they said yes, they pulled away waving and smiling at all the firefighters sitting on the wall. He returned to the group gathered at the wall and said, "Watch this."

About five minutes later the same group of girls pulled up on the ramp again. They yelled at him, "Hey, what's going on! We're right back where we started!" He walked back over toward their car, smiling from ear to ear, and said, "OK, I just wanted to make sure you girls could follow directions." I think he got one of their phone numbers!

Most people who stop for directions are extremely polite, but there are always exceptions. Some people will pull up in front of the station in the pouring rain and motion for us to come out to them. We'll just shake our heads and motion for them to come in and talk to us. One day a guy was persistent about us coming out to him. One of the firemen gave in and braved the rain. He thought that maybe this gentleman was handicapped and couldn't get out of the car – he wasn't. He told the fireman that he was late for a business meeting and that he needed to find an office building that was supposed to be located near the firehouse. The fireman told him that he had just passed it. He said, "Just back up and take this ramp. It will take you to the rear of the station and the parking lot of the building you're looking for." The guy just rolled up his window and began to back up. No "thank you" or anything like that. Hey – he was in a hurry!

When the guys in the station saw the man drive down the ramp next to the station they were confused. This ramp led to the Police Headquarters' parking area and was restricted access. It was also a very tough place to turn around, as it was a very cramped area. About ten minutes later a very angry civilian pulled back up the ramp and passed a bunch of laughing firemen standing in front of the station. He beeped and gave them the finger!

The firehouse downtown, the LaSalle Square station, was a unique place to work. It was an old cavernous building that housed the fire station (with four pieces of apparatus), the Fire Department Headquarters, the Fire Prevention Bureau, the Police Department Headquarters, locker area, Detective Bureau, Traffic Bureau, the cellblock, the Commissioner of Public Safety's Office, Providence Municipal Court, and the Housing Court. All in a single building! The building has been in decay for as long as I've been on the department. Plaster was falling down, the plumbing was shot, usually there was no hot water, and there were not enough parking spots for the working firefighters. The entire building was on a single heating zone – which was located on the police department side of the building. This often resulted in the dormitory feeling like an oven in the wintertime. The heat would be constantly clanking the old radiators while the windows in the dorm would be wide open – even on the coldest nights. I remember waking up some nights while working there and my head and chest being drenched in sweat, while at the same time, my feet being numb with the cold from being in a draft from a window. For these reasons, I never enjoyed working in this station. Some guys loved it, however, and spent their entire career at this firehouse. It took a special breed.

Most of these guys seemed to like being in the hub of the city. Most of the cities office buildings were located downtown, as were the clubs and restaurants. There was always something going on around them. These guys also loved to play. I remember one of the new guys was working there one night on Engine 3, and he was eager to impress his officer. He made himself a real pain in the ass, following the officer around all night and asking all kinds of silly questions. When the Lieutenant of Engine 3 finally went to bed, the officer of Ladder 1 grabbed the kid and handcuffed him to the railing of a stairway on the other side of the building! He then proceeded to go up to his room and to bed. As usual, most of the runs that night were for Engine 3. The Lieutenant had no idea why this kid was missing the truck. He checked the dorm, but nobody had seen him. It wasn't until the next morning that someone found him asleep on the stairs. After that, whenever he worked there again, he kept his mouth shut and didn't annoy anyone.

The guys at this station also had some interesting games going on at different times. One of the games involved shooting water balloons from the open windows of the dormitory and keeping score. They used an old inner tube, which was nailed to the window frame, as a slingshot to launch these missiles. The dorm was on the second floor so this helped with the trajectory. They would aim at things such as buildings, windows, buses, parked cars and signs. The smaller the target or the further the distance, the higher the point value for a hit. I understand that the 'bulls-eye' was when they would hit a moving piece of fire apparatus from their own station either responding to or returning from a call. This game was usually played at night, when there wasn't too much pedestrian traffic around the station – there were also less Chiefs around. These guys would have mini-tournaments in between calls.

This old building was huge, and the Police Department offices were to the rear of the building. Another game that some of the firemen who were stationed at this firehouse years ago used to play involved bottle rockets. They would set up a launching site in the parking lot next to the station and fire the rockets at the open windows of the police station. Again, the point value increased with size and distance. This went on until a rocket exploded in the office of a high-ranking Police Officer and he complained to our Chief.

These experiences will never be repeated – at least not by the firefighters stationed downtown. The city finally moved them out of this rundown old building. They built a new, state-of-the-art Public Safety Complex that houses all of the agencies that were located in the old building – and more. The building is a climate-controlled environment. None of the windows will open! This is one way to teach the kids to behave!

Fire stations in the city seem to be a magnet for the down-and-out and the mentally challenged. Most people scorn these members of society or simply choose to ignore them. Firemen will often take the time to talk to them and give them a helping hand. Very seldom have I seen a fireman give any of these people money, because it would never stop. What we do is offer them a place to warm up or rest occasionally. We'll also let them use the public facilities or make a phone call if they need to. For the mentally challenged we'll often give them little odd jobs around the station such as sweeping floors or washing windows. We'll pay them by including them in our meals or giving them a department tee shirt. Needless to say, these guys are always coming around and they feel like a part of the firehouse. Some of these guys know the firefighters at *their* station extremely well – where they've worked before, what they do part time, and even their kids' names and ages. I know of firefighters who have invited one of these guys to a family party. I know that they used to be included in a lot of station gatherings off the job, such as ballgames, company parties, and official departmental functions. Things have changed a lot over the past twenty years or so, and this kind of open-house situation in the firehouse is rapidly becoming a thing of the past. The violence on the streets and the epidemic growth of diseases such as HIV/AIDS, Hepatitis and TB have sent most stations into a lockdown mode, keeping strangers out and keeping us in. This is really a shame.

There was a guy named Johnny who used to hang around the Broad Street station years ago. He seemed to always be there and knew all of the firemen there. He was always doing odd jobs and running errands for us. He wanted more than anything else to be a Providence fireman. He was a great guy, very friendly and curious. He was also 40 years old, mentally challenged and stuttered. He had been abused as a child and took to the friendly, safe atmosphere around the firehouse. He would always ask the guys if he could talk on the radio. He was fascinated by the fire channels on his scanner.

In those days, Fire Alarm would conduct a radio test for all the apparatus in the city at the beginning of each shift. Johnny had finally talked one of the firefighters from Engine 11 into letting him answer the radio test. The fireman, Dan, told Johnny, "OK, just say Engine 11 OK, but don't fuck up!" Johnny eagerly awaited his chance as the dispatcher went through the companies – Engine 1 – Engine 2, etc. When it came time for Johnny to answer, he keyed in the microphone and proudly said, "E-e-e-ng-g-gine 11 O-o-oK." He then turned to Dan and said, "Hey, D-d-d-an, I didn't f-f-f-fuck up!" The only problem with this was that he had forgotten to release the key of the microphone and this had transmitted over our department frequency for everyone to hear! Everyone on the fire department knew whose voice this was, and for the rest of the night the phones at the station rang off the hook – all asking, "Is J-j-j-j-ohnny there?"

A lot of the practical jokes played on this job victimize the new guys. Usually this is because they're inexperienced and eager to please. Although sometimes opportunities arise to pull one off on a more veteran firefighter – even an officer! One such opportunity used to be on lockouts. When people lock themselves out of their apartment they usually call the fire department to help them gain entry. If there is no one else in the apartment, such as a sleeping baby, this is not really a true emergency. Because of this, the dispatcher would not sound the alarm and dispatch a truck over the vocalarm. Rather, he would call the officer in charge of the ladder truck in the district and verbally apprise him of the situation. The officer would then have to round up his guys and respond to the location. To pull this joke off you needed to have a new Lieutenant who was assigned to a new firehouse. It also helped if the firefighters on the ladder were guys who had been assigned there for a long time.

One night, when I was a firefighter on Engine 2, I called the Lieutenant of Ladder 3 and pretended to be one of the dispatchers from Fire Alarm. This new Lieutenant was a friend of mine who had pulled a couple over on me over the years. "Loo," I said, "this is Fire Alarm. We have a second floor lockout at 426 Admiral Street." It was about 2:00 AM so he had to go into the dormitory, find his guys in the dark, and wake them up. The guys from Engine 12 were also sleeping, so he was careful not to wake them in the process. His firefighters both had more time on the job than he did, so he had been trying to gain their respect and show them that he was capable of leading them. When he woke them, they all stumbled down the stairs to the apparatus floor and climbed onto the truck. The driver started the truck and pulled out of the station. He then asked the Lieutenant what the address was so that he'd know which way to turn. "426 Admiral," the officer said. The firefighter stopped the truck, put it in reverse and backed into the station once again. "Loo, someone's busting your balls," he said, "this is 426 Admiral Street." He then climbed down from the truck and went back up the stairs and to bed. The Lieutenant called Fire Alarm and started screaming at them. They told him that they hadn't called him at all that night. I'm not sure if he ever found out who had called him, but I do know that this story spread around the job very quickly. We have a saying on the department that says, "the three quickest ways to spread gossip are: telephone, telegraph and tell-a-fireman."

When I was brand new on the job most of the 'old hands' were extremely patient and helpful in teaching me some of the tricks of the trade. Some of the older guys, however, would look at the new guy with disdain. There was one such guy on Ladder 7 that I worked with one day. We had a small fire in an apartment house and the Chief told our company to search the floor above the fire. We split up the company and I went with him. He told me, "I'll show you how it's done, kid." The apartment was smoky but you could still see fairly well. As I entered the first bedroom, he watched as I searched the floor and the closet. I then got on my hands and knees and looked under the bed. It took a few seconds to lift the sheets up and direct my light under the bed to get a clear view of the floor underneath. There was no one there and I left the room. He gave me a condescending look, led me to the second bedroom and said, "Stay at the door and watch how it's done." He entered the room and quickly searched the floor and the closet. He then moved quickly toward the bed, dove on the floor and slid his shoulder under the bed frame. In one motion he lifted the bed and felt the floor underneath. I was totally impressed! This was much quicker than I had been in the first room. We entered the third bedroom and he proceeded to slide toward the bed. I heard a loud thud, and a groan. This bed was a platform waterbed and it wasn't about to be moved. I helped him down the stairs and to the Rescue. He had separated his shoulder! When the guys on the Rescue asked us what happened I just shrugged and walked away. He never acted smug toward me again. I had a good laugh at his expense, but not in front of him!

Another time, years later, the roles had been reversed and I was the veteran showing a new guy how to search an apartment above the fire. There was a small fire on the first floor and I took him up to the third floor to search. Everything went well and there was no one in the apartment. Our Captain joined us and told us to open up the windows to ventilate. As we began, the new guy began to open a window just as I caught a glimpse of an air conditioner on the sill. I tried to stop him, but it was too late! As he opened the window the air conditioner began to fall to the driveway below. He looked at me in shock and I quickly poked my head out the window as I heard the crash below. I saw the Chief jump a mile as the unit landed about a foot away from him! I quickly pulled my head back inside the window and told the rookie to look and see where it landed. He stuck his head outside just as the Chief had gained his composure and looked up to see where it had come from!

Back in 1982, when I was stationed on Engine 2, we backed into the station one day after a run. As we did, we noticed that someone had put up a small tripod on the median strip in front of our firehouse. A woman and a man were standing to the side, talking. When we got off the truck we looked over at them and they just kept on talking. As we started to close the overhead door we noticed that the woman walked up to the tripod and began to fiddle with the camera. Our station had four red overhead doors in the front. One for each company stationed here – Chief 3, Ladder 7, Engine 2, and Rescue 3. My Lieutenant, Joe, opened a different door to see what she was doing. As it began to open, she backed away from her camera. That was all we needed to see. Apparently she was trying to take a photograph of the fire station and wanted all the doors down. We quickly shut the door just opened. Again she began to approach her tripod. We didn't even need to look out the window anymore. We had the timing figured out. Pete, Joe and I would take turns in opening and closing the various doors for the next few minutes. As soon as one would completely close, another one would begin to open. Sometimes it doesn't take much to keep a fireman amused!

After we did this for awhile, the doorbell rang. She had sent her assistant over to ask us if we could put all of the doors down – or all of them up. He explained that her name was Rebecca Zurier and that she was traveling all around the country trying to take photos of different types of American firehouses for a book she hoped to publish. We obliged by putting them all down. She would send him over from time to time and ask us to try other combinations with the doors. When her book was published, *The American Firehouse*, I noticed that she had chosen a picture with the two middle doors open and the outside doors closed. I also noticed that she had captured our station mascot, Cocoa, lying in front of the station.

Cocoa was a female Dalmatian with a white coat and brown spots. She was just about six months old when one of the firefighters at our station found her and her brother roaming around on the highway. He stopped his car and corralled them. When he brought them back to the station we located the owner and returned them. About a week later, the owner showed up at the station and said that they were getting out of his yard too much and that he had to get rid of them. He asked us if we wanted to take one of them. We did. Our station had just lost its long time mascot a few months earlier – a male Dalmatian named Freckles. We kept Cocoa. She served us well and stayed until we had to put her down about 12 years later. There are now two headstones located next to the flagpole just outside the front door – "Freckles" and "Cocoa."

She had her share of mishaps but always bounced back, at least until she got too old. She tried to ride the trucks and was pretty good at it, but when a truck would take a sharp turn you'd sometimes hear her claws scratching on the diamond-plate of the engine compartment as her paws would go a mile a minute trying to keep her balance. Sometimes she would succeed; sometimes she would not. When an alarm came in and the firemen would slide the pole, she would chase us to the pole hole. When the floors had just been waxed she sometimes misjudged the distance she would need to stop. Again, you'd hear her claws scratching on the floor as she tried to put on the brakes. Again, sometimes she'd succeed and sometimes she wouldn't. She took the 20-foot-plus plunge on more than one occasion. She survived it all with no major injuries. I'm sure that all these bumps and bruises took a toll on her in later years. Life is not easy around the firehouse – for firefighters or for dogs.

The funniest incident I remember involving Cocoa happened when she was in heat. We let her out of the station to run around the cemetery across the street all the time. One day we saw her with another dog and realized that she was in heat. We tried to keep her in the station from then on, but it was difficult with all the activity around the firehouse. Back in those days, from 2100 hrs. to 0700 hrs. (9:00 PM to 7:00 AM) our stations would run on "night-time-operations." This meant that we didn't have to monitor the radios to listen for an alarm. Our dispatchers would trip the alarm at individual stations from Fire Alarm by flipping a switch. This would open the vocalarm at that station, strike the bell, turn on the lights, and open all of the overhead doors. Three minutes later the lights would go out and the doors would close automatically.

One morning when Cocoa was in heat, an alarm came in around 5:30 AM. When we slid the poles, there had to be at least twenty male dogs chasing Cocoa around the apparatus floor. They were all hanging around the station, and when the doors opened, they rushed in. We were being dispatched to a report of a building fire, so we had no choice but to get on the trucks and go. All of the trucks in the station were leaving. When the doors shut three minutes later, Cocoa was trapped in the building with about twenty dogs with just one thing on their minds. When we returned (about an hour later) we chased all the dogs away. We had to carry Cocoa up the stairs! She couldn't even stand up! She never went into heat again. We had her spayed at the earliest opportunity.

Most firemen I know are animal lovers. As with any group of people we all have our own preferences in this area. Some of us prefer cats, some of us prefer dogs, and others prefer the more exotic pets such as snakes or reptiles. Regardless of our 'petual preference', we care about saving your pet when there's a fire in your home. We do have to prioritize our actions, however. Our mission, as a department, is to: save life and protect property. Obviously the choice between a human life and an animal life is an easy call. The choice between an animal's life and the protection of property, however, is not always that clear. Take the classic case of the old woman who calls the fire department because her cat is stuck in a tree. She's worried sick about her cat and wants it down now! Firemen in the past have gone to the cat's rescue and retrieved the cat by climbing the tree or using a ladder to reach it. Some firemen have also been hurt when the cat being rescued doesn't want to be rescued and claws the fireman, causing him to fall. This has led most departments to forbid their firefighters from attempting this rescue. Some people think this is heartless, but the fact is, the cat will eventually come down on its own when it's hungry enough. After all, when was the last time you saw a feline skeleton in a tree?

We responded to a fire in an occupied apartment building one day and found heavy fire in the front of the building and smoke throughout. There was a report of an old woman trapped on the second floor. As the first engine company was stretching a hoseline to attack the fire, two members of the first ladder company went in the back stairs, found and rescued the woman. They carried her down the stairs and out to the rescue in front of the building. The initial report was that the first floor occupant was at work. As another company did a primary search of the first floor they found six kittens. They quickly grabbed them and brought them outside. The kittens seemed fine so they put them in the back yard and returned to continue the search. When the two members who had rescued the woman returned to the rear door to continue their search of the second floor, they stopped at the doorway to put on their masks. While one of the firefighters was putting on his facepiece he took a step backwards. He felt something under his foot and jumped. He tore off his mask and to his horror he had stepped on one of the kittens, killing it. This bothered him so much that he was unable to continue at this fire. Even though he had just saved the life of a woman five minutes earlier, all he could think of was this poor kitten.

At the Department's Medals Day ceremony later that year, this firefighter received a medal for his bravery at this fire. As he went to the stage to receive it, a chorus of "meow" could be heard throughout the auditorium. Firemen never let you live anything down!!

Chapter 4
...Sometimes You Cry!

Sometimes this job can get the best of you. Hard work, long hours, low pay, dangerous working conditions, understaffing, cold, heat: these are some of our 'normal' working conditions. Firefighters know of these factors before joining the fire department. Although these things can wear you down, they seldom break you. In my experience, I've found that two factors more than any others, contribute to firefighter 'burnout' and low morale – failure and lack of appreciation.

Firefighters *hate* to fail. I know that most people aren't too thrilled of failing. This is human nature. We'd all like to succeed at whatever we attempt. Firefighters are no different in this respect. Where we do differ, however, is in the depths of our failures. Our failures usually mean that we lose a building, or worse – a life! Lose enough of these battles and it takes its toll on your spirit. Add to this a lack of appreciation (or respect) from your commanders and you have a burden that can break the strongest of men, leaving them questioning why they continue to put themselves through this.

The year I reached my 20th anniversary on the job I went through just such a time. That year we had a long hot summer. We were short on manpower and when the vacation season came, the overtime was there for the taking. It wasn't uncommon for an officer to work 48 straight hours, have 24 off, and then do another 48 straight. The long hours, combined with more exposure to smoke due to responding to more fires, can wear you down. This took its toll on me, and by August I had developed pneumonia. I initially went to see my doctor for this during my time off, and because I wasn't transported to the hospital directly from work, the department denied my claim for injury status for the pneumonia. I fought this, but they wouldn't budge, and it eventually cost me over $10,000 out my pocket. I was out of work for about three months. The lack of support from the front office was terribly disheartening. The Chiefs, although part of the administration, are supposed to have an understanding of the dangers and the possible illnesses firefighters face as a result of our constant exposures. Part of the problem in the Providence Fire Department is that the Chief who makes decisions regarding injuries had only about a year of front-line service on the trucks. He just has no understanding of what this job can do to you physically, or emotionally. This situation leads to low morale in the department, and makes us wonder why we continue to risk our lives and jeopardize our health by aggressively fighting fires employing an interior attack. All fires will eventually go out if we "surround and drown" the fire – pour water on the building from the outside without going inside. There will certainly be more damage to the property, but they will eventually be extinguished, and we'll still pick up our paychecks on payday. Pride is the reason we operate the way we do. Pride in ourselves. Pride in our companies. Pride in our department. Pride, and the satisfaction of knowing that we're protecting our community and its citizens as well as we possibly can. When the pride in the department is taken away, it causes low morale and burnout in the front line firefighters. This was my state of mind when I returned to work after being legitimately sick, but being treated like I was a common thief – trying to steal money from the city under false pretenses. Burnt out.

I returned to work in December, and it was cold and raw. I worked both of my day shifts without any significant calls. My first night shift was a different story, however. It started out easy enough, a couple of minor rescue runs before midnight, and then it seemed to get quiet all around the city. It was a very icy night on the roads, and most of the earlier runs were fender-benders involving people returning from the malls. People seemed to want to get home quickly from their Christmas shopping and stay out of the cold night air, choosing to stay inside their nice warm houses and do some gift-wrapping or just take a break from the holiday hustle. It was a Thursday night, a little over two weeks before Christmas.

I was hoping to stay inside that night also. I was scheduled to work the next two nights and I wanted to have a couple of easy shifts, because my fiancée and I were planning to decorate the house this weekend and buy a Christmas tree. When things quieted down, an hour or so after the stores closed, it seemed very promising.

It must have been a cozy night for the three families living at 24 Hymer Street also. The house was decorated for Christmas and gifts had already been wrapped and put under the tree of each apartment. This was an old three-story building with a large apartment on each level. It looked larger, though, because it was constructed on top of a five-foot wall. It was on a corner lot, but the house to the left was only about ten feet away. Many of the older houses in

Providence are very close together. From the turn of the century until around the 1970s space was at a premium in the city, and builders tried to cram as many people as possible into the smallest amount of space. As with many older cities in the Northeast, this condition has made fighting fires in this area of the country very difficult. There always seems to be an 'exposure' close enough to the fire that requires us to first 'contain' the fire before beginning to extinguish it – stopping it from spreading to other structures.

On this night, the families on all three floors were at home. A family of three on the first floor, a family of two on the second, and a mother and her five kids on the third. Whatever festivities were going on in the different apartments that night, by 1:00 AM everyone in the house was fast asleep, safely tucked into their own beds. It was bitterly cold that night and as in most of these old houses, the drafts blowing through the old windows tend to overwhelm the tired, old heating systems. Many families living in these types of houses have to resort to space heaters to keep the chill out of the rooms. Such was the case for the family living on the first floor. They had a colorfully-lit real Christmas tree in the front room, sparkling through the front windowpanes – shining holiday cheer to the street below. The lights to the tree were plugged into an extension cord, which ran under a carpet to a wall socket. Plugged into the same wall socket was another extension cord, which ran to a space heater, warming the next room.

The mother of the family on the third floor had returned from a church function earlier in the night with her five kids. They ranged in age from 3 to 16 years old. She put the kids to bed and called a friend to talk for a while on the phone. A short time later she decided to turn in herself. I imagine her going to each room checking on her children as they slept, the way most parents do each night, silently thanking God that they're all good kids and not in any trouble. Most of all, though, thanking Him that they're all at home and safe.

Around this same time I was just going to bed at the station. I had stayed up to finish some reports that I had been putting off from runs earlier in the night. I needed to finish them before going home in the morning, and I've always worked better at night than first thing in the morning. The last thing I wanted was to wake up with paperwork hanging over my head. I'm definitely not a morning person! I set the alarm, shut the light, and climbed under the covers. I could hear the wind howling outside my window and I was glad it had been a relatively easy night. As always, I left my portable radio turned on to hear what else was going on in the city. There hadn't been much chatter on our frequency in the last couple of hours.

Right around 1:15 AM there was a small 'pop' in the first floor living room of 24 Hymer Street as one the extension cords heated up and shorted out. This caused the wall socket to overheat and begin to burn. No one seemed to notice the small amount of smoke in the front of the house. The short caused the other extension cord to heat up and begin to melt the plastic coating around the wires, which in turn, began to burn the carpet. Little by little the fire was moving away from the wall, and toward the rest of the room. When the flames reached the curtains and the gifts, the fire gained momentum and quickly spread to the tree. "Like an explosion," according to one of the first floor occupants, the flames consumed the tree in an instant and engulfed the entire living room! The blast woke the family all at once and because the apartment was rapidly filling with smoke, they immediately knew their home was on fire. There was no time to call 911 – only time to escape through the rear door. The teenage boy ran up the rear stairs to alert the other occupants, screaming "fire, fire!" and banging on the doors of the second and third floors – before running down the stairs to escape the fire.

The fire had 'blown out' the front windows and the fresh oxygen was feeding this ever-growing fire very rapidly. Also, when the family had exited the first floor apartment they left the rear door open, causing a crossdraft that sucked the fire right through the apartment. The family on the second floor narrowly escaped, before the flames reached the rear stairwell. The teenage boy, who had continued to the third floor to warn the occupants, was caught in the fire as he pushed his way down the last few stairs to the back yard. He sustained second and third degree burns on his hands and his back. He survived, thankfully, and his heroism certainly saved the lives of the second floor residents. The family on the third floor opened their rear door to try and follow the boy down the stairs, but must have been driven back by the intense heat coming from below. When a fire is burning on a stairway below, the stairway itself becomes like a chimney. Because heat rises, the top of the stairs quickly becomes unbearable. The mother turned around and guided her kids toward the front stairs.

When the flames exploded out of the front windows, it must have awakened many of the neighbors in this congested neighborhood. Someone called 911 to report a fire.

I was just drifting off to sleep when the radio and the vocalarm echoed together, in stereo, as all the lights in the building came on. "Attention Engines 12, 2, 15; Special Hazards; Ladders 3 & 7; Rescue 3; and Battalion 3; a Still Box – a reported house fire." I immediately jumped up from bed, stepped into my pants, and began to get dressed – just as about 24 other firefighters across the city were doing the same. I slid the pole, put on my bunker pants and climbed onto the truck. When Fire Alarm dispatched the second round, they gave the address: 24 Hymer Street. I wrote it down on the pad on the dashboard, and we were out the door and into the cold. This was about the same time the mother on the third floor was leading her family to the front stairs.

"Fire Alarm to Engine 12." "Engine 12," they answered. "We've received numerous calls on this," Fire Alarm said. "Engine 12 received," they answered as they sped to the scene. This was beginning to seem serious! I had already figured that we had a fire by the fact that Fire Alarm had dispatched the full complement of trucks for a working fire right from the beginning. When they send Special Hazards and a Rescue right away, it's a good sign that the dispatchers believe there is a serious fire. Numerous calls at 1:15 AM is a sure sign of a significant fire, and at this time of the morning, fires often get a good head start. At this time, the family was beginning to descend the front stairs. The fire had already burst through the front windows of the first floor and onto the porch. Once the porch was going, the flames began to engulf the entire front of the building.

"Engine 12, we have a report of people trapped on the third floor," Fire Alarm squawked over the radio. The Lieutenant answered, "Received." "Engine 12 to Fire Alarm we have a heavy smoke condition," he said. This was rapidly escalating to a real 'worker.' Every firefighter on every piece of apparatus responding to this fire was monitoring the radio and could sense the situation growing more and more serious by the moment. The adrenaline kicks in, and you completely forget that a minute ago you were fast asleep! The mother led her kids to the bottom of the stairwell. There was no place to go! Outside the door, the porch was a wall of flames! She tried to lead them back upstairs, but one by one they collapsed in a heap in front of the door. She tried to pull them up, but collapsed right next to them. The 16 year old made it back up to the third floor landing before collapsing from the smoke and the heat.

Engine 12 turned onto Hymer Street and saw the house completely engulfed in flames. "Code Red, three-story, occupied, fully involved," radioed Engine 12, "give me a second Alarm." We came to the corner of Hymer Street just prior to Engine 2, so we hooked into the hydrant to supply the water to Engine 12. Engine 12 and Ladder 3 immediately rushed to the rear stairs to try and make their way to the third floor. In these types of buildings the front stairs sometimes only go to the second floor, but the rear stairs always go all the way up, so when trying to gain access to the third floor we always take the rear stairs. There was heavy fire throughout the stairway and they tried to take control of this exit by hitting the fire with a 2 ½" handline. This large diameter hose delivers more water than our normal attack lines and can knock down much more fire. Even with this amount of water, however, they weren't making any progress. Meanwhile, Engine 2 had a line in front of the building trying to keep the flames from spreading to the house on the left. This house was occupied also, and we didn't know at this time whether the occupants were in or out of the building. We laid 'feeders' to Engine 12, then took a line to the front of the building. We had to knock down the flames from the outside of the building because the fire was too intense to gain entry from the front. The first Ladder company, Ladder 3, couldn't get their truck in position to use their aerial because of cars blocking the road, so they put ground ladders to the windows of the second and third floors on the right side of the building. Firefighters quickly climbed up these ladders to enter and search these apartments as other firefighters manned hoselines to protect them by keeping the flames back from the ladders. Ladder 6 entered the second floor and Special Hazards entered the third floor. Each of these companies was only able to search the kitchen area before being driven out by the extreme heat, scrambling back to the safety of the ladders.

When they were driven out of the upper floors, it became apparent that we were going to have to extinguish this fire from the bottom up. The Chief ordered us to take our line into the first floor via the front door. This was where the fire was most intense. Here, and in the back stairway. When the fire on the porch was knocked down, we began to advance our line into the first floor. There were two doors entering the building from the porch. The door on the left went directly to the first floor apartment, the one on the right led to the stairway to the upper floors. As we began to advance, I noticed that there was some fire on the stairway. I told the nozzleman to follow me into the stairway before entering the first floor. I wanted to quickly knock down the fire in the hallway before it traveled too far up the stairs. This area hadn't been engulfed by fire yet, and I wanted to keep it that way. The fire on the stairs had been started by radiated heat from the flames on the porch, after the heat had burst the glass in the upper part of the door. I tried to push the door open with my shoulder. It wouldn't budge. Apparently it was locked. I tried again, but still it wouldn't budge. I told the nozzleman to hit the fire through the opening in the door. After he had knocked it down, we began to move into the first floor. We made good progress in pushing back the flames from the front of the apartment, but the rear of the building was getting worse.

Ladder 7 had taken their truck around the block to gain position to use their aerial to vent the roof. They then tried to enter the third floor rear window via their aerial. The intense heat wouldn't allow them to enter. As the fire gained control of the upper floors, the exterior wall began to lean outward. The Chief pulled everyone out of the building, in case of a structural failure and collapse. We spent the next hour or so pouring water on the building from the outside. We were cold, wet, tired and extremely frustrated. We still didn't know if anyone was still in the building or not. We only knew that if anyone *was* still in the house, they couldn't have survived.

When the Chief gave us the OK to re-enter the building, we took our line back to the first floor, where we knocked down the rest of the fire in that apartment from the inside. While working here, I began hearing that they had found a body on the stairs. This seemed to confirm that someone had been trapped. We had all been hoping that the reports of "people trapped" were unfounded, as is the case most times at these types of fires. Shortly, I heard that there were five bodies…then six! A mother and five kids. My heart sank! I know that everyone there felt the same way. A mother and her kids!!!! Shit!! We hate to lose anyone to a fire, but a whole fucking family is the most bitter of defeats!

When we had finished extinguishing the fire on this floor, the Chief told me to take my crew up a ground ladder in the front of the building to the second floor to knock down the remaining fire there. When we backed out to the porch to go to the ladder, I saw some firefighters beginning to set up a tarpaulin to cover the front door to the stairway. I poked my head through the opening in the door and saw the mother and two kids laying against the door. Two other kids were lying on the stairs just above them. One of the boys was about the same age as my 9-year-old son, Teddy! This was the same door I had tried to force open earlier!! Now I knew why it wouldn't budge. When I think of this family being *ssssoooo* close to escaping with their lives, it makes me want to cry! It makes me second-guess myself; and my actions that night. I ask myself, "what if"??! If only I had concentrated all the efforts of my company on that doorway when we first arrived on the scene. I'm sure the officer of Engine 12, Brian, asks himself the same questions. If only we had known they were right there!!!!!

The reality is that there was no way for us to know this when we first pulled up to the scene. The reality is that Brian and I, as well as the other officers and firefighters on the scene, made the right choices, given the circumstances. We played the odds – took an educated guess. We acted exactly the way we were trained to act – it just didn't happen to be the best possible action for this particular fire. Hindsight is always 20/20 – especially after a fire. When the smoke clears, and the emergency is over, it's easy to walk through the scene and say we should have done this or we should have done that. Unfortunately, we have to act immediately when we first arrive at the scene. There's no time to hesitate when it comes to attacking a fire or attempting a rescue. You make an educated guess as to what your best plan of attack is, and you immediately put it into action. No hesitation. No looking back. We can't afford that luxury. When we lose, as we did on this night, we have to be able to put it out of our minds. We have to console ourselves with the knowledge that we did the best that we could. If we don't, it will eat us up inside, and we'll be worthless the next time we're faced with similar circumstances.

Although we have to put it out of our minds, this is easier said than done!!

We proceeded to the second floor, and then the third. On the third floor landing, at the top of the stairs, I saw the oldest boy. We had to walk past him to gain access to the apartment. This seemed somehow even sadder. He was alone! He must have already known that the rest of his family wasn't going to make it, but he was desperately trying to find somewhere to escape the heat and the smoke. I can only imagine the terror he must have felt in those last moments. You could see the claw marks in the soot on the top few stairs where he had dragged himself to the landing!

We were there for a few hours more, extinguishing the 'hot spots', packing up the hose and removing the bodies. Normally this is what we refer to as the 'social hour.' The pressure of the fire is over and all the guys catch up on department gossip and bust each other's balls. This night everyone was very quiet. All of us were drained – physically and emotionally! All of us were thinking of our own kids – safely tucked into their beds, completely unaware of what had just happened. Me? I was thinking that I was going to tell Nancy and my stepson, Bobby, we were going to get an artificial tree this year!

It was an emotional week following this tragedy as the news was told over and over again on the television and in the newspapers. The department brought in counselors to talk to the firefighters involved, to help us deal with the emotions we were all going through. The next week we all returned to work and tried to go on as usual. The best way to put something like this behind you is to get back into your normal routine. This is what we tried to do.

On my second day shift back to work I was offered a 'callback.' This meant

I would be working the night shift also. I stayed right in my own company, so this was ideal. It was another cold and miserable night, so I wasn't going to be doing anything that night anyway. I'd probably be just sitting at home watching TV. I could do that here – and get paid for it! The guys on this shift always treated me well. They were good at their jobs, and they fed me well. What more could you ask for? We had a macaroni and sausage dinner and watched the Bruins hockey game. We even saw most of the game, being interrupted only once or twice by rescue runs. After the game I made up my bed and turned in.

About 2:00 AM the bell tipped. Fire Alarm was sending out the 'full complement' to a reported building fire – and we were first called! When we slid the pole and got on the truck they gave us the address – 88 Erastus Street. This was only a couple of blocks from the station. We were going to get there quickly. We'd barely have enough time to get our gear on enroute. As soon as we left the firehouse you could smell something burning. About 30 seconds after that we were turning onto Erastus Street. The night sky was illuminated by flames that shot out into the middle of the street, melting the electrical wires in front of the house and causing them to arc. There was a crowd of about thirty people in the street frantically waving us down. I radioed, "Engine 15 to Fire Alarm, Code Red, two-story, occupied, heavy fire showing on both floors."

We stopped the truck before reaching the house, because of the flames and the crowd in front of the building. The chauffeur readied the pump to give us water, and the firefighter on the side went to the rear of the truck to get the hoseline. I went to the front of the building to do my 'size up.' Before I could gather enough information by visually checking out the extent of the fire, to determine whether or not to call for more companies, I was 'jumped' by a hysterical young woman! She literally jumped on my back and started screaming that her baby was in there! I had to quickly take control, and shake her to find out where her baby was. "First floor," she cried. I radioed that I had a report from a mother that her baby was trapped on the first floor, and started to enter the front door. I was told later, by the guys who were responding, that they could just barely make out what I was saying. All they could hear was the mother continuing to scream in the background. Hearing this, they realized they were rolling into a bad situation. When we monitor the radio calls while en route to an emergency, it's not just the words being spoken that we pay attention to. We listen to the tone of the voice and the peripheral noise being picked up by the microphone – anything to help us gain an insight as to what's going on at the scene.

I tried to open the front door, but it would only open about an inch. I tried to push it again, but still it wouldn't budge. I tried to rush the door and bash it open with my shoulder but all I succeeded in doing was injuring my shoulder. Ladder 6 was pulling up to the scene and I told them to "take down this fucking door!" They quickly ripped the door from its hinges and tossed it aside. There was a full-sized bed just inside the doorway, that's why it wouldn't open! The heat, smoke and flame poured from the open doorway as we opened up our line and crawled over the bed and into the front room. The nozzleman knocked down the fire as the rest of us pushed as far into the apartment as we could get, all the while feeling for anything that could possibly be a child. We couldn't see anything but the glow of the fire in front of us. We learn to search by feel. When we got to the back of the room someone came upon the frame of a bassinet that had burnt. We feverishly searched this area of the floor. Carefully moving the burnt debris trying to feel for a baby – all the while hoping that it wasn't there!

When another hoseline was put into operation from a different entrance, we began to make better progress at pushing the fire back. We entered the next room and began the search process all over again. And the next room. We were searching the third room when one of the firefighters from Ladder 2 said, "I think I've got something!" A few of us crawled over to him and shone our lights on the area he was digging. As he carefully removed what seemed like a ton of debris from the floor, the lights shone on the small, charred, lifeless body of an infant. He quickly picked up the child and brought him to the doorway where the rescue was waiting. They desperately tried to revive the child – even though it was obvious to everyone at the scene that there was no hope. I followed him out of the building, as I was almost out of air. I'll never forget the anguished screams of that mother as they rushed her baby into the back of the rescue!

Another cold, wet night spent in defeat! This was exactly one week after the fire at Hymer Street. It was only two weeks since I had come back to work from pneumonia, and it was just ten days before Christmas. So much for a happy holiday season!

This baby was only six months old! Sometimes, when I lie in bed at night, I can still hear that mother's wails.

Chapter 5
Lieutenant Gloom & Doom

There was a particular group of guys with whom I sometimes worked that seemed to bring me nothing but bad luck. These guys swore it was the other way around. The company was Engine 12 and they were quartered with Ladder 3. They called me Lt. Gloom. Our Groups corresponded in such a way that whenever I worked with them it would be a night shift.

Firemen primarily judge the difference between a good night and a bad one by the number of runs after midnight. When you ask a fireman how his night was he might answer, "Great! We didn't turn a wheel after midnight." Or he might answer, "It sucked, we had 5 runs after [midnight]." We don't mind running around and keeping busy during the day or early evening. Once we go to sleep, however, we'd rather not be constantly awakened – especially for a nonsense run such as a false alarm at a street box, or an EMS call for a bloody nose. It always amazes me that someone walking the street at 3 AM suddenly decides that since he's up at this hour he'll wake up the firemen, too. I guess misery really does love company.

It seemed that every time I worked with these guys, we would have a terrible night. We would inevitably have five or six runs after midnight. On one occasion we had eight runs between 1:00 AM and 5:30 AM and were grumbling to each other as we climbed the stairs to head back to our beds to try and catch a few extra minutes of desperately needed sleep. Just then, the vocalarm blasted: "Attention Engines 12, 2, 7 - Special Hazards 1 – Ladders 3 & 7 – Battalion 3 – a still box." When a dispatch is sounded in this manner, we know we can expect a working structure fire upon our arrival at the scene.

We all did an about-face on the stairs and wearily climbed into our gear and onto the truck. When the dispatcher gave us the address of the alarm we were slightly encouraged, as this was a big mill building in the district that was common for false alarms – maybe this would be a short run. When we arrived on the scene we found nothing obviously wrong and began to check the building from the exterior. We spent about five minutes looking for signs of trouble from the front and sides. I also sent another company to check the rear of the building. As I was just about to call my dispatcher to ask if they had any further information on this call, one of my guys said "Loo, is that smoke up there?" When I looked at him, I followed his pointing finger to the top of a six-story spire connected to the front of the building, which covered an exterior stairway. At the very top of this spire, you could see tiny wisps of what appeared to be light gray smoke. As we stared at this for a moment, you could see the smoke increase ever so slightly when the wind picked up. "Yeah Steve, I'm afraid it is," I said. I didn't have to turn around to look at them to see their faces in my mind. I knew they were as discouraged as I was, due to our lack of sleep. These are the times you silently curse those people who pulled the false alarm boxes, or lit that dumpster fire at 2:00AM that kept you up all night. This was going to be a real pain-in-the-ass job, and we were going to need all our energy to make sure we stopped this fire before it could spread to the main part of the building.

Normally when such a small amount of smoke is visible the first-in officer would go to the source and investigate the cause before stretching the hoselines and dragging equipment into the building. I would usually have one firefighter with me carrying an extinguisher. Many times this is all that's needed to extinguish the fire. Operating this way can save us a lot of unnecessary work and minimizes the damage done to the property. Normal operations go out the window when the property is a six-story mill building. With any size fire in a mill building, you have to assume the worst and over-attack. With the heavy timber construction and oil-soaked floors of this type of building, even a small fire can quickly escalate into a fire that is beyond our resources. You must attack aggressively and quickly to keep it contained.

I ordered everyone to don their SCBA's and that the 250' bed of 1 ¾" hoseline be stretched to the building. Each engine company in this city carries four beds of pre-packed 1 ¾" attack hoselines ready to pull off the truck and immediately be charged with water and put into use. Three of these beds have 200' of hose. This length is sufficient to reach the seat of the fire in most fires to which we respond. The majority of building fires we fight in Providence are in 3-deckers. With 200' of hose, we can stretch it to the rear stairway, up three flights of stairs and through the apartment to the front of the house. Because of the weight of a charged hoseline,[1] and the difficulty in maneuvering it through the twists and turns of an apartment house, you don't want to have any more length than you might need. One bed on the truck is pre-packed with 250.' This is pulled when the situation calls for extra length to insure you reach the seat of the fire.

As we were readying ourselves to enter the building, members of Ladder 3 forced the door at the bottom of the spire. When the door was opened you could see a haze of smoke throughout the stairway. We began the first of what seemed like a hundred treks up the six flights of stairs to the summit of the spire. We found a small smoldering fire in the peak of the roof, which we quickly extinguished. Although it was a small fire, we still needed to open up the area all around the involved section of the roof and walls to ensure there was nothing left smoldering which might lead to a re-ignition a few hours from now. This part of the operation is called 'overhaul.' This is one of the bull-work parts of firefighting, as it consists of chopping through heavy timber with axes and saws and pulling ceilings and walls with hand tools called plaster poles. In many instances, this process lasts much longer than the actual extinguishment of the fire. That was certainly the case on this morning. This process was especially thorough and lengthy in this case because we were dealing with a high fire hazard property – an old mill building.

About two hours later we returned to our quarters exhausted, sweaty, and soaking wet. Most of the guys cleaned up to go home or to their part-time jobs. I didn't even have time to clean up, as I had to throw my gear into my car and rush back to my normal assignment at Engine 15 – to begin my day shift. Before I could make it out the door I heard one of the guys from Engine 12 yell, "Hey, Lt. Gloom, the next time they offer you a callback on Engine 12 – say no thanks." He was laughing when he said this but I knew he was only half joking.

This became my new title with these guys. I worked with them a few more times over the next year or so with no other major incidents or problems. We had some busy nights, but nothing out of the ordinary. Still, every time I walked into the building someone would inevitably say, "Shit, it's gonna be one of those nights. Lt. Gloom is here!" We'd all laugh and I'd tell them that I'd been given no other choice of companies at which to work. "This would be my last choice of places to work," I'd say. The truth was, most times I *was* given a choice, but I enjoyed working at this station. This was a good group of guys; and they were good firefighters.

This is the way things stayed between us until one hot July night a year or two later. This is when I earned the second half of my title – doom. When I showed up at their station that night, we all went through the same kidding that we always did about the luck I was bringing to the firehouse that night. One thing about firemen is that they never let one of their own live anything down. Even up till that point, if I ever met up with one of these guys on the street thirty years from now, chances are that I'd be greeted, "Hey, Lt. Gloom." That's just the way we are. Our Local Union newsletter even printed a list of many of the nicknames we have for each other a few years back. There were more than a hundred names listed, and many were titles the guys would love to forget. There's no such luck on the fire department.

That night began as a very ordinary summer night at the firehouse. We began by going to market to shop for our evening meal. Big steaks, baked potatoes, salad, corn on the cob, and ice cream for desert. We always eat well at the station. The wives of many firemen say that they feel inadequate in the kitchen because their husbands eat so well at work. Although I never did much cooking at the firehouse, everyone is expected to be able to prepare a meal if need be. I've been fortunate enough over the years to have worked with many great chefs who prepare great meals every day – from basic to gourmet. The basic requirements for a firehouse meal are: 'hot and a lot.'

After we had enjoyed our meal, we settled in to watch the Red Sox on TV. Although we went on a few runs during the course of the game, we did get a chance to watch and enjoy most of it. Some of the guys went out to sit on the wall in front of the station while others went to bed. I went into my office to finish up the reports for our previous calls. It was turning out to be a good night. I remember thinking to myself that maybe I'd broken my curse at this station. I finished the reports around midnight and turned in for the night. I was hopeful that I'd get a good sleep tonight.

At 1:15AM we were awakened by the station bell and the vocalarm: "Attention Engines 14, 15, 12; Special Hazards 1; Ladders 6 & 3; Rescue 4 and Battalion 3 a still box." At that time of the morning and upon hearing that a Rescue was being dispatched, we all had the sense that this was probably a working fire. On the second round of the dispatch they added the address and "...a possible structure fire in an occupied dwelling." Our movements, although quick from the beginning, took on an added urgency as we all shook out the cobwebs and began to mentally prepare ourselves for what we were rushing into. We went from a sound sleep to sliding the poles, getting dressed in our gear, climbing on the trucks, and heading out the door in less than a minute. On the way to the scene all firemen try to take the time to go over in their minds what they might find upon arrival, and what their first course of action should be. The officers of the trucks, especially, have to be sizing up the situation while responding, trying to prepare their plan of attack. Once we arrive at an emergency scene, we don't have the luxury of taking our time to formulate the best course of action. Most emergencies are time-critical. We have to act appropriately; and we have to act quickly.

The size up of any situation begins when the bell tips. The first clue you have is the time of day. You build on this with every bit of information you're given. The order in which companies are dispatched gives you an idea of what may be expected of your company when you arrive. In this particular case, as we were called third, we began to prepare for a search and rescue operation above the fire floor, as well as having to place the second hoseline into service. A good fireman has to prepare himself for the job at hand before he gets off the truck; but a good fireman also has to be able to change tactics as quickly as the situation changes. At an emergency scene, things often change very quickly.

On this night we were the third engine truck called, but the location of the reported fire was at an area in the city where the first-due districts of all three engine companies dispatched came together in a two block radius. As we raced through the night with sirens wailing and lights flashing, we began to sense a faint smell of burning wood. Just about a block before the turn for the street called, we crested a small hill and began our descent. As we started down the hill I noticed that the first-due engine was still a couple of blocks away and heading toward us. We were going to beat them in. This changed our plan, as we now had to take on the responsibilities of the second engine company. When my chauffeur took a hard right onto the street, I realized that we were going to be first in. I could also see a large amount of fire blowing out of the first floor, front picture window. I gave the initial report, "Code Red, two-family, wood-frame, occupied, heavy fire showing first floor, Side 1." As my firefighters stretched the hoseline to the front door, I asked the people gathered on the sidewalk if anyone lived here. A woman who claimed to be the second floor occupant said no one else was in her apartment, but she hadn't seen the man who lived on the first floor. She screamed, "I think he's still in there!"

The pump operator charged our hoseline as we opened the front door and donned our masks. I radioed the incoming Battalion Chief that I had a report of a person trapped, and yelled to the men that we needed to do a primary search ASAP. A primary search is a quick search of the fire building for possible victims. This is done floor by floor, and room by room, as quickly as possible. This is standard procedure at all house fires – even vacant buildings. This crew knew what it was doing and I really didn't need to remind them how to do their jobs. I guess knowing that in this situation the odds were high that the occupant was still in the apartment, I thought it best to remind everyone of the obvious. As the fresh air from the doorway fed the fire, the flames leapt out to the night sky over our heads. We kept low as the pipeman opened the nozzle and started pushing the flames back with the 125 gallons per minute of water our truck's pump provided. He kept advancing the line as he knocked down more flames, and very quickly had the bulk of the fire in the front of the apartment knocked down. As he did this, I moved to his side as we entered the fire room and started the process of the primary search. The 4th fireman on the truck humped hose for the nozzleman until he had enough line in the building, then started the primary search from the opposite side of the room.

Very quickly this firefighter yelled through his mask, "I think I've got a foot!" The pipeman shut down the nozzle, and he and I converged on the area where the muffled voice was heard. We had found the victim, and he was unconscious. I radioed the Chief, who was now on the scene, to have the rescue meet us at the front doorway. The three of us picked up the victim. Two of us picked up a leg and the pipeman grabbed the shoulders. As we neared the doorway, the light attached to the pipeman's coat shined on the face of the victim. In a startled reaction he pulled back and dropped the victim to the floor. Their faces had been less than a foot apart, and he was not ready for the shock of what he saw when the light revealed the condition of the victim. We put his legs down and I used my handlight to examine the body. There was no sense in taking the body out to the sidewalk for the neighbors to see. This person was obviously dead. He was burnt beyond recognition. His skin was completely burnt black and there were splits in the toughened skin that revealed the pink underlayers of fat and muscle. This is what we not so tactfully refer to as a crispy critter. I guess this is a fireman's attempt at dark humor.

I met the Chief and the rescue at the doorway to inform them of what we had, and to get a sheet from the rescue to cover up the deceased. We covered the victim and went back to knocking down the rest of the fire. Despite the previous reference to 'crispy critters', we try to show as much respect as possible to any remains we may encounter. We try – but sometimes things just happen.

While we were making entry to the apartment and initiating the search the first in ladder truck, Ladder 3, was raising their aerial to the roof to ventilate at the peak. This is done to allow the heat and smoke (which rises) to escape, allowing the engine company to advance more rapidly into the building, and giving any trapped victims a couple of extra minutes in which to be rescued. After they've accomplished this, their members normally come into the fire building with their tools to help pull walls and ceilings to search for hidden fire. As we went back to work knocking down the remainder of the fire we were facing the rear of the apartment. Just then, one of the firefighters from Ladder

3 came in the front door to give us a hand and walked right onto the sheet we had put over the victim. He stopped right in the middle and we heard him yell, "Tell me this isn't what I think it is!" As we spun around we caught a quick glimpse of him standing on the sheet with his plaster pole in his hand like a staff before he quickly jumped off. We told him later that he looked like Jesus trying to raise Lazarus from the dead. He didn't appreciate our attempt at humor when we made the sign of the cross on our foreheads every time we were near him for the rest of the night.

We found out later that the victim was more of a victim than we had realized. He had been shot in the face five times, stabbed in the chest twenty-seven times, and then set on fire. The murderer then stole his car. As far as I know, the case has never been solved. The police found his car a couple of days later but have never made an arrest.

After we had finished packing the hose on the truck, we all went to the Canteen Truck to get a cold drink before going back in service and heading back to quarters. As we stood around drinking, my chauffeur said in a loud voice, "OK, that's it. This is fucking ridiculous. You're now officially Lt. Gloom *and Doom!*"

Chapter 6
Kids, Kids, Kids

Kids. You gotta love 'em!

Isn't that the way it goes? Well I do love 'em. I've got three of my own, two stepkids and a grandkid. Each and every little kid is unique in his/her own way. We could learn so much from kids if we only took the time to watch them interact with each other and explore the world. Instead, we are the ones that teach them. We teach them our language. We teach them our customs, our religion, our hopes and dreams. Unfortunately we also teach them our hatreds...our prejudices. I think we've got it backwards.

In my occupation, I wish the only time I had dealings with kids were when they came to the fire station for a field trip, or I visited their school for a talk on fire safety. We post the thank you letters from the kids who visit the firehouse on the bulletin board with pride. Most of us have kids of our own, and it's like taping up their artwork on the fridge at home. As we drive our trucks down the streets of our district and pass kids on the sidewalk, most of them raise their right hand into the air and making a pulling motion like they're ringing a bell. Most adults probably don't know what I'm talking about, but if you know a kid between the ages of 3 and 16, ask him. He'll tell you. They're trying to get us to blow the airhorn. We usually try to oblige.

Any time we're dispatched to a run where a child is involved we run a little faster to the truck, we drive a little faster to the scene and we rush that child to the hospital with a little added urgency. Tragedies involving kids are always the hardest to shake off. Those are the ghosts that haunt my dreams. That being said, not all incidents involving kids are tragic.

One day, when I was riding the rescue, we got a call to respond to a home where we had a report of a boy stuck in a fence. These types on runs are fairly commonplace. A kid gets stuck in *something* and the parent is too afraid of hurting the child to free him. Usually it just takes a little brute force and a lot of patience to remedy the situation. Many times it's the panicking parents that present the biggest obstacle to firefighters on the scene. This time was a little different. As we walked up the driveway, we saw a boy of about seven or eight *on top* of a chain-link fence, with what seemed to be his whole family gathered around him. No one was screaming, or seemed too upset, so we assumed the boy had freed himself and they were going to thank us for coming, but tell us everything was all right. When we reached the top of the driveway, the rest of the family moved away and left the boy's mother holding her son, while he balanced on the top of the fence. I noticed that some of the kids in the crowd were snickering. When we asked mom what was wrong, she started to tell us, but the boy screamed at her not to tell. This went on for a minute or two before we convinced the boy that we couldn't help him if we didn't know what was wrong. He looked at his mother and shyly nodded. She slowly lifted the leg of his baggy shorts to reveal that two prongs of the top of the fence had been caught on the boy's scrotum. They had pierced through the outer skin and were caught inside his sack. The Lieutenant and I looked at each other in a pained expression, then started assessing the situation. The fence was impaled in such a way that there seemed to be no way we could extricate him without doing further damage. We decided our only option was to *cut it off*, and transport him to the hospital. That is – cut off the top of the fence. I gave mom a break, and held the boy still until a ladder company was called with bolt cutters to clip the fence. I had some chewing gum in my pocket so I gave him some. We had a bubble-blowing contest while we waited. This seemed to keep his mind off his embarrassment and pain a little. We then, carefully, transported him to the ER. The amazing thing about this was that this boy never cried or complained at all! What a brave little man.

On another occasion we were called to an accident on Interstate Rte. 95. We had a report of a multiple car pile up. When we arrived on the scene there were about six or seven cars involved in the accident, with various degrees of damage. One car was tipped over on its side. Another car had been rear-ended in such a way that the car that had hit it wedged itself under its bumper and lifted its rear end up onto the hood. The nose was pointing down toward the pavement, and the driver's door was open. The occupants had been extricated prior to our arrival, so we immediately began checking for injuries. The woman who was driving the auto that was rear-ended was hysterical and kept screaming and pointing at her car. She was speaking Spanish, so no one understood what she was trying to say. When I tried to ask her if she was hurt, she still kept pointing at her car. When I looked at the car, I noticed two things: the rear wheels were still spinning because the car was still in gear, and there was a car seat in the rear of the car. Her baby was still in the car! That's why she was so hysterical. I climbed on top of the bottom car and tried to reach the gearshift of her car. Her car was tilted away from me, so I couldn't reach the shift. I had to carefully climb into the driver's seat to shut down the car. I then climbed into the back seat to discover a three-month-old child, sound asleep. I unlatched the car seat and carried it down to the waiting mother. I never understood what she said to me as I handed her baby to her, but I know she was very grateful.

We have groups of kids come by the station, all the time, on field trips and visits. Elementary and pre-school classes, scout packs, and many neighborhood parents bring their kids in to see the trucks. We show them the firehouse, all the equipment and let them climb all over the trucks. Most kid's favorite part of the visit is seeing the fire poles. If they're small enough, we'll usually have a firefighter hold them while he slides the pole, otherwise we'll just let them watch as one of us slides it alone. It's very important to us that these kids, especially city kids, grow up trusting firemen. Too often they're taught to distrust policeman and that's a real shame. But the police have two jobs – protect people and enforce the laws. This sometimes means that a child's first experience with a police officer may be a negative one. Firefighters, on the other hand, have only one job – protect. We try to encourage positive contacts between firemen and the kids in our area at an early age.

When I started in this business, firemen could respond to violent situations without fear of being targeted by the assailants. There seemed to be an understanding that we were responding to *help* – keep hands off. In the past ten years or so, an increasing number of firemen have come under attack while trying to render assistance. This has led to a delayed response on our part, as we wait for the police to respond and secure the scene. The best way to avoid these attacks on us is to promote a positive interaction between firefighters and kids that builds their trust in us. Although most of us are uncomfortable with the 'hero' label, I believe it's very important for these kids to have someone they can turn to outside of their family circle. The more these kids understand our purpose, and the more they get to know us, the closer we'll be to gaining this trust.

I spent a Sunday afternoon in July at a birthday party for my niece about seven years ago. It was a typical family cookout with what seemed to be a hundred kids laughing and playing and eating hot dogs and hamburgers. My mom and dad and all my brothers and my sister were there. And all our kids!

It was the perfect way to spend a summer day. I could have stayed there enjoying this gathering forever, except I had to work a night shift that day. That meant I'd have to leave around 4:00 to get to the station before 5:00. You end up having to leave many parties early, or missing them altogether, when you're a fireman. This is probably the worst aspect of the job. Nights, weekends, and holidays are no different than any other day for us. Someone *always* has to be on duty.

As soon as I stepped in the doorway of the firehouse we were being dispatched to a second Alarm of fire at a small mill building in the jewelry district. I grabbed my turnout gear from my locker and raced to the truck. I met the day shift Lieutenant, took the portable radio, and we headed out the door. The first alarm companies had done a good job at containing the fire so we didn't really have a lot to do. We did have to stretch a hoseline into the building, however, and this means that we had to break down the sections of hose after we were done, drain it and repack it on the truck. This is what we consider 'social hour' during the good weather. Firefighters from different trucks helping each other repack the trucks while catching up on the latest gossip. In the cold winter months this task becomes pure hell. You can spend hours soaking wet and packing hose in sub-zero winds. Often, in these conditions, when we return to the station we're covered in ice. So much so, that when we get out of our gear we can stand our coats up on the apparatus floor and they'll remain standing on their own – just like a statue!

While we were packing our hose I heard the dispatcher at Fire Alarm (our dispatch headquarters) send a rescue and another engine company to a report of "a child shot" in our district. I radioed the dispatcher that we were clearing this incident and we were "able to respond." I knew that, because of where the other engine was coming from, that we'd get to the scene much faster. He cancelled the other company and we started racing towards the location given for the shooting. As we were pulling up to the scene the police were just arriving. Our normal operations at a reported shooting would be to 'stage' about two blocks away until the police confirmed that the area was secure. As I said earlier, when there's a child involved we 'step everything up' in our response, so we pulled right up behind them and jumped off our apparatus immediately. We observed a large group of people crowded around a five-year-old girl lying in a pool of blood on the sidewalk in front of a candy store. The scene was extremely chaotic. People were screaming, and crying, and trying to crowd around the little girl. This is one of those moments where we have no time for tact or diplomacy with the onlookers, whether they are family or not. We pushed our way to the girl and began to assess her injuries. She had a gunshot wound to the lower abdomen. A single entry wound and no exit wound. This meant that the bullet was still lodged somewhere inside her little body.

She had already lost a lot of blood and was unconscious. I radioed this information to the responding rescue as my men began to try to control the bleeding and stabilize her on the ground. If the bullet has already done damage to her spine or is lodged next to it, we need to keep her from moving and doing more damage. Also, with a gunshot wound to the abdomen, we don't know what organs may have been damaged and bleeding internally. The only chance we had of saving this precious young life was to get her to a surgeon as quickly as possible. When the rescue arrived, we quickly stabilized her on a backboard, packed her into the rescue, and 'screamed' to the Trauma Room. We're fortunate in the City of Providence to have six major hospitals within our city limits – one of which (Rhode Island Hospital) has a fully staffed Trauma Center. The proximity of this center has led to a favorable outcome for many trauma patients, who otherwise would have had a very slim chance of survival. Thankfully, this was one of those cases. When we arrived at the Trauma Room a full Trauma Team was already awaiting us. They took her from us, stabilized her and sent her directly to the Operating Room where the surgeons repaired the damage done by the bullet.

Unfortunately, the bullet was too close to her little spine to safely remove. She recovered fully and is living a normal life, thus far, but she still carries that bullet as a reminder of how close she came to being just another victim of gang violence. If the bullet moves any closer to her spine she may face more risky surgery to remove it once and for all. She's not out of the woods yet.

This 'accident' was the result of a botched drive-by shooting on a crowded city street, involving rival gangs. No one has ever been charged with this shooting. These gang members have no concept of life and death. They have no consideration for innocent bystanders. They have no conscience. They have no courage. All they have is their 'tough guy' reps. "You piss us off – we'll hit you. You hit us – we'll hit you back." They don't seem to understand very much more than this. As far as I'm concerned, it's nothing more than a complete waste of life, waste of potential. With most of these kids, their tough guy images are just that – just an image.

A perfect example of this was an incident that took place on a cold winter night in 1995. Four 16- to 18-year-old, gang members committed a home invasion in a neighboring city and threatened the occupants with a gun. When the police responded, these kids hopped back into their car and fled. The police gave chase and the resulting high-speed pursuit zigzagged its way through two additional cities before coming to an abrupt end in Providence. By this time, police from four cities were involved in the pursuit, and the news media were monitoring the situation over their police scanners. During the course of the chase these kids had evaded police roadblocks, and at one point had tried to run down a police officer. When their car was finally forced off the road in Providence, it ended up 100 feet off the street and on the front lawn of a Catholic Church. The police say that the youths wouldn't get out of the car when ordered to, and that someone in the car made a threatening motion toward the police.

The police on the scene responded with a hail of bullets toward the car. All four of the kids were hit, some more seriously than others, but none had life threatening wounds. As we were dispatched, we were told to stage around the corner from the church. When the police called us in and we turned the corner, I couldn't believe my eyes. There were more police cars than I've ever seen at one time, completely surrounding the scene. There was at least fifty cars crowded around this church, and we couldn't get our apparatus any closer than a block away. With all the twinkling lights from the strobe bars of the different police cruisers lighting up the cold dark winter night it looked absolutely surreal. It looked like the biggest Christmas light display I had ever seen.

As we walked up to the scene, the police guided us to the most seriously injured of the four kids. He had been shot four times, but none of the wounds were that serious. He was handcuffed and walking and being escorted by a policeman. We took custody of the kid and continued to walk him to the rescue truck, which had fought its way a little closer to the scene. By this time the news media was there with cameras rolling and recording every step we took. This kid looked directly into the camera, spit in its direction, and proceeded to shout something like – "watch out 'cause me and my boys'll be comin' to get ya." As soon as we put him in the back of the rescue he started screaming in pain and crying like a little kid. He literally called out for his mommy. My point is not that he cried like a little kid – hell, he was only 16 – he was a little kid. My point is that as long as there was an audience he had to maintain his 'tough guy' image.

The last thing I heard about this case was that all four kids were released from the hospital and doing fine. I don't know what they were charged with or the disposition of those cases. I do know, however, that mommy was suing the various police departments involved because her little boy shouldn't have been shot at. I wasn't there when the shootings took place so I can't personally justify the use of deadly force by police in this particular case. I can, however, personally vouch for the fact that a police officer shot by a 16-year-old kid dies just as dead as he does when shot by a 50-year-old man.

While it's true that kids have an amazing ability to bounce back – I've been to a couple of incidents involving infants falling from second or third floor windows and sustaining only scratches – they are not invincible. Young children and teenagers sometimes believe they are, however. This often leads to tragic accidents. I was working one Friday, years ago when my kids were younger, and had only about an hour to go on my shift. I was looking forward to going home, as we were planning on leaving that night on a family trip to Cape Cod for the weekend. I had arranged for someone to cover for me on my scheduled night shifts – Saturday and Sunday. It had been a while since we had been to the Cape, and the kids were really looking forward to it. They were probably more excited about the stay in a hotel room than being at Cape Cod, but I was excited by their enthusiasm.

This is when the call came for us to respond to an old shipping company for a report of a person trapped in an elevator. We get these calls all the time so this didn't seem like anything out of the ordinary. We usually find an elevator stuck between two floors – with or without people inside. If there turns out to be no one in the elevator we simply shut down the power and tell the building manager or owner to contact their elevator service company. If there is someone in the elevator we shut down the power, open the doors, shore up the elevator and assist the occupants to safety. As soon as we arrived, however, we realized that this was not an ordinary elevator emergency. The people on the scene were extremely distraught. One young girl was particularly upset. She was a 17-year-old part-time worker there, and had just come in to pick up her paycheck. She had brought her 12-year-old brother with her. It seems that while she was in the office talking to one of her co-workers, her little brother had wandered off to do some exploring. He had ridden the freight elevator down to the basement. This was an old building and an old freight elevator with no gate – just an open front. The shaft was made of old masonry stone with big fancy archways at each level. While he was in the basement exploring, someone must have pushed the call button on an upper floor. It appears that when the elevator began returning to the upper floor, the boy must have panicked about being left alone in the basement and tried to jump onto the moving car. When we were led to the basement we found him still trapped between the floor of the elevator and the top of the archway. We sent someone to shut the power and quickly freed the child using a crowbar and brute force. He had sustained a massive crushing injury to his upper torso and had no heartbeat or respiration. You could clearly see the imprint of the stone arch on his back. We began CPR and rushed him to the hospital even though we knew from the outset that this was a fruitless endeavor. This 12-year-old kid couldn't recognize the danger he was placing himself in, he merely realized that he was too afraid to remain in the basement alone.

I returned to my family a little late that night, but we left for the Cape as planned. We had a great trip – the beach, miniature golf and ice cream. The kids had a ball. I had a good time too, but my enthusiasm was tempered by thoughts of this little boy who wasn't able to go on vacation this weekend.

Sometimes I look back and realize that times like that probably caused problems in my marriage. At a time when I should have been enjoying a wonderful family experience, I was somewhat distant and detached. I know they could sense it. I'm sure this type of situation, repeated many times over the years, contributed to my wife and I drifting apart. We divorced after 22 years of marriage. I miss having the kids around every day. It saddens me to realize that I'll never be able to recapture that time. I don't, however, regret the divorce. We had become strangers to each other, and sometimes even enemies. I'll share some of the responsibility for drifting apart. I tended not to share my feelings about these things, and when I did, she seemed not to be interested. What I came to learn most from this situation is that even when you might feel all alone in this world and you feel helpless – there's always hope. I met a beautiful woman, Nancy, who is about to become my wife. We share *everything*. I don't want to repeat the mistakes of the past. She is also the best listener I have ever met, so she makes it easy for me. "Everything happens for a reason," she tells me. I believe her.

To teenagers, however, affairs of the heart seem to be a matter of life or death. Some of them don't have the ability to see the long road ahead when love ends. All they see is their world crashing down all around them. This is so sad. If they'd only give themselves the opportunity they'd realize that love would come again.

I was 'detailed' to a different company one night and was working in a station that had a reputation of being very busy. This engine company was first-in on many fires, so I was looking forward to a rocking night. As my luck would have it, on this night the truck seemed to have square wheels. We didn't move. Not until we went to bed. At about 2:00 AM we were sent to a reported shooting. When we arrived there were no police, and no one to guide us to the victim. The address given was a darkened 3-decker, on a street with no working streetlights, in a terrible section of the city. As we entered the alley between houses, a woman came from the doorway of the darkened house and told us that she heard a gunshot from the apartment on the third floor. As we followed her into the stairway it was pitch black. She said that the kids broke the lights as fast as they were replaced. When we reached the third floor doorway it was locked. We banged on the door but got no response. Just then, another woman appeared below us on the stairs. She said her 16-year-old son was the only one at home in the apartment. She started screaming that he had been threatening to commit suicide because his girlfriend had broken up with him earlier that day. She opened the door and pushed past us screaming his name. She calmed down a bit when she quickly checked the rooms and found no sign of him. We continued to check further, however, to make sure there was no problem before we left the scene.

When I checked the boy's bedroom I saw pictures of his girlfriend scattered on his bed and on the floor. I walked to the closet and opened the door. When I looked into the closet I could see a pair of skinny legs toward the back wall. I crawled in and dragged out the limp body of a good-looking young boy dressed in jeans, with no shirt. As I dragged him across the hardwood floor, a small handgun rolled from his lap. He had a single gunshot wound to his chest. He had no pulse and wasn't breathing. I immediately started chest compressions to artificially keep his heart pumping, but every time I would compress his heart, a stream of blood would shoot straight up at me from the chest wound. As I was doing this, the other fireman with me was searching the medical bag for the bag mask we use to give artificial respirations. As it happened, the previous shift had used it earlier in the day, and not replaced it. This was a major sin. This firefighter was not going to let this kid die if he could help it, so he got on his knees and started mouth-to-mouth resuscitation on him. We had to continue CPR and carry him down three flights of stairs in the dark to get him to the rescue truck. We kept this up all the way to the hospital, while we were bouncing around in the back of the rescue truck. When we transferred his care to the doctors at the hospital, we thought he still had a chance of making it. Unfortunately, the bullet had punctured his heart and they were unable to save him.

Sometimes, the good die young.

One night, just past midnight in a public housing complex, a young woman was returning home from work. She worked second shift as a nurse's aide in a nursing home. As she got out of her car and headed for her door she was attacked by a local drug addict. Apparently trying to score money to feed his habit. He threw her down to the pavement, grabbed her purse, and started kicking her, as she screamed for help. When he found only $7.00 in the purse he became enraged, pulled her up by her hair, and began beating her. She pleaded for him to stop, and continued to scream for help. Some of her neighbors called 911. One of her neighbors, a 16-year-old boy who was sitting on his couch watching TV rushed outside to her aid. He grabbed the junkie, pulled him off the battered woman, and began to beat him. The addict pulled out a knife and stabbed the young boy in the stomach. When the boy fell to the ground the junkie fled. That's when we were called.

When we arrived, we found the boy conscious but lying in a large pool of blood. The woman who was originally attacked was holding a towel over his wound, trying to stop the bleeding. The boy wasn't crying or screaming but I could tell that he was scared to death. His eyes were wide open and they looked like two white china plates gazing up at me, pleading me to tell him he was going to be alright. I did. This was the first of many lies I told this boy on this night. I bent down and grabbed his hand to take a pulse. He squeezed my hand so tight that I could feel my ring dig into my fingers. As we worked to get him onto the gurney and into the back of the rescue, he wouldn't let go of my hand. The Rescue Lieutenant told me to ride with them to the Trauma Room and keep him calm, so I climbed into the rescue, never letting go of his hand. All during the ride to the hospital this young boy just kept staring up at me and asking, "Am I going to die?" I kept on telling him, over and over, "No, you're going to be fine. We're going to get you to the hospital and the doctors are going to fix you up." Judging by the amount of blood he had already lost, and the deepness and location of the wound, I knew this probably wasn't going to be the case – but what else could I say? When we got to the hospital and wheeled him into the Trauma Room the nurses had to pry his finger open to free my hand. As I left the room I said to him, "You're going to be alright, you're going to be fine."

The next morning, as I was having coffee at the station, I got a call on the department phone. It was the Rescue Lieutenant from the night before. "Tommy," he said, "I just thought you'd want to know that the kid who was stabbed last night didn't make it." I thanked him for letting me know and hung up. I went back to my coffee and the conversation about the Patriot's chances this Sunday, but I was overcome with a sense of helplessness. Why couldn't we have done more to save him? Why him and not the junkie, who's killing himself slowly anyway? Why did this *child* go out in that parking lot, anyway? There were too many questions, but no answers. I had another question that popped into my mind – what was his name? Somehow, this seemed important this morning. It was another question to which I'd find no answer.

This is the way it is with most of our experiences. We never know very much about them as people – they're simply "the victim" or "the patient." Maybe it's best this way. We simply respond to the scene, render whatever assistance we're able, and return to our station. All business and no attachment. No emotional baggage following us home.

Sometimes, though, it's impossible to remain emotionally detached. Two rescue calls immediately come to mind in this area. One tragic and one uplifting. On occasion it is possible to crack the tough veneer of a hardened fireman.

I was working the night shift and we were having one of those rare 'good' nights – a couple of runs early in the night but nothing after midnight. I was still sleeping at about 6:00 AM when the vocalarm sounded, "Attention Rescue 4 & Engine 15 a still alarm, report of a baby not breathing." This kind of alarm tends to wake you up in a hurry. We slid the poles, jumped on the truck and were out the door in no time at all. We rushed to the scene and arrived just a moment before the rescue. When we entered the apartment we found a woman crying hysterically, "Look what they've done to my baby!!" She was pointing at her husband, who was lying face down on the living room floor. It was still dawn and there were no lights on in the house, so we were having a difficult time seeing clearly. This wouldn't have been the first time I had encountered a situation where a 300-pound man was someone's "baby," so we still weren't sure what the problem was. I bent down over the man so that I could see, and touched him to see if he was breathing. As I did, he rolled over to reveal his 6-month-old daughter lying motionless beneath him. He was sobbing uncontrollably. He hadn't been unconscious; he had been leaning over his baby trying to protect her. When I crouched closer to her I was horrified by what I saw. Her nose and part of her face had been chewed off. It was then that I noticed that there were pit bull puppies in the house. The baby was not breathing, and was obviously dead, but we just couldn't accept this outcome. I picked up the baby and handed her to the Rescue Officer who was right behind me. He rushed her to the truck and we sped her to Hasbro Children's Hospital as fast as our trucks would take us. To no avail.

We found out later, from the police investigating the death, the mom and dad had gone to bed after having a little too much to drink. When the baby cried in the middle of the night, the father got up to feed her. He placed her on the living room rug and held the bottle to her mouth as he lay next to her. He must have dozed off and rolled over onto his daughter, smothering her. When he rolled back off her, she was already dead. She must have had formula smeared over her face. The puppies must have smelled this and began to eat it up.

When I went home that morning I squeezed my five-year-old son and wouldn't let him go. When my wife asked me what was wrong I started to tell her what had happened but I broke down. I fell back into the corner of the kitchen and cried like a baby. During the course of the rest of the day she didn't ask me about this again – and I didn't volunteer any information. When I returned to work that night I asked the other guys on the truck if anyone thought they might need counseling for this incident. They all said no, they were fine. I did too. That's what we do best (or so we think) – put it behind us and move on to the next run.

On another occasion, while working a day shift, we received a call for "a baby choking." When we arrived at the scene we were led to a second floor apartment. There was a language barrier as no one in the house spoke English, but we saw a woman screaming and clutching a small child. The child was not making any sounds and had begun to turn blue. We tried to remove the baby from her arms but she kept rocking and wouldn't let him go. We pried the baby from her arms and began CPR. I radioed the responding rescue that we had a pedi code (a child with no vitals) with a possible airway obstruction, and that we'd meet them on the street. When the rescue arrived we put him in the back of the rescue and one of my guys drove their unit. As they sped to the hospital, with us following behind, the rescue men continued CPR and suctioned the toddler to remove anything blocking his airway. They were successful in removing the food that was lodged in his windpipe and the boy began spontaneous respiration. By the time we arrived at the ER he was on his way to recovering, and the doctors needed only to monitor his progress for a couple of hours before releasing him to his family. Sometimes things do have a happy ending.

When the department's EMS Chief responded to the hospital I was standing outside having a cigarette and I greeted him "Hi, Chief." He said, "Hi, Tom. Are you OK?" I hadn't realized it, but I was crying. I guess I was thankful that things had gone so well and that we had been lucky enough to save this little child. My mind was also thinking of my first little grandchild who would be born later that month. These were tears of gladness and relief. "Yeah, I'm OK, Mike. I just got something in my eye." I turned and walked back to my truck.

Chapter 7
Is this a Fire Truck or a Rescue?

In the past few years it seems that most of our runs are EMS (Emergency Medical Service) calls. The fire service has, over the past twenty years or so, had a dramatic rise in the number of medical assistance calls we receive, especially when compared to the modest rise in fire calls. During the civil unrest and urban riots of the late sixties and early seventies, it sometimes seemed that the whole city was burning down at once. My dad, who was a Providence fireman from 1955 until 1977, and a number of the old fire-eaters I met when I first joined the department, used to talk about jumping straight from one fire to another during that time period. They would sometimes go to three or four in a single night. Although I've had a few nights like this, they're not a common occurrence any more. Chances are that if I come home in the morning after being up all night, it was either because I had one 'good' fire or because I had multiple rescue runs. In my father's day, rescue calls probably accounted for about 10% of his runs. Last year I would guess that closer to 50% of my calls were EMS related.

The EMS side of the fire department has become increasingly more specialized. Paramedics, EMT's and EMT-C's (Emergency Medical Technician – Cardiac) are fairly new to the fire service – compared to the long tradition of firefighting. Prior to my joining the department, many rescue units were called "meat wagons." The firemen assigned to these trucks didn't necessarily have any specialized training. They just provided basic first aid and transported the patient to the hospital as quickly as possible – they called this "scoop & run." Although most people in Providence associate the rescue with the fire department, not everyone makes this connection. Many times we'll pull up to someone's home with the engine truck and we'll be told, "I called for a rescue, not the fire department." We have to explain that we're all part of the fire department and that the dispatcher sent us *along with* the rescue. We explain that there are more engine companies throughout the city and we'll usually get there faster. We further explain that we can begin treating the patient prior to Rescue's arrival.

Whether or not a person understands the relationship between the rescue and fire trucks, they do understand that they can call the fire department at any time, and that we'll respond quickly. They also know that we'll either lend them the assistance they need or contact someone who can. This was the case one night while I was a Firefighter assigned to Engine 8. We were a busy company with many first-in fires. One area to which we'd responded numerous times for fires was Bridgham Street. One night, after midnight, we were dispatched to a street box alarm – Bridgham & Fales. This means someone pulled the fire alarm box located at the corner of these two streets. Most times a street box is pulled, it's the result of a malicious false alarm. In some areas, however, these alarms turn out to be our first notification of a 'working' structure fire. This was one such area. When we arrived at the scene, we found a tall thin black man standing out in the cold awaiting us. He told us to hurry, that his wife was having a baby. We followed him to his apartment, which was a few houses away, and into the living room. There, we saw a woman, obviously pregnant, pacing nervously and holding her belly. She would pause every couple of minutes and quietly moan as her contractions came. The room was full of concerned family members. There had to be at least fifteen people crowded into this small room. My Captain radioed Fire Alarm to dispatch a rescue to the scene and advised them of the situation. We monitored the woman and timed her contractions until the rescue arrived. We helped her down the stairs and onto the truck. The husband thanked us and shook all our hands before climbing into the rescue with his wife. He explained that their phone had been shut off, and that he had no car. He didn't know what else to do except pull the fire alarm box to get his wife to the hospital.

The next night we were sitting at the station watching the Tonight Show when the vocalarm crackled, "Engine 8 respond to Box 3354, Brigham & Fales." As we slid the poles and climbed onto the truck, I said "I guess they sent her home last night." We were all thinking the same thing. We figured this was going to be for the same reason as the previous night. We were wrong – sort of. When we pulled up to the box, we found the same thin man from the previous night waiting again. When we asked him if he pulled the box for his wife again tonight he said, "No, no she had a baby boy last night!" We all congratulated him, and then asked, "So what's wrong tonight?" He lead us back to the same small room where we found the same people gathered around. He pointed to another woman who was obviously pregnant and said, "My sister-in-law is having a baby." From that time on, Brigham & Fales was known to us as the 'baby box.'

Not all maternity runs are as easy – or as pleasant. Years later, when I was a Lieutenant on Engine 15, we were called out in the middle of the night for a possible maternity. We pulled up in front but saw no lights on in the house. It was a large 3-decker on a corner lot. We knocked on the front door and rang all three bells but still no response. I went around the corner to the back door. I yelled in the darkened stairway, "Did someone call for a rescue?" I swear, it must be a city ordinance in Providence that rear stairways in 3-deckers cannot have working lights! It always seems to be that way.

I heard a voice from the third floor say in a foreign accent, "Baby, baby, baby!" Another of those city ordinances at work – if someone needs to be carried out in a stretcher, it has to be from the top floor. We groped our way up the stairs and were met by an old Hispanic woman and a cute little girl of about five. Neither of them spoke English, but the old lady kept saying, "Baby, baby" and led us to the bathroom. When we followed her to the door we saw a woman on the toilet. We entered the cramped bathroom and started to ask her what was wrong. She just shook her head to let us know she didn't understand and stood up. She had delivered the baby into the toilet! The toilet was full of feces and the baby was lying face down in this water. The umbilical cord was still attached to the baby and still inside the mother. She hadn't delivered the placenta yet. One of my guys pulled the baby from the toilet and followed us as I helped the mother to the kitchen. Both of us were being extremely careful not to tear the cord. There was blood everywhere. We laid the mother down, cleaned off the baby and cleared it's airway. We put the baby on the mother's belly, clamped and cut the cord and covered them both with a blanket the old lady had given us. I had sent my other firefighter out to meet the rescue and help them bring up the stretcher. By this time they were entering the apartment. We bundled the mom on the split[2] and struggled down the darkened stairs. I let the firefighter who had dug her out of toilet, Joe, carry the little baby girl. We all transported mom and baby to the hospital. As we wheeled mom into the ER, Joe followed the gurney carrying that newborn baby like a proud father.

We cleaned up a little at the hospital and returned back to the station. We stopped at a 24-hour store on the way back and I bought cigars for everyone. We stayed up for a while and smoked our cigars. We reflected on the fact that even though this run was a real ordeal, it was always worth it when the outcome was so positive. We then changed our bloodied clothes and went to bed. I think we all went to sleep that night with inflated egos, feeling like we did good!

About an hour after we had gone back to sleep I was awakened by the department phone. It was the Lieutenant of R-4. He said, "Tommy, I just wanted to let you know that the mother on our last run was HIV positive." I didn't wake the other guys. Let them enjoy their night's sleep. I'd tell them in the morning.

When I had been on the department for about two years and assigned to Engine 2, I had one of the strangest runs I've ever been on. Maybe I should say two of the strangest runs. We were having a quiet night at the station and I was playing cribbage with a fellow fireman from Engine 2, Pete. Our Lieutenant used to call us "15-2 & 15-4" referring to the counting of the cribbage points at the end of each hand. We'd spend hours playing that game. I loved it. It's funny, but since I left that station, over seventeen years ago, I don't think I've played even once. We were quite the team, Pete and I; we were the best of friends. We still are, although we don't see that much of each other these days. He tore his rotator cuff at a fire in 1989 and never returned to the department. He went through two surgeries and a year of physical therapy trying to regain his firefighting position, but the doctors couldn't clear him for fire duty.

Anyway, on this night we were playing cards when we were dispatched to a street box alarm. It was about 1:00 AM. We responded to the box location to find a man lying on someone's front lawn and covered in blood. My Lieutenant immediately called for a rescue and the police, and we got off the truck to attend to the victim. He had been stabbed in the shoulder, beaten, and he had scrapes all over his face and body. He was semi-conscious. We asked him what had happened. He told us that someone had kidnapped his girlfriend. He said that he and his girlfriend were at a bar having a few drinks and that they started talking to some guy who was sitting next to them. He said that when the bar was closing he asked the bartender to call them a cab. This stranger offered to give them a ride home, and they accepted. While on the way home the stranger pulled into a parking lot across the street from the box location. He stopped the car, pulled out a knife, and stabbed the boyfriend. He then walked around to the passenger's side, pulled the boyfriend out of the car, beat and robbed him. He threatened the girl, and told her to get into the back seat saying, "*Now* we're going to have a good time." As the car sped away, the boyfriend held on to the passenger door and was dragged about 100 feet before letting go. He said he banged on doors in the neighborhood to get help but no one would answer. That's when he saw the street box and pulled it.

We waited with him until the rescue arrived and transported him to the hospital. We then returned to our cribbage game. Eventually we went to bed and drifted to sleep. At around 4:00 AM the station bell tipped and we were sent to the same street box. This box was one that came in all the time so we didn't think this was strange. We responded sleepily. No need to wake up completely if we were only going to have to wind the box and return. We'd be back in bed in five minutes. As we approached the box we could see the figure of something on the same lawn as earlier. When we got closer we could see that it was a woman, bare-ass naked, and covered in blood. When she realized we were there she got up and ran to the truck. Pete put his fire coat around her, and my Lieutenant called for a rescue and the police – again. She said she had been banging on the doors in the neighborhood for help, but no one would answer. The people of this neighborhood were having a great night! She told us that she had been kidnapped earlier. She told much the same story as her boyfriend and said the stranger then drove her to a secluded field and repeatedly raped her at knifepoint. He then drove her back to the same parking lot and pushed her out of the door without even slowing down. She was covered with scrapes and lacerations from head to toe. As the rescue drove away transporting her to the hospital, I thought to myself that she could have easily ended up killed this night. In one sense she was lucky, but I couldn't help but feel a deep sadness in my heart for what she had been through. I had a wife and daughter at home and I'd be devastated if some animal had done to them what he did to her.

The thing about this job, however, is that you can't let these feelings linger or you'll be worthless on the next run. You have to put it out of your mind like it never happened. We went back to the station, put on a pot of coffee and started a new game of cribbage; 15-2, 15-4.

Another aspect of the job I experienced while assigned to Engine 2 was responding to motor vehicle accidents (MVA's) on the highway. This is a whole different type of run than an MVA on a city street. The potential for a greater loss of life and for greater destruction, be it vehicle or body, is in direct proportion to the greater rate of speed. This fact, along with the potential for chain reaction pile-ups, makes the highway a unique response area for a firefighter.

One night, as we were having a little going-away party for a member of the station who was being transferred, we received a call for an MVA on Rte. 95 North. We left the station, with the rescue following behind us, and headed for the highway. It was about 10:00 on a Thursday night so we knew there wasn't usually much traffic on the highway at this time. The weather was clear and dry so there was no reason to suspect a multi-car pile-up. These are usually the result of poor visibility or wet roads. It was also too early for the bar crowds to be drunkenly weaving their way home from their favorite watering hole. That was our usual 1:00 to 2:00 AM crowd – sometime after 'last call.' These are some of the things that go through our minds as we roll to an accident. We try to prepare ourselves for what we are about to face. The more information we can gather concerning this particular run, whether from visual inspection of the scene or from prior experience, the more effective our response will be. We can get an idea of where we may want to park the apparatus, how to approach the scene, or what type of injuries we might expect. Knowing these factors prior to 'blindly' pulling up to the accident could save time, effort, and even lives.

As we approached the scene, we could see a surprisingly large crowd of people gathered around a large truck that was parked in the breakdown lane. The flatbed trailer attached to the rear of the truck was carrying a large backhoe. There was a new minivan crumpled around the left rear corner of the trailer. When we rolled to a stop behind the scene of the accident, an off-duty Providence firefighter approached my Lieutenant's door. "Joe," he said, "you better call for Special Hazards because you're going to need the 'Jaws' on this one." Our "Special Hazards" truck is a heavy rescue vehicle similar to those used by FDNY. It is equipped with many different types of specialized equipment for use in just about any unusual situation we may encounter. The 'Jaws of Life' is one such piece of equipment. This is used to cut or pry open a vehicle so that we may extricate the victim without further complicating his injuries.

When we walked up to the vehicle, we could see that the entire front passenger area of the minivan was wrapped around the corner of the truck. We could also see that there was only one victim – the driver. He was completely pinned in the van and wasn't moving. We couldn't reach him from the outside of the vehicle and we couldn't tell the extent of his injuries – although we could safely assume that they were pretty severe. We had to get someone inside to reach him. We cleared the remainder of glass from the already broken rear window and I climbed into the rear compartment. I carefully squeezed my way into the back seat (I was much thinner then). When I reached the front, I found that the victim still had a pulse. I relayed this information to my Lieutenant, then held the man's head straight (applying traction) to avoid any further possible spinal or cervical damage. In a major trauma such as this, once you ascertain the victim is alive and breathing on his own, the next step is to guard against any possible spinal damage. This is done by immobilizing the victim *and* maintaining constant immobilization until he is transported to the Trauma Center. It takes two people to properly apply a cervical collar to stabilize the victim's neck – one to maintain traction by holding his head straight, and one to apply the collar. As no one else could reach this man, I needed to remain here and maintain traction until the extrication of the victim. This process took about forty-five minutes. It was a warm summer night and I had been wearing my heavy fire coat when I entered the van. When the extrication was completed, and someone was able to apply a collar, I was drenched in sweat.

We transported the man to the Trauma Center and although his injuries were severe, he did survive. It turned out that this man had just left a bar and was intoxicated. The driver of the truck had pulled over to the breakdown lane to check a noise from the rear of the trailer. While standing in the back of the truck, he noticed a van swerving "all over the road" as it approached him on the highway. He had to jump out of the way to avoid being struck. The driver of the van probably avoided being killed because he didn't even realize he was going to strike the truck. We've noticed that many intoxicated victims have surprisingly minor injuries, compared to what we might expect when surveying the damage on the vehicle. We believe it is because the victim is not aware of what is about to happen and is completely relaxed, therefore more flexible, at the time of impact. There's an old saying that goes, "God watches over the children and the drunks." I believe this.

I wish the same could be said of motorcyclists. They don't have the protection of a vehicle surrounding them while they're on the road. This makes them particularly vulnerable to serious injuries when they're involved in MVA's. I hate going on calls that involve motorcycles. When I hear a motorcycle roar by the station, I'll often mutter under my breath, "Just make it to Engine 14's district before you lose control." I know this sounds horrible, but if I never go to another motorcycle accident in my career I'll be very happy. I cringe when the dispatcher says "…a report of a motorcycle accident." Sometimes it's nothing more than a person with scrapes and bruises; but there's just too much potential for serious, life-threatening injuries to the rider. Especially on the highway.

From the window of the sitting room in Engine 2's firehouse we could look out and see Rte. 95. This always gave us a chance to check the traffic before heading home. If it was backed up with bumper-to-bumper traffic, we could take an alternate route and avoid the highway altogether. It could also give us an indication that there was an accident on the highway, and that we would be dispatched soon. Such was the case one warm day in early March. It had been a terrible winter, with snow right through February, so people had begun to get "spring fever" during a recent warm spell. I looked out the window and saw the traffic backed up on 95 South. I began to say, "I think we're going…" But before I could finish my sentence, the station bell tipped and the dispatcher said, "Attention Rescue 3, Engine 2 and Engine 3 a still alarm." He was sending us to a report of a motorcycle accident on the highway. We were out the door in less than a minute, with the rescue right behind us – 'riding our taillights.' We had to fight our way through the traffic to reach the scene of the accident. It never seems to fail that when traffic backs up, people start using the breakdown lane. They don't seem to realize that this lane is for cars that "break down" – and for use by emergency vehicles. My guess is that these people are the same ones who bitch and moan about how long it took us to get there when they're the one's waiting for the rescue. But don't let me get started on that!

As we rounded a slight curve in the highway we came upon a large tractor-trailer in the middle of the roadway. It was stopped and people were gathered around. A motorcycle lay on its side about 50 feet in front and to the left of the 18-wheeler. When we got off our truck, people frantically motioned for us to come to the trailer. We hurried over to the area and saw a man lying on his back, in a pool of blood, directly under the trailer. The man was conscious, but obviously in a lot of pain. There was a woman squatting over him and holding a blood-soaked white towel over his belly. She told us that she was an ER nurse and that the victim had a massive hole in his abdomen, and that we needed to get him to the hospital *right away*. She was shaking so much the towel was moving. I thanked her and took over the direct pressure she had been applying. When the Lieutenant from R-3, Bob, arrived a moment later, he pulled the towel back to examine the wound. I was shocked to see that his internal organs were exposed. He had a hole in his belly the size of a watermelon! I could clearly see the underside of his heart as it continued to beat. We returned the towel and wet it down with saline to keep the area as clean as possible. I have to say that this biker was one tough old bastard! He was conscious the whole time we worked on him, but never once screamed out or complained. We were concerned about him going into shock, so we worked as quickly as possible to stabilize and transport him to the hospital. He was still talking to us as we rolled him into the ER. The doctors prepped him and sent him up to surgery. I understand that he lived to ride again.

We found out later that there had been a small fender bender about a quarter-mile ahead of the tractor-trailer. This is what had originally halted the traffic. Prior to taking the curve on the highway, the motorcyclist had no idea that there was a backup ahead. In the middle of the curve he saw the traffic, and he tried to come to a quick stop. Sand on the highway, still there from the last snowstorm, sent his bike on its side and into a skid. He slid under the trailer and was impaled on one of the metal legs of the truck, as the bike continued on. He was lucky to survive!

Another motorcycle rider I worked on was not so lucky. I was working on Engine 8 a few years later and we were sent to Rte. 10 for a report of "a man down." This type of call on the highway is usually the result of a person being struck by an auto. We were heading northbound, and as we approached the location we saw that there was a commotion on the southbound on-ramp, just opposite us. We exited the highway and started down the on-ramp toward the crowd. There was a young man in his twenties lying face down in a large pool of blood, which was flowing down the grade of the asphalt toward the road below. A crowd had gathered, and a couple of people were tending to him. There was another highway that ran parallel to this ramp, about thirty feet above our level. A large concrete wall separated the two roadways. I noticed, as I exited the cab, that there were people watching from the expressway above – hanging over the guardrail. I thought this odd but turned my focus to the victim.

We still believed that this was a case of a person being struck by an auto. That is, until the people tending this man moved aside for us, and we saw that he was wearing a motorcycle helmet. I should say - half of one. It was then that we were told that the victim was riding his motorcycle on the ramp above. A man driving a van cut through two lanes of traffic when he thought he had missed his exit. He struck the cyclist and pushed the bike into the guardrail, throwing the rider to the pavement thirty feet below.

He had massive head trauma and multiple broken bones. This is what we could see on initial assessment. He probably had serious internal injuries as well. He had no chance. However, we found he did have a weak pulse and slight respirations upon this same initial assessment. We don't have the authority to pronounce someone dead. We also don't have the authority to decide that someone is better off dead. We were bound by protocols set by the State to treat and transport this patient to a hospital. We stabilized him the best we could and assisted his breathing by using a bag mask connected to oxygen. It was difficult to 'seal' the mask to his face due to the severe trauma, but we did our best. When we arrived at the ER the doctor saw the condition of the patient and asked us, "Why the hell did you transport him? He's gone."

I have the utmost respect for doctors, especially those who work in the ER. It's a tough job with long hours and not much money (for a doctor). They're usually overworked and under-appreciated. They can also be awfully fucking arrogant at times to Rescue personnel. They bitch about protocols not being followed. They bitch, as in the case above, about protocols being followed. The fact is that they have no idea what it's like to work on a patient in the street. Treating a patient at a chaotic scene or in a moving Rescue is much different that treating the same patient in a well lit, sterile trauma room.

A couple of years ago Engine 15 was dispatched (along with Special Hazards, Ladder 6, Rescue 4 and Battalion 3) to "…an elderly man who has fallen from a second floor window." We climbed onto the truck and waited for the location. When the address was given over the vocalarm we realized it was our 'local hospital.' While enroute, Fire Alarm directed us to enter via the ER. This seemed strange to us – if the patient were already there, why would they need us? We responded as directed, however, and entered the ER through the ambulance door. There didn't seem to be any doctors around, and that seemed a little unusual. The nurses frantically directed us down a hallway to the Communications Room. This is a small windowless room of about 15' by 15' with two switchboard operators behind large desks. This is also the room that houses the hospital's main Fire Alarm Panel, so I was very familiar with this area. The operators pointed to a door in the right-rear corner of the room. The door led to a tiny bathroom with just enough room for a toilet and a small sink – and a window.

When I entered the bathroom and looked out the open window I saw three ER doctors working on an elderly man who was lying on the ground. They were standing in an enclosed dark alley that was about 6' wide by 15' long. They had put the man on a backboard[3] and had applied a cervical collar. When I informed them that we were here, they started to lift the board and said, "Good, help us get him out of here." I said, "Whoa doc! You know that *protocol* calls for him to be 'packed' before we can move him. Put him down and get the hell out of there! We'll bring him to you." We helped *them* out of the alley then climbed in to 'pack' the victim.

Packing is the process of strapping a patient securely to a backboard, and 'packing' either small sandbags or specialized foam inserts around the victims head and neck. This prevents any movement of the spine or neck during the transport of the victim. Protocol requires that we do this prior to moving the patient in *all* suspected spinal or cervical injuries. In this case, however, it was essential that we do this because we would have to stand the backboard up when we slid him through the window, in order to make the 90-degree turn to the bathroom door. As we slid the man into the window, Ladder 6 and Special Hazards stood him up, turned him around, and carried him out the door. Before I climbed back into the bathroom, I looked up to see a ripped screen in a second floor window just above the alley. How, I wondered, had this elderly gentleman fallen through that window?

As we left the hospital through the ER, we passed the Triage Desk where two of these doctors were talking. They never even looked our way.

The prize for the strangest rescue run I've been on, I believe, would have to go to the old Japanese woman who tried to commit hari-kari. We didn't know this when we first arrived on the scene however. We had to piece it together as we gained more information. Many times this is the case. We respond to find someone injured, treat and transport, and never know how the person sustained the injury.

In this case, we responded to a report of "a woman unconscious." When we pulled up to the house we were met by an attractive young Japanese girl in her late teens. She said she'd been knocking on her grandmother's door for the last ten minutes and had gotten no response. She told us she was sure her grandmother was home, and told us she heard her yelling about a half-hour ago. The old woman lived on the first floor of a two-family house. We tried the front door but it was locked, so we went around to the back stairway. This door was locked also, but as we tried to 'jimmy' the lock we heard groaning from inside the apartment. I kicked in the door and we found a little old lady lying on the floor, in the middle of the kitchen. There was blood everywhere, and small amounts of brain matter mixed with the blood on the floor.

I radioed for Fire Alarm to send the police.

The most obvious wound was a deep gash toward the back of the woman's head. There was no way to move in the kitchen and avoid the blood. By this time, the rescue was with us and we knelt around the woman and started to treat her wounds. We saw a large bloodstained meat cleaver lying on the floor next to the woman. We had to move it out of the way to keep from kneeling on it. While rescue was bandaging her head wound, someone said, "Did anyone check the apartment to see if the assailant is still here?" No one had. I radioed for the police to step it up and started to check the other rooms with one of my firefighters. The police showed up a minute later. As they searched the rest of the apartment, we returned to the kitchen. When we rolled her over, we could see that she also had multiple stab wounds to her abdomen. We bandaged these too, packed her up, and transported her to the Trauma Center.

On the way back from the hospital we returned to the house to pick up some equipment we had left behind. By this time the police had searched the crime scene and interviewed the granddaughter and the victim's husband, who had returned home from work. It seems that the woman had a history of depression and had attempted suicide on numerous occasions in the past. She was supposed to be on medication for this, but the police had found her prescription bottle and suspected that she had stopped taking them a week or two ago. The police also found a pair of long scissors taped to the stove. It appears that the abdominal wounds were the result of her trying to impale herself on them. As unbelievable as it seemed, apparently the wound in her head was self-inflicted with the meat cleaver.

When I joined this department 23 years ago I had no idea that I was going to be spending so much time on medical calls. I hated rescue runs. They're still my least favorite part of the job, but I've gradually gotten used to them. The best part of these calls is in knowing that you've helped someone. To take someone from death's doorstep, stabilize him, and get him to a hospital where he can be saved is a *great* feeling! The doctors and nurses are the ones who *save* people. It's our job to give them the opportunity.

Still, after a long night of EMS runs every hour on the hour, you can sometimes hear me radio Fire Alarm as we try to sneak into the station, "*Rescue* 15, in quarters and off the air."

Chapter 8
Hayward Street

One of the things that's never ceased to amaze me is the depth of the brutality that one human being can show to another. Just when you think you've seen the worst that man has to offer, someone steps up and shows you that you're mistaken. People who commit a crime at the spur of the moment, in a fit of passion are not the worst that society has to offer. Not in my opinion. Neither are people who are mentally incapable of knowing right from wrong. As horrible as their crimes may be, they have no understanding of what devastating effects their actions will bring. Likewise, people who set in motion a chain of events that results in more destruction than they could have reasonably foreseen don't belong on this list either.

Take an equal measure of hatred, anger, indifference, and selfishness. Toss them into a bowl and mix thoroughly. Pack tightly in a paper made of hopelessness, poverty, and lack of opportunity. Light fuse. Stand back. This is my recipe for the worst mankind has to offer.

Murdering someone in cold-blooded, premeditated revenge, without a thought of the innocent people being harmed is a perfect example of the worst that man has to offer.

We had just such an act in Providence when I first made Lieutenant.

Things started out as a pretty average Friday night. It was the beginning of the last weekend in February and it was cold and damp outside. I was assigned to Ladder 7 as a new Lieutenant. I had been sworn in to my new rank just five days earlier, and I was looking forward to a nice honeymoon period to get my feet wet at commanding a fire company. I had two things working in my favor toward accomplishing this. One, I had been stationed at this firehouse for six years when I first came on the job, on Engine 2, so at least I knew the district. This makes things much easier than being in a strange area – there's one less thing to worry about. Two, Ladder 7 was not a busy company. We didn't usually do much fire duty. I knew that I'd eventually want to get back to the 'action', but for right now I was content with breaking in slowly.

It had snowed earlier in the day. Just a dusting, but it left the air with that chill that New Englander's know so well. The chill that makes you believe winter is never going to end. The chill that makes you want to take up residence in Florida…at least during the winter! This was a good night to be on Ladder 7. Chances were that we wouldn't turn a wheel. We had gone on only one run during both of my day shifts, so staying in tonight was a good possibility. We had finished our meal early and had settled in to watch some of the Stanley Cup playoffs. At about 10:00 PM we heard the dispatcher at Fire Alarm send a rescue and an engine company to Hayward Street for a report of "a hit and run, pedestrian struck." We didn't give it much notice at first. This was a common type of call. It was also on the other side of the city. My interest was tweaked, however, when Engine 10 arrived on the scene and radioed for the rescue to "step it up." This signals the rescue, and everyone else monitoring the radio, that the victim has serious injuries and needs medical assistance right away. It turned out that the victim was standing in front of his house when a car coming down the street crashed into his parked vehicle. When the victim started yelling at the driver and running toward the accident, the driver turned the car toward him, and ran him down. The victim was dragged over 400 feet before being freed from the car. His buttocks had been scraped off, almost completely, right down to the bone. He also had a severe head injury.

Rescue 1 and Engine 10 worked as quickly as possible to pack the victim and transport him to the Trauma Center at Rhode Island Hospital. This was no easy task, however, as the victim was in severe pain. Normally, in the case of a possible spinal injury, the victim would be put on a backboard face up. In this case they had to secure him to the board on his side. Doing it this way makes it more difficult to secure him to the board in order to keep him immobilized. We didn't know the extent of his injuries at that time. The next transmission we heard after the 'step it up' was when they were transporting the patient to the hospital. The whole incident was over in the span of about twenty minutes. A couple of firefighters at my station who didn't know where Hayward Street was, had gotten up and looked it up on the map when the incident started. Although the street was on the other side of the city, and we wouldn't be responding, a good fireman will often take an opportunity like this to learn the location for future use. All of our stations have a large street map of the city on the wall for just such a purpose. When we look at the map, and find the location, we are better able to see the area in our heads. We can picture the types of buildings in the neighborhood and spot the main streets nearest the location. We also mentally drive to the location, planning the best route from our firehouse. I had just been transferred to this station when I was promoted, and Hayward Street was in my old district. I knew where the street was and how to get to it, but it was good feeling to see my guys get up and go to that map. It meant they were interested in learning. I hadn't worked with these guys for long and we hadn't been 'tested' together yet, but this was a good sign. Before the night was over, we would be tested. And they'd pass this test – with flying colors!

We settled back into the hockey game on TV, the hit and run no more than a small distraction. When the game ended, some of the guys drifted into the dormitory to go to sleep while the rest of us switched the TV to David Letterman. I watched the monologue and decided to turn in. By the time I had settled into my room and slipped into bed, it was just about midnight. I always sleep with my radio on. I like to listen to the activity around the city. It also gives me a heads up if something is going on around my district to which we might be called on to respond. If you hear the call, you can get yourself prepared – grab a new battery for the portable radio, look up the street, go to the bathroom, or whatever else you might need to do before responding. Once the bell tips, it's too late to do any of these things. You're sliding the pole and getting on the truck immediately. Firemen learn early on in their careers never to put off nature's calls. There's no time when the bell tips, and you never know how long you'll be tied up. If you gotta go – go!

About ten minutes after I slid under those nice warm covers I heard the call go out, "Attention Engines 10, 3, 8; Specials Hazards; Ladders 5 & 1; Rescue 1; and Division 1, a Still Box." Fire Alarm sent them to a report of a building fire at 54 Hayward Street. The dispatcher added that they'd received numerous calls on this and that they had a report of people trapped on the third floor. The way this was sent out I knew this was going to be a working fire. As for the report of people being trapped, you never know until you search the building. Many times, we work through an entire fire still searching for occupants who are "definitely in there," only to have this person show up at the scene after the fire is out.

I got up from bed quickly. I knew that there was a good possibility that we were going to be moving – not to the fire, but to another station. Engine 2 and Ladder 7 were the "relocation companies" for that side of the city. This meant that whenever there was a major fire in that area, that was going to tie up a lot of companies for an extended period, Fire Alarm would send us to cover one of their stations. This certainly sounded to me to be shaping up as a major fire! I got dressed and started for the sitting room to tell the guys who were awake what was going on – to give them the heads up. Too late. Before I reached the sitting room, Fire Alarm tipped the bell and told us to relocate to the Broad Street Station. Sending us before the first companies were even on the scene is unusual, I thought, they must have received numerous calls. When a company is sent to 'relocate,' it does so as quickly as possible, so as not to leave the district to which they're responding uncovered any longer than necessary. There is another reason for rushing toward the district to which you're relocating – if the companies on the scene call for more help and you're close to the area, Fire Alarm will send you. If you're still closer to your own station, they'll send someone else – someone closer to the fire. There's nothing most firefighters hate more than to 'baby-sit' someone else's station when there's a big fire going on a short distance away! We were already out the door and rolling toward Broad Street when Engine 10 reported, "Code Red, three-story wood, occupied, fully involved." I told the chauffeur to head to the highway. This was the quickest way to the station, and it would take us right by the fire scene.

Engine 10's Lieutenant reported that there was a man down on the street, in front of the building with multiple injuries, who had jumped from the third floor. He requested Rescue 1 to respond to the front of the building immediately upon their arrival with their gurney. He also radioed that he had a report from this victim that there was still six people trapped on the third floor. We were getting on the highway heading in that direction. Fire Alarm relayed E-10's report to Rescue 1 and Division 1. We were a little closer now and could see a large glow in the sky in the direction of the fire. We were still quite a distance away, however. Engine 3 jumped in on the radio to report they had a frozen hydrant and would have to grab another one. Fire Alarm relayed this to Division 1. We were closer still; we could now plainly see the flames rising above the rooftops of the buildings in our line of sight. Division 1 radioed Fire Alarm that he had received Engine 3's message and added, "Give me a second Alarm!" We were almost at the exit we needed to take to get to the scene so I radioed Fire Alarm, "Ladder 7 and Engine 2 are approaching the Atwells Ave. exit." "Roger Ladder 7. Engine 2 and Ladder 7 head for 54 Hayward Street." We headed for the fire.

When the victim of the hit and run was transported to the hospital earlier in the night, his family members weren't sure if he was going to survive or not. They only knew that he was seriously injured and being brought to surgery. They kept a vigil at the hospital. One of his cousins had witnessed what had happened and rushed to the hospital. He found that no one had any news on his cousin, but he knew that the driver of the vehicle that had run him down had left 54 Hayward Street just prior to the incident. He left the hospital and picked up a friend. They drove past the house and began planning their revenge. They were going to burn the house down while he slept. Apparently they didn't give a thought to the other people who would also be sleeping. This was a large, three-family house and all three apartments were obviously occupied. If they had cared to look they would have seen lights on all three floors. It would have made no difference.

They got a five-gallon gas can from someone and took it to a service station a few blocks away. One of them filled the can with gasoline and the other asked the clerk for a couple of books of matches. They returned to the scene and took the front stairs to the third floor landing. At this point it was obvious to them that all three floors were occupied. It was also obvious to them that there were children in the house as there were toys in the hallway. This would not deter them. They were here for one reason – revenge. They weren't going to let a little thing like killing some innocent kids stop them. They began spreading the gasoline on the landing and worked their way down the three flights of stairs. When they reached the outside door on the street level they lit a match and tossed it into the hallway. *Sssswwwooooooooooooosshhhh!!!!!!*

The flames must have shot up that stairway like a cannon shot! Instantaneously the whole front of the house was ablaze. Right from the start there was absolutely no way to escape from the front of the building. It sounded like an explosion, and the noise awakened most of the occupants in the house. They only had a few seconds before their apartments were filling with smoke from front to back. This told them that they would have to escape through the rear hallway. Two brothers in their thirties lived on the first floor. One of them was paralyzed and unable to walk – his brother carried him to safety. On the second floor a 46-year-old woman lived with a 14-year-old daughter, a 12-year-old son, and a 5-year-old nephew. She said later that she had heard a loud crash and the banging of feet from the upstairs apartment and assumed there was a disturbance going on. She was going to call the police, but when she went to the front of her apartment to get her phone she saw that the house was on fire, and the entire front of her apartment was filled with dark smoke. She woke up the kids and quickly got them out through the back door. A family of seven lived on the third floor. A 41-year-old father, 40-year-old mother, and four kids 18, 16, 13 and 6 years old. The father's 37-year-old brother was also living with the family.

When the fire broke out, the 6-year-old girl was asleep in her bedroom at the rear of the apartment. The rest of the family was in the front living room assembling costume jewelry to make some extra money. When they heard the loud noise from the front stairway, the 16-year-old son opened the front door. Flames, heat and smoke immediately rushed into the apartment. There was no way to get close enough to shut the door. The family stumbled toward the back door, with the heat and thick black smoke following them. The flames were moving quickly toward the back also. The door was locked! A deadbolt was in place and the only way to open it was with the key. With the smoke in the apartment they were unable to locate the key! As the uncle groped around the apartment he lost track of the rest of the family. The heat was intense and he couldn't breath or see. He happened to find himself at a front window and knew that he was going to die. He forced the window open and in a last attempt to save himself, dove out the window to the street, three floors below. He broke his leg on impact and began to scream in pain. He also started yelling that the family was still in the apartment. He screamed this to the Lieutenant of Engine 10 when they pulled up on the scene.

Engine 10 took a 2 ½" hoseline to the front door and tried to knock down the fire in the stairway to gain entry. (A 2 ½" line is a larger diameter hose than the normal 1 ¾" attack line used at most fires. The larger hose supplies more water, which is needed for larger fires.) They tried to push back the flames but the fire was too intense, they couldn't make any progress. They poured the water onto the fire and darkened down the flames, but the fire greedily retook the area it had just given up. If they advanced at all, it was inch-by-inch, not foot-by-foot. Their focus was the third floor. They had no way of knowing that the front door of the apartment was opened and that the fire had already found its way in. They had no way of knowing that it was already too late. They knew in their hearts that it was probably a futile effort, but these guys were not the type to quit unless the situation was 100% hopeless. Meanwhile, Ladder 5 had positioned their apparatus to the left of the building and quickly extended their aerial toward the third floor windows. These guys, too, had but one thing on their minds – rescue. They used the tip of the aerial to knock out a couple of the windows and almost immediately had two of their members ascend the ladder in hopes of being able to sneak in the window and search for victims. They, too, knew it was almost assuredly hopeless already. They were fighting the flames licking out of the windows, and the furnace-like heat! They never backed down, however, and finally were joined by an engine company with a hoseline snaked up the aerial. They were hoping against hope to push back the flames enough to make a quick entry to the apartment. They were hoping against hope that someone had found some kind of shelter inside this inferno and was still clinging to life. That's the nature of a firefighter: we don't give ourselves the opportunity to step back and analyze the situation to realize that it has become a hopeless situation. Our minds may know already, but in our hearts, we cling to the smallest possibility that we might be able to change the terrible outcome. These guys continued to push, and in the process the tip of their aerial was exposed to too much heat and began to bend. The intense heat also scorched some of their turnout gear.

While this was going on in the front and side of the building, Engine 8 had taken a hoseline to the rear stairway to secure this means of egress. They encountered smoke and heat, but no fire as they made their way to the third floor. They stopped at each level and did a quick search of each apartment on the way. They had to be sure they weren't passing a savable human life, but their focus was on getting to the third floor where reports of a family trapped had echoed over the radio. The first and second floor apartments were clear but the flames were already beginning to advance toward the rear stairway. They closed the door behind them as they re-entered the stairway to keep the smoke and fire from chasing them up the stairs. When they reached the top of the stairs, they found the landing choked with debris and garbage. They had to pull the clutter off the landing, item by item, and toss it behind them, in order to clear a large enough path to crawl over the mess and reach the door. They too found the door locked, and the Captain could *hear* the intensity of the fire just on the other side of the door. No sound of any voices or screaming, just the hissing and popping of the fire. No one could possibly be alive on the other side of that door! Their turnouts were beginning to steam! They tried to cool the area with their hoseline but the water turned to steam as quickly as it left the nozzle. They had to back down!

As this was unfolding, Engine 3 had successfully hooked up to another hydrant and supplied 'feeders' to Engine 10's pump operator. Feeders are a pair of large (3") diameter hoselines connected from the hydrant to the engine company's pump. The engine company takes in the water, diverts it to its pump, boosts the pressure, and sends it to the firefighters fighting the fire, through their smaller diameter hoselines. The simple fact is that the engine company 'pumping' at the fire can't supply more water than it's taking in. With the size of this fire and the number of lines it was pumping to, Engine 10 would need additional feeders. That also meant locating another hydrant, as Engine 3 had also laid feeders to their own truck from the original hydrant to supply their handline and Ladder 1's 'ladder pipe.' A ladder pipe is a large nozzle attached to the aerial or bucket of a Ladder truck, which is capable of putting out large volumes of water to attack the fire from the exterior. When I reported to Division 1 upon our arrival at the scene, he assigned me another company and told me, "Get Engine 10 some more water!"

We found a hydrant that was not being used around the corner on Broad Street about 400 feet behind Engine 10. I told one of the guys to go and 'dress' the hydrant.[4] The rest of the guys 'humped' (dragged) the 3" hose from Engine 10's hose bed, 400 feet down the street to the hydrant. When they reached the hydrant I 'broke down' the hose at the truck and helped the pump operator connect the lines to his intake valve.[5] By splitting up the tasks, we had water flowing to Engine 10's pump amazingly fast. While the others returned from the hydrant, I checked the lines for 'kinks' or leaks. Kinks are folds in the line that can restrict the flow of water. There were none, but what I did notice was that the 'charged' (full of water) hoselines were too close to the fire building. This house was "fully" involved. There was fire throughout the entire building – all three floors *and* the basement. The intensity of the fire was threatening the structural integrity of the building and the feeders were in the 'collapse zone' in front of the structure. The 'collapse zone' is the area, on all sides of the building, which could be buried in the event of a catastrophic collapse. The feeders, if left in place, could be jeopardized. They could be buried under the rubble, cutting off the water supply at a crucial time in the operations. I told the guys who were returning from the hydrant to grab the feeders and help me move them to the middle of the street and out of the collapse zone.

While we were doing this I noticed that there were blue flames licking along the ceiling of the basement. This meant that natural gas was leaking from one of the pipes inside the cellar. We needed to shut this down immediately. I informed the Chief of this fact and he told me that the gas company and the electric company had already been summoned to shut down the utilities from the street. He then assigned me to meet the gas company representative and assist him in securing the shutoff. When he arrived on the scene I informed him of the situation and told him that we'd assist him in any way possible. He informed me that the remote shutoff was on the sidewalk right in front of the fire and that, "I'll be damned if I'm going that close to that fucking building!" The flames were shooting above our heads and into the street from the first floor windows. I, along with another firefighter began to search for the small metal lid on the ground that would indicate the gas line remote shutoff. We had to search through the dusting of snow on the ground and some overgrown grass along the sidewalk. I found the lid amid the grass, turned to the gas company man and said, "Here it is! Now get the fuck over here and shut this down!" He warily approached and attempted shutting off the gas as the other firefighter and I stood next to him. The lid on the sidewalk lifts to reveal a pipe about 2" in diameter which goes straight down approximately 8 feet to the gas line entering the building. The gas company has poles with a special attachment on the tip that grasps a shutoff valve on the line that allows them to stop the flow of gas into the building. There was a problem, however. Someone, a vandal or a kid playing, had pried open the lid at some time and dropped a bunch of rocks into the pipe. This prevented the man from the gas company from being able to terminate the gas in this manner. He told us he couldn't help us and retreated to his truck about a block away.

We still needed to try to shut the gas off because the gas lines throughout the building were beginning to fail – especially in the basement. More and more the blue flames were evident. Another firefighter who had seen what was going on, Tim, came up to me and said, "Loo, the gas meters are right inside that window," pointing in the direction of the window directly in line with the remote shutoff, "I think I can reach in and shut the gas off at the meter." I had witnessed and been aware of many courageous acts this night already, but none any more so than what this fireman was proposing! I looked at the window and saw that there were no flames coming from it right at this moment. It was also evident by the charring around the frame that there had been flames present earlier. I moved to window, crouched down and examined the gas meters. There were three of them lined up side by side just inside the exterior wall. The first two would be reachable from here, but the third one was uncertain. Flames continued to roll across the ceiling of the basement impinging on the gas lines that were exposed, continuing to leak blue flame. I said, "OK, let's do it!" I grabbed the other firefighter, Scott, who was helping me with the man from the gas company, and told him that I wanted him to grab Tim from the opposite side and that we'd both hold him as he leaned into the basement. We proceeded to get a good grip on him, at which time I told Tim, "Go ahead, and be careful!" He leaned in and shut the first meter off easily. He then stretched as far as he could while we held his coat and just managed to shut off the second meter. He wasn't going to be able to reach the third one, I thought. We pulled him back and tried to figure out how to reach it. I checked the status of the flames in the basement. They were still staying far enough away from the window to give us room to work, and still leaking blue. Scott and I were almost overcome with the smoke and the heat coming from that window, however, and I had to wonder how Tim was holding out. I asked him, and he said, "I'm OK, Loo. I think I can reach that last one if you and Scott hold my legs." I agreed, but told him that if he felt himself going too far to stop, because if he fell into the basement we'd never be able to get him out alive. "Don't worry about that," he said, "I'm not going to slip, and you guys aren't going to drop me, right?" I just laughed. He lay down on his stomach and crawled through the opening. He tried to pull himself along, as well as balance himself, by pulling on the pipes along the wall. As he disappeared further into the smoke, Scott and I lay across his legs and leaned into the window to hold him by his waist. When he had successfully shut down the last meter, we pulled him out onto the sidewalk. As the three of us were lying on the ground catching our breath, I slapped him on the shoulder, "Great fucking job!" I said.

We got up and got the hell away from the collapse zone. I notified the Chief that the gas had been terminated. "Good," he said. I don't think he ever found out how we did it. I know that I didn't tell him that night. There was still too much going on and too much to do to waste time talking about how things were done. Firefighters are bottom line kind of people. He assigned me the job of getting the gas shut off. It was off. That was the bottom line. He then assigned us another job.

At about this same time, while Engine 8, Engine 10 and Ladder 5 were trying to gain entry to the apartment, the roof collapsed into the third floor. This effectively ended the 'rescue' portion of the operation. There was no way to get them out now, and we all had to face this fact. This also confirmed that there was sufficient structural damage to the building to cause it to collapse at any time. We were forced to back out, gather outside the collapse zone, and begin a defensive attack. This means pouring large amounts of water on the fire from a safe distance until the fire is knocked down enough to safely re-enter the house.

When the fire was put out and the 'hot spots' were wet down, it was time to begin body recovery. The Chief looked for volunteers. I volunteered my company because I felt we hadn't taken as much of a beating as the guys from the first Alarm companies. The Chief was about to agree when the officers of those companies spoke up and said they *had to* see for themselves where the victims were located. They *had to know* how close they were. The Chief understood. He allowed them to enter the apartment and search for the victims and he let the second and third Alarm companies go. We helped pack up as much hose as we could – that which wasn't still being used, and headed for the Broad Street station. It was about 5:00 AM. It had been a long, cold night for us, and we were soaking wet. I needed to stop for a dry pack of cigarettes before returning, so I told my chauffeur to stop in front of a 24-hour gas station around the corner. When I went it to buy the cigarettes, the clerk asked me about the fire. I told him that I couldn't talk about it because it was under investigation. He told me that last night, just before midnight, two kids came in and bought gas, filling a five-gallon container – and they asked for matches! I returned to the scene and found the investigator. I told him about the clerk and he said he'd go over and talk to him. We then went to the station, washed up, and put on a fresh pot of hot coffee.

When we left Broad Street at 7:30 AM to return to our own firehouse, the guys from the first Alarm companies were still on the scene. They were helping the Medical Examiner recover and bag the bodies. They then loaded them in Stokes baskets and lowered them to the ground in Ladder 2's bucket. Those guys had been out in the cold for an additional 2½ hours and ended up staying an hour more. They had to be completely exhausted, and frozen to their bones.

A couple of them told me later that it took them about a half hour of searching the apartment before they located the five victims who were trapped in the kitchen. The bodies were so badly burned that they blended in with the charred debris on the floor. The companies had to crawl on their hands and knees to closely examine the floor before they recognized a victim. Some members crawled right on top of them without even realizing it! They then had to 'dig' the victims out of the rubble. The sixth victim, the 6-year-old little girl, was still lying in bed in her corner bedroom. This room was largely untouched by the fire, so she was easily recognizable – she looked as though she were still sleeping. A strangely peaceful picture amid a horrific scene!

I have to add one thing about this incident.

When the fire first broke out, the noise alerted some members of an American Legion Post who were still lingering at the hall after a function. They immediately called 911 and rushed to the scene, which was only about 100 feet away, and tried to lend assistance. They assisted the man who jumped from the window and tried to get up to the third floor to help the family out of the building. They were driven back by the heat and the smoke before they could reach the third floor. They were met at the back doorway by the crew of Engine 8, who were on their way to the third floor. They told me later that they never felt so helpless in all their lives. These guys ended up helping a great deal that night! They opened their hall for the firefighters to go and get out of the cold. They provided us with coffee and drinks. They also provided us with sandwiches and doughnuts. I know that all the firemen on the scene that night were extremely grateful to these guys for being so generous during this terrible night.

Chapter 9
The Unknown

Few things are as frightening as the unknown. Think about the last time you saw a horror movie. The most frightening parts of the movie were when you didn't know what was coming next, or when something completely unexpected surprised you in a flash. The unknown. The unexpected. The unforeseen. These are scary things to most of us. Firemen are no exception. I think I can speak for all of us on this point. I do know that the unknown is what scares *me* the most when I enter a building that is burning, and full of deadly smoke. Give me a 3-decker, with fire showing upon arrival, and I'm confident with my knowledge of these types of fires to feel comfortable. I assume that the same would be true of NYC firefighters pulling up to a brownstone, which is so common in that city. Although these types of fires can still surprise us with the unexpected, the familiarity of the buildings brings a certain amount of predictability – but not always.

One morning when I was a firefighter on Engine 2, we were awakened by the bell at about 5:00 in the morning. We were being sent to a report of a building fire in our first-in district. Most calls at this hour are legitimate reports. At this time of morning most of the cranks are sleeping. This, along with the fact that there were a lot of open buildings in the area, due to a large-scale restoration project in the neighborhood, made us believe that we were going to have a 'worker.'

It didn't take us long to be proven correct. We hopped out of bed, grabbed our pants, stepped into our shoes and slid the pole. While we were running to the truck to don our turnout gear, the doors were opening to a morning just beginning to allow the light of the new day filter its way to the ground. Even in this darkness we could plainly see the column of dark smoke rising from the top of the hill where the building fire had been reported. The location was only about a minute from the station, so I turned my attention to checking and donning my gear. We were going to be on the scene very quickly and I was riding the side of the apparatus. This meant that I was going to be the pipeman.

I was responsible for pulling the 200' of hoseline off the truck and bringing it into the building to begin the initial attack on the fire. Most firefighters will tell you that this is the best job on the fire department. That's always been my opinion, anyway. This is the part of firefighting that I miss the most since I've been promoted to Lieutenant.

When we arrived we found a three-story building, in the process of a complete renovation, with fire showing on the first floor. The doors and windows had been removed. The fire was getting a good head start, due to the large amount of fresh air in the building feeding the flames. This also meant that we were going to have to attack this fire quickly, because the flames were licking out of the windows and igniting the right side of the building. I grabbed the line and climbed the stairs to the porch, where I donned my mask, flaked out the unneeded length of the hose, and started crawling into the dark smoke. My officer and I crawled deeper into the apartment, searching for the seat of the fire. We knew it was on Side 4 (the right side of the apartment), but it was difficult to make our way to the back of the apartment. We were being slowed by obstacles on the floor. We had no way of knowing what was there. We had assumed there was no furniture, because the house was under renovation. When we were close enough to see the fire, George called for water. I cracked open the nozzle and braced myself for the surge flowing through the hoseline as the pressurized water from our pump made its way to us. When the water came, we began to push forward, keeping as low to the floor as possible. As the stream would hit the fire, the water would turn to steam, rise to the ceiling and begin to bank back down on us. This is the part of the attack where firefighters are most vulnerable to thermal burns – mostly on the ears and neck. The lower you stay, the more tenable the atmosphere.

We knocked down the fire room by room as we crawled down the hallway, which divided the apartment into two equal halves. While we were advancing our line deeper into the building, other companies were beginning their attack on the fires on the outside of the building and on the upper floors. Due in large part to our rapid extinguishment of the seat of the fire, the extension to these areas was minimal, and the other companies quickly had it under control. When we knocked down the last of the fire on the first floor, the apartment began to clear of smoke pretty quickly, due to the influx of fresh air through the missing windows. George and I were curious about what the obstacles we encountered in the kitchen area could have been. We shut down the line, walked back down the hallway, and saw crates containing window frames, countertops and other assorted building supplies, piled on the floor. Now we understood why we had such a problem navigating through this area.

While I was still looking at these crates I heard George say quietly, "Tommy, come over here and look at this." He had gone back down the hallway and was checking out the rooms toward the rear of the apartment. I walked over to him and he pointed into a room that was right across the hallway from the room where the fire started. When I looked into the room I almost shit! There had to be at least ten large acetylene tanks standing against the wall. Sitting next to them were a couple of 5-gallon containers of gasoline. There were also a number of other pieces of equipment – saws, torches and other building supplies. Obviously the company doing the renovations on the buildings in the neighborhood was using this apartment to store many of their supplies. We didn't have a clue these tanks were here when we entered the apartment. What if the fire had been in this room!? I don't want to even think about that!

That's an example of the unexpected. Usually, it's the type of situation that we might discover during routine district inspections. Unfortunately for us, the renovations hadn't been going on that long and none of our companies had inspected this building since it had begun. The building should have had 'Hazardous Materials Placards' at the entrance, but it didn't. The placarding system is designed to give emergency workers a warning that these dangerous substances are present. No matter what we do, we can't be aware of *all* the dangerous conditions in our districts. This is why we must be constantly prepared for the unexpected.

Some hazardous conditions are a little easier to predict – at least to the veteran firefighters. We were dispatched to a fire in a small warehouse when I was a Lieutenant on Engine 15. One of the guys on my truck at that time was a firefighter who didn't have a lot of fire experience. When we arrived at the fire, the Chief told me that they had knocked down the fire, but that he wanted me to take my crew and search the second floor in the rear of the building for any possible victims overcome by smoke. We made our way to the stairs that led to the rear loft. I told them that we were going to stick together and search as a team. The smoke had lightened since the fire had been knocked down, but there was still a small amount lingering in the air. The second floor was a storage area with a grated metal floor. As the smoke rose from the first floor, it passed right through the grate. We couldn't see the floor clearly. As we began to move toward the back wall one of my firefighters, the inexperienced one, began to get ahead of me. "Hold on, Joe," I said as I grabbed his shoulder, "if you can't see where you're stepping, use your axe as a probe and check for holes or stairs." We went back to searching, probing the floor in front of us with our tools. Joe hadn't taken more than two steps when he stopped suddenly. "Holy shit," he yelled. We all stopped, and then inched toward Joe. We strained to see the floor in front of him. What we saw was an opening in the grate that was used to lift large pieces of equipment to the loft. The drop was 25' straight down to the concrete floor below! "Thanks, Loo," he said quietly, "I would have went right through if you hadn't stopped me."

Holes or pits in floors of commercial buildings can be anywhere. These buildings are not like residential buildings where dangerous conditions like this are very seldom present. An experienced firefighter will realize that conditions such as these may be present. We can't know for sure that they'll be present or predict where they'll be, but knowing that it's a possibility gives us the warning we need. The warning is – be sure of every step.

This lesson was drilled into my head at the Training Academy. Like many lessons learned at the drillyard, however, it had drifted to the back of my mind. Like many other lessons I've learned in my years on the fire department, it didn't fully stick with me until I almost made a fatal mistake on the fireground. I was operating a hoseline from the bucket of a tower ladder one day at a fire in a vacant building. The fire had started on the first floor and was burning pretty good when the first company arrived. It had burned out the stairway to the third floor. The fire had spread to the third floor and we had been told to knock it down from the bucket, and chase it in through the window. When we had knocked it down from the outside, we had the operator of the bucket bring us to the window. I shut down the hoseline and began to enter the apartment through the window. My Lieutenant stopped me. "Wait a minute," he said, "Put the line in the window first. When you climb in the window, hold onto the line until you're sure the floor is safe. Don't let go of that line until you're sure!" I did what he said and sure enough, my feet never touched flooring. It had been burnt right through! If I had just climbed right in, as I had begun to do, I would have fallen right through to the second floor. With the weakened condition of the interior of this building, I could have easily gone right through that floor also – possibly all the way to the basement. It's lessons like that which stick. I'm sure Joe won't be walking through any more smoky rooms without probing in front of him with a tool.

When I was new on the job, in the early 80s, there was an epidemic of arson rampant in the Northeastern U.S. Many building owners would hire professional arsonists, or sometimes neighborhood kids, to burn their unwanted property. The properties were often insured for more money than they were worth. This made arson a very profitable business. In cities or towns where the fire departments had a primarily 'surround and drown' approach to fighting fires in vacant buildings, all the arsonist had to do was get the fire started and wait. The building would end up as a total loss for insurance purposes, and the owner would collect his money. In cities that had an aggressive interior attack policy on vacant buildings, the arsonist's task was more difficult. He would sometimes have to torch the same building numerous times. He would light them and we would go in and put them out.

Eventually some sick bastard had the bright idea that if he made these vacant buildings more dangerous for the firefighters, we wouldn't attack them so aggressively. He began sawing halfway through stairs and floor joists, so that when the firefighters put their weight on the area, it would collapse. He also began to punch holes in an upper floor and put balloons filled with gasoline in the space just above the ceiling of the floor below. When a firefighter was in the room below and pulled down the ceiling, searching for hidden fire, the balloon would fall from the ceiling space and douse the firefighter with gasoline. If there were a heat source in the area, such as smoldering debris, it would ignite the gasoline and burn the firefighter. This became a common practice among many arsonists. Again, knowing that this was a possibility kept the veteran firefighters on their toes when pulling ceilings in a vacant building. This sort of thing was totally unpredictable, however, especially for the first few firefighters who were victimized.

I was on Engine 2, years ago, and we had a fire in a restaurant. It was a three-story building with the restaurant on the first floor, and two apartments above. The fire was on the first floor, but the smoke filled both apartments above. We were the third engine company on the scene. Our job was to take a line to the second floor to check for any victims trapped above the fire, and check for any extension of fire. We entered the staircase from the front of the building. It led directly to the door of the apartment and was filled with smoke. When we reached the landing and tried to open the door, we found that it was locked – we would have to force it. When I kicked in the door, I was quickly knocked to the floor. I didn't know what the hell had happened. I thought I heard the faint sounds of growling as I was falling. When I looked down the stairwell, I saw two large Dobermans scrambling, as fast as their legs would carry them, toward the exit – and the fresh air. I picked myself up and followed the rest of the company into the apartment. We found out later that these had been attack dogs that guarded the restaurant at night. Under normal circumstances they would have made a meal out of me if I had knocked down the door to that apartment. Apparently they were too scared to think of anything but getting the hell out of there. It was just another case of firemen rushing in as everyone (and everything) else rushes out.

All these cases were unexpected. In all these cases the unknown could have resulted in serious consequences. In truth, there is the potential for unforeseen happenings at every emergency scene. That's one of the reasons we don't rush when we arrive on the scene. In many of these situations there are clues to be found, prior to entering a building, which could alert the firefighter of potential dangers. That's why the first-in officer's size-up of the scene is so important. Is it a commercial building? Have there been prior fires here that might affect the structural integrity of the building? How long has it been burning? Is it occupied? All these questions, and a hundred more, go through an officer's mind as he's pulling up to a fire scene. The more information we can gather prior to entering a building, the more likely we are to have a favorable, and safe, outcome. Once you step inside the building, you don't get another chance to survey the exterior, to look for clues on the layout of the building, or the location of the fire.

I responded to a house fire one New Year's Eve where the first-in officer's observations proved to be a lifesaver – literally. As he climbed out of the cab he called a "Code Red" over the radio and then continued his size-up. He tried to pinpoint the location of the fire. He noticed that the fire seemed to be predominantly on the exterior of the building. When he further observed that the fire was located near the electrical service wires entering the building, he told his crew to hold their ground for a minute. He traced the wire back to the pole with his eyes. He saw that a high service wire was draping over the service wire causing it to overheat, and ignite the exterior of the house. He also noticed that the high service wire was draping over the metal fence in front of the building. He called for the electric company to respond to cut the power to these lines, and transmitted a warning to all responding companies to avoid contact with the fence, and to stand by with their hoselines until the power had been cut. His thorough size-up and quick thinking probably saved the life of one of his men. He carefully led his company through the rear door to make sure the house was evacuated. He then positioned his line on the interior of the building, in the area of the exterior fire, and awaited word that the power had been shut down. I took my company to the driveway on the side of the building where the fire was located, and stood by in that position until the power had been cut. You have no idea how difficult it is for a fireman to wait and do nothing as someone's home is burning in front of his eyes. Luckily the electric company responded very quickly, and we had the situation under control promptly after that.

Electrical wires can pose a real hazard at building fires. All the power lines in the City of Providence are above ground, mounted on telephone poles. Most of the houses in the city were built within ten feet of the street. This means that there are high-tension power lines very close to most buildings. This creates a couple of potentially dangerous situations for firefighters operating at a building fire. If a fire breaks through to the exterior of a wood-framed dwelling, the flames can frequently impinge on the wires in front of the building. This can cause the rubber insulation to melt, and the exposed wires to arc. Without the coating of the rubber, these wires are even more dangerous – electricity has the ability to jump ten feet or more, looking for a conductor to connect it to the ground. Also, without the added strength of the heavy rubber coating, these wires will eventually snap. The wire can remain 'live', even while lying broken on the ground – seemingly harmless. If a firefighter doesn't avoid walking, or even stretching a hoseline, under these wires, he can be electrocuted if a live wire snaps. A live electrical current can travel right along a wet hoseline to the firefighters operating at the nozzle. A live wire in a puddle of water can also be a deadly trap for the unsuspecting firefighter. When electrical wires are involved at a fire or other emergency scene, we need to be extremely vigilant.

Power lines can also be a hindrance to aerial ladders trying to reach the roof of a building. When the first aerial ladder arrives on the scene of a house fire, its first responsibility is to ventilate the building above the fire level. All the superheated gases and smoke, produced by the fire, rise. When the heat and smoke reach the uppermost point of the structure, they begin to bank down throughout the rest of the building. This makes it difficult for the engine companies and other ladder companies to gain entry. It also makes it virtually impossible for anyone still trapped in the house to survive. Venting above the fire allows the heat and smoke to escape, and makes it easier to enter the building in search of survivors. The best place to ventilate, therefore, is the peak of the roof. This is the highest point in the dwelling. Power lines frequently block any clear path of an aerial ladder to the roof. This often means that the heavy aluminum aerial is often placed very close to the high-tension lines. If a firefighter comes in contact with the power line, he will be electrocuted. At many fire scenes, the firefighters climbing the aerial to the roof must crawl under the power lines while ascending and descending. Another problem could occur if the aerial comes in contact with the power line. In this case, the entire truck would become 'live', and anyone who touched the ladder truck, while also being in contact with the ground, would be electrocuted. Firefighters are aware of these dangers and we are extremely careful around electricity. Even so, accidents with electricity take the lives of firefighters every year.

As I stated earlier, the unknown hazards are what scare me most on this job. It would be nice to arrive at the scene of every emergency and be given a list of all the possible hazards we may encounter. Unfortunately, this doesn't happen. We try to ascertain as much information as possible regarding an incident – previous inspections, size-up, and reports of witnesses – prior to beginning operations. Once we begin a course of action, we put the unknowns to the back of our minds.

We think about the unknown. We worry about the unknown. We don't dwell on it.

Me, at 1 year old, with an antique fire truck.

Branch Avenue Fire Station

Front (L to R): Bob, Joe, Cocoa, Jerry
Rear (L to R): Al, George, Pete, Joe, Me

My family at my father's promotional ceremony.

L to R: Terry, Danny, myself, Dad, Julie (on his lap), Mom, Timmy, and Kevin

My oldest daughter, Joy, in my fire gear.

My daughter, Caitlin, and me at the Fireman's Ball.

My son, Teddy, sliding the fire pole at the station.

Me, while assigned to Engine 2 in the early 80s.

Me driving Engine 2 (before any accidents!)

Messer Street Fire Station

Front (L to R): Capt. Ray, Joe, Bucko, Me
Rear (In bucket): Dan, Brian, John

Me, with white stripe on my fire coat, operating the deck gun at a house fire while on Engine 8.

Me rappelling at the drill tower
during my assignment to Engine 2

Engine 8 after I had wrapped it around a tree.

The Providence Firefighter's Little League Team

Firefighters L to R: Rick, me, and Doug
My son, Teddy, is standing in the cab door.

A fire while I was assigned to Engine 8 around 1987. We were operating on the 3rd floor, just below the visible fire.

Nancy and I at the Fireman's Ball.

Entering the front door at 88 Erastus Street, where we lost an infant. I'm in the doorway with the interupted stripe on my back (my air pac).

My son, Teddy, and my grandson, Kalif, sitting on the
bumper of Engine 15.

The 'Worcester Six' memorial.

Me, turned toward the camera in center, marching in the
FDNY memorial parade for the WTC victims.

Me visiting Ground Zero in October 2001.

Nancy in my firecoat!

Engine 15 leaving the station at Warp Speed!

Chapter 10
Chiefs
(The Good, the Bad & the Ugly)

This chapter would be a lot easier to write if I were already retired. I'm going to tell it like it is – from my perspective. Sometimes Chiefs don't like to hear it like it is. Sometimes they get a little pissed off when someone talks of their shortcomings or their mistakes. Sometimes there's retribution from a Chief on someone who would dare to openly criticize or even question him. So be it.

First of all, let me begin by saying that the type of Chief mentioned above is the exception – not the rule. I've worked with well over a hundred different Chief's during the course of my career and I would have to guess that the number of 'Bad' Chiefs I've encountered would be less than 10% of the whole. The problem is that they are out there, and they will bite you in the ass. I'm not telling any unknown secrets here. Every firefighter knows that these Chiefs are out there...and every firefighter knows exactly who they are!

Most Chiefs I've worked with have been good men, good firefighters, good fire officers...and 'Good' Chiefs! In order for me to respect a Chief, he must have respect for himself. Respect for the Department. Respect for his position. Respect for his superiors. *And* respect for the men under his command! I judge a Chief by two criteria: competence, and how he treats subordinates. If he is lacking in either of these areas, in my opinion, he is not a good officer.

Competence in any job is important. You wouldn't want a bad mechanic working on your car, would you? In the fire service it's even more important than that – it's very literally life and death. Firefighters, especially officers, are often called upon to make decisions which could have life and death implications – when to pull your men out of a fire building, when to let them continue to push inward, when to risk your own life and the lives of those under your command to try to save the life of a perfect stranger, and when to give up on a search. These are not easy decisions, by any stretch of the imagination, but if you are not ready to make them at a moment's notice, you are not ready to be an officer in the fire service!

I believe it's the job of every firefighter to be ready and eager to do his job as aggressively as possible, at every single incident to which he is called. I also believe that it is the job of the commanding officer, by virtue of his knowledge and experience, to allow his men to go forward, direct them when necessary, and rein them in when conditions warrant. A company officer does this with his company; and a Chief does this with all the companies under his command.

The way a Chief (or any officer for that matter) treats his subordinates is a very important measure of his strength or weakness as an officer. The fire service is a complete team effort. No one man, no matter how good a firefighter or officer he may be, is able to put out a building fire by himself. A company officer must be able to delegate responsibilities and tasks. He can't take care of every detail himself. This is even more true of a Chief. By the nature of his job he is no longer a firefighter; he is a coordinator. His job is no longer to go in and *fight* the fire room by room; it is to see the big picture, and organize companies in such a way as to effectively allow *them* to fight the fire. Any Chief who micromanages (over-directs) an incident is not doing his job properly. To delegate responsibility is to pass it on to someone else and forget it. As a Chief, you must have confidence in your fire officers, and allow them to do their jobs. Just as a company officer must have confidence in his firefighters. Every good Chief I've worked for has said that it was the company officers, and the firefighters riding the trucks, which made him look good. That's because he'd delegate a task and know that it would be done. He didn't waste time or energy telling us exactly how to get it done.

Let me explain how it is that a person becomes a Chief in the Providence Fire Department. A Chief's job is a political appointment. The Mayor normally chooses a Captain and promotes him to the rank of Chief when a position opens up. There is no exam to take and pass for this position. There is a promotional exam for the rank of Lieutenant and there is a promotional exam for the rank of Captain. Captain is presently the highest rank attainable in the Providence Fire Department strictly on your own merit. Under the current format, any firefighter who reaches the rank of Captain, in my opinion, deserves the same respect as a Chief. Some Chiefs forget this, unfortunately. They forget where they came from, and think they're someone special. I respect the man for making Captain, and if he successfully plays the political game and becomes a Chief – good for him!

Once in a while a firefighter skips the ranks of Lieutenant and Captain and is promoted directly to Chief. I have no respect for these individuals as Chiefs. This only means that they were that much *better* at the political games than the rest of us – usually at the cost of other firefighters! We currently have one such Chief on our department. He had one year assigned to a Ladder Company, a few years as a Chief's Aide, and about ten years as an investigator. He was then promoted to Investigative Chief – the Providence Fire Department equivalent of Internal Affairs. He is now in charge of investigating our actions and our injuries. How can any firefighter have respect for a *guy* like this! He had about four or five fires as a front line firefighter in his entire career! Promoting him to this position was a truly ugly move.

We have another Chief on the job who is neither competent nor respectful of his subordinates. He is smart enough – he passed the promotional exams for both Lieutenant and Captain – so he has my respect for that. He seems to think, however, that it is his job to protect the department from the hijinks of some of its firefighters. He seems to have forgotten some of his own hijinks when he was a firefighter! Like backing the apparatus into a wall inside the station and going back upstairs to sleep without even realizing what he had done. Now he acts like it is a personal issue if a firefighter's hair is too long, or if a sick day is called in too late. He's just forgotten where he came from. He's a good enough guy, but I'm glad I don't have to work for him anymore! I worked for him for quite a while!

He's the type of Chief that drafts up a pre-plan with meticulous detail, only to throw it out on the fireground. He knows what he wants to do but it seems that he blanks out from time to time and forgets what he's told you to do. On many occasions he's told a company officer to do a job, then asks him, "Why the hell did you do that?"!!

I remember responding to a small boiler fire one day when he was the working Chief. Engine 15 was the second engine at the scene, so we hooked up to the hydrant and ran feeders[6] to Engine 14's pump as they stretched their attack line into the basement. The next engine on the scene, Engine 12, took the second hoseline into the house. They took it to the first floor. The Chief ordered me to take our line to the cellar, to back up Engine 14. After the fire, he ripped the officer of Engine 12 a new asshole for not taking his line to the basement to back up Engine 14. Technically, he was right. The department's S.O.P.'s call for the second line into the building during a cellar fire be deployed to the basement, to back up the first line. "But Chief," the officer said, "it was only a small fire, and I wanted to make sure it hadn't gotten to the first floor." This Chief didn't want to hear it. The rule is the rule – no exceptions. By the book! That is, unless it's his decision to break the rules.

This same Chief was in charge of Battalion 2 one night about three months later when Engine 15 pulled up to a fire fully involving the basement of a six tenement apartment house at 2:00 AM. "Code Red, three-story, six-unit, occupied building. Heavy fire in the basement," I reported to Fire Alarm. I placed my firefighter at a cellar window with our handline and instructed him to knock down as much fire as he could from the outside, while I searched for a way into the basement. I climbed the three stairs of the porch on the right side of the building and opened a door. It was to the hallway between the front and rear apartments, and the stairway to all of the upper floor apartments. It also led to the basement stairway. The fire was already consuming the cellar stairs and beginning to threaten the main stairway of the building! I called my pipeman, John, to the porch. We crouched low, donned our masks, and I pushed the door open. The hallway was a sheet of flames, which licked out of the door above us impinging on the underside of the second floor porch. John opened the pipe and pushed back the flames. We stayed at the doorway to completely extinguish any visible fire in the hallway. This was our first priority! Keep this means of egress open for the occupants of the building, and keep the fire from traveling up the stairway!

Fires are fought one step at a time. The first priority is always saving a life! By keeping the exit open, we could allow the residents on the upper floors to escape. The second priority is saving property. By containing the fire, and not letting it claim any more of the building, we were keeping property loss to a minimum. The third priority is extinguishment. Once the fire is contained, we can begin to advance on it, and begin putting it out.

As we crouched at the door fighting the advance of the fire through the hallway, the fire in the basement was escaping through a cellar window below the porch. It was right below our position, and was igniting the boards on which we were kneeling! Engine 14 stretched their line to the side of the porch and protected us by knocking down the fire at the window. After we had secured the hallway, we began a slow descent into the basement, reclaiming the stairs step by step, as we went along. The heat was intense! The basement was still fully ablaze and the stairway acted as a chimney for all the heat and smoke to rise. Now I knew what Santa Claus felt like when someone left a fire going in the fireplace on Christmas Eve! As we descended into the basement I would yell at John, in a muffled voice through my mask, to make sure the next step was secure before putting his full weight on it. I reminded him of this on *every* step! The fire had been burning below us quite intensely for quite a while, and if he put too much weight on a fire-weakened stair, we could both be dumped into the basement below – and into the flames! I was clenching his coat in my fingers. If he had begun to fall forward, I would have pulled him back to my step.

Engine 14 had moved their line into the doorway, to the top of the basement stairs – backing us up. If we fell through the stairs, they would 'cover us' with the hoseline, and try to rescue us. This is the reason for a backup line in a cellar fire!!! When we finally reached the bottom of the stairs we could turn the corner, ever so slightly, and begin to knock down the fire in the basement. We were making slow but steady progress.

All of a sudden we heard a rumble in front of us! We couldn't tell what it was, but it was getting louder and getting closer! The heat began to get more intense, also. We had to back up onto the stairway again, sheltering ourselves from the heat with the stairway wall. As we climbed onto the bottom of the stairs, I looked up and saw that our backup line was gone! We 'dug in' at the bottom of the stairs, and slowly darkened down the rest of the remaining fire in the basement.

When the fire was knocked down I told John to shut down the line and go outside for a break. I tracked down the officer of Engine 14 on the street and asked, "Dave, what the hell happened to you guys?" He shook his head and started ranting, "Shit, I'm sorry, Tommy, but that fuckin' asshole ordered us out of the building and repositioned us at the cellar window to knock down some fire!! I know we were pushing it all back on you, but I had no choice. He ordered me to!!"

That explained a lot. The rumbling we heard was their hoseline hitting the ductwork of the heating system in the basement, and the increasing intensity of the heat was because they were pushing the fire back at us! This same Chief who had ripped the 12's a new asshole a couple of months ago for not backing up the company in the basement, had just broken two cardinal rules of firefighting! You never take away a backup line, especially in a cellar fire, and you never pour water on a fire from outside the building toward a company working on the inside! I guess the rules only apply when he wants them to.

I had yet another fire with this same Chief a couple of months later. It was about 1:00 AM when I was awakened by the sound of the bell, and the glare of the 'blow lights[7].' As I jumped out of bed and began getting dressed, the voice over the vocalarm squawked, "Attention Engines 15, 14, 6; Special Hazards; Ladders 6 & 2; Rescue 4; and Battalion 2, a Still Box. 16 Covell Street for a reported building fire." The address was only a few blocks from the station, so we had to don our gear quickly as we responded. There was no time to wake up gradually – we were on the scene in about a minute! When we turned the corner onto Covell Street I could see a crowd of people at the end of the street waving frantically at us. I could also see heavy fire reflected in the windows of the building across the street from the reported address! As we pulled up to the scene I could see that the entire back side of the building was ablaze. "Code Red, three-story, occupied, heavy fire in the rear of the building," I said on the radio. There were just three of us on Engine 15. The chauffeur, Al, would have to stay with the truck and run the pump to provide us water. That left Rick, who was riding the side, and myself to stretch the line from the truck and begin to knock down the fire. I told him to grab the 2 ½" handline. This line was bigger than our normal attack line. It would give us more water to knock down the fire at the rear of the building, as quickly as possible. As I was putting on my air pak, an old man came running up to me crying and tugging on my coat. "You've got to save her! She's on the second floor landing of the rear stairs and she was screaming!! She's gonna die! Save her! Save her, please!!" I told Rick to grab the 1 ¾" line instead and "follow me in." "Engine 15 to Fire Alarm," I said into the radio, "I've got a report of a woman trapped on the second floor in the rear." Rick walked to the rear of the truck to grab the line, as I walked to the rear doorway.

The house was a 3-story dwelling with a single-story addition on the back of the building. The addition was fully involved in fire, as was the entire rear exterior of the main building. The flames were beginning to lap around the left rear corner when I got to the small porch that led to the side doorway. The doorway was on the left side of the building about 10 feet from the left rear corner. When I reached the doorway and looked inside I could see that fire had already made its way into the cellar beneath the stairway to the second floor. There was heavy smoke coming from inside the door and the heat was intense. I knew that if the woman was on the second floor landing of this stairway I only had a minute or two to get her out alive! I looked back toward the truck and saw that Rick was having a tough time getting the hoseline through the crowded driveway.

It doesn't happen often, but I was really scared of this one. No backup yet. No hoseline yet. I didn't know if the stairs would hold out, and the exterior fire was almost to the door. I thought about my fiancée, Nancy. I thought about my kids, Joy, Caitlin and Teddy. I thought it was possible that I might not be seeing them again! I also thought that this is what I get paid to do. This is my job. I chose this profession. I also thought that if you talk the talk, you have to walk the walk. It was time to walk! All these thoughts went through my head in a split second, as I was donning my mask. I went in and began to crawl up the stairs, feeling my way for the next stair and hoping to feel the woman who was trapped in this building. I couldn't see my hands due to the blanket of thick black smoke. I stayed along the wall of the stairway to follow the curve up the stairs, and to keep my weight on the strongest part of each stair. I made my way to the second floor landing – no one was there. I felt my way up to the third floor door – still nothing. The door was closed, so I assumed she had gone back into the second floor apartment. I crawled back down the stairs to the landing and met Rick and a firefighter from Ladder 6, Jermaine. I yelled through my mask that we were going to search the apartment. When we entered, Rick could get just inside the doorway before the hoseline wouldn't go any further. It had snagged up on the cars outside in the driveway, which were now on fire.

When I had entered the building, Rick was trying to squeeze down the driveway with the line to the rear door. He followed me into the house about a minute later, and Jermaine followed right behind him. The officer of Engine 14 tried to follow Jermaine into the doorway but just at that time, the entire doorway was swallowed up by the advancing fire, and he was pushed back! He told the Chief that Engine 15 was trapped inside the building. In reality we weren't trapped, we could have escaped through the front of the building – working away from the fire. The Chief ordered Engine 6 to take a 2 ½" hoseline and secure the doorway. They took their hoseline and knocked down the fire around the door and stairway. They also put out the fires burning in the cars in the driveway. They then knocked down a considerable amount of fire to the rear of the building.

Rick couldn't advance into the apartment, so Jermaine and I started searching room to room. I told Rick to stay put and to keep yelling. "What do you want me to yell," he asked? I said, "I don't care, just keep yelling!" I just wanted him to make noise so that we could use his voice as a guide so that we could tell which direction we were facing. When you're crawling around a strange apartment in complete darkness, it's very easy to become disoriented. By having Rick yell, we could gauge where we were and where the exit was. Rick held his ground and kept yelling. As I circled one room in the apartment, I knocked over a mattress and box spring that had been leaning against the wall. They fell on me and momentarily trapped me underneath. When I freed myself, I listened for Rick, to readjust my bearings and finished the search of the room. We had finished searching the back half of the apartment when our masks began to vibrate, indicating that our air bottles were beginning to run out. I ordered everyone out of the apartment to get fresh bottles.

As we descended, we found that the middle of the stairs had been burnt out, so we stepped to the side of the stairs and carefully made our way down. When I got to the street I met the Chief and informed him that the Primary Search was complete in the rear of the second floor and that it was negative. I told him that we were returning to complete the front half of the apartment. He just said, "O.K., Loo." He didn't say another word to me that night. As I was talking to the Chief, Al was removing my old bottle from my back and replacing it with a fresh one. When we had the fresh air bottles, we returned and finished the Primary Search of the apartment. There was no sign of anyone.

I found out later that while we were doing our first search of the apartment, Special Hazards had spotted a woman in the front window of the third floor apartment. She had made her way to the top of the rear stairs, and gone through the third floor apartment to the front, but she couldn't open the window to get out. Special Hazards climbed the fire escape, broke the window and pulled her to safety – right in front of the Chief! The Chief never told me that the woman had been removed. Even when I talked to him while changing bottles!! He allowed me to return to the second floor with my crew, believing that someone was still unconscious in the apartment.

When we returned to the station, I found out how difficult it had been for Rick to hold his ground at the doorway. When he removed his bunker pants he saw that he had sustained second degree steam burns to his knees. That's how hot it was on the floor of that apartment! Jermaine and I were moving, but Rick was kneeling in one spot the whole time. He had to be transported to the hospital and relieved of duty.

The next night I got a visit from the Chief. He asked me to follow him to the kitchen so that we could talk in private. He said he wanted to discuss the fire from the night before. He told me that he wanted to let me know that I should have ordered the 2 ½" line pulled – a lot of fire, a lot of water. I told him that I had originally ordered the 2 ½," but when I found out there was someone trapped, I decided to take a line that we could maneuver more easily, so that we could reach her as quickly as possible. He didn't agree. He said that I should have taken the larger line and secured the doorway until the next company arrived on the scene, and made entry. I said, "Chief, it took over a minute for the next company to get there. In my opinion, if the woman was where she was reported to have been, she would have only had about another minute to be rescued alive."

He still didn't agree. He said that he had gone home after the fire and had looked up the priorities of the fire department in our SOP's. "The number one priority is life safety," he said. He further explained that under life safety, firefighter safety takes precedence over civilian safety. I told him that although I don't believe in taking unnecessary chances, I do believe that sometimes we have no choice, that's a part of our job. When there's little to gain – risk little. When there's a lot to gain – risk a lot. He didn't go for that either. "You put the lives of firefighters at risk," he said. He told me that Engine 6 had taken a large line and secured the doorway, and that he was going to put them up for commendations. He then just walked away – our conversation was over.

I couldn't believe it! I certainly don't do this job for medals, but this was a slap in the face. Engine 6 gets written up for commendations and I get my ass chewed out! They never even went into the fire building. That's not a knock on their company; that wasn't their job that night. I went straight upstairs to my office and wrote up recommendations for commendations for my guys!

Chapter 11
Stealing the Fire

In the initial stages of any emergency, the actions of firefighters are always racing the clock. In both the time it takes us to respond to the scene, and the time it takes us to apply our tactics once we arrive, speed is crucial. If there is an opportunity to successfully mitigate a situation – be it rescue someone or control the fire – there is a finite number of minutes in which to do so. If our plans are put into action too slowly, the opportunity could be lost. Managing the time or *beating* the clock, therefore, is a critical part of our responsibility. That is why we are endlessly training and pre-planning every aspect of our job – from learning the streets (to cut down on our response time), to training with our equipment, to analyzing our tactics and strategies, to inspecting the buildings in our district, to... etc.

There is no easy way to teach someone to be a firefighter. Much of our career is spent in on-the-job training. Every call is a different situation with its own unique set of circumstances, and every call is in a different location. The general public can't imagine how many hours of preparation, as well as how many years of experience, it takes the firefighters in their city to be able to respond to their homes and take the actions necessary to save a life or to protect their property. Although it's impossible to predict the circumstances of any emergency, we train using a basic *strategy* common to most situations and allow our instincts and experience to dictate the specific *tactics* for each case. 'Strategy' is that which we want to accomplish – put out the fire by putting water on it and cooling it down. 'Tactics' are the specific actions employed to successfully carry out the strategy – bring the hoseline into the rear stairway and up to the third floor. We have to be flexible enough in our duties that we can immediately adjust to a changing situation, but our basic plan of attack is the result of carefully thought out tactics and pre-planning. We have no time to sit down and draw up a plan of operation at the scene of an emergency. The initial size up of a situation by the first-in officer is done within the first ten seconds on the scene. From this analysis he decides what type of tactics to employ at this emergency.

Speed is a factor in many of the things we do. From the simple and obvious things such as backing our apparatus into the station to allow us to get out quickly to conducting large scale mock disaster drills, which include the police and area hospitals. We continually plan for the improbable, while practicing and honing our skills for the 'normal' day-to-day operations we encounter at our most common calls. A firefighter quickly learns that the fireground is no place to develop his skills with his equipment. He may hone his skills with each instance he uses them, but he must be fully competent in their use prior to trying to employ them at an emergency. There is no time to develop skills at an emergency – only to put them to use.

As time is such a large factor in our actions, response time is the first area in which this comes into play. Fire companies pride themselves on getting out the door and to the scene of an emergency quicker than anyone else. Most of the better companies are those in which the members are more aggressive. These two factors lead to a fierce competitive attitude between fire companies. It is always a feather in a fire company's cap to "steal the fire" from another company. In Providence, this is especially true with the engine companies. Our normal procedure is to have an engine company lead and the ladder company follow when responding to a reported building fire. The engine will proceed just past the building and the members will pull the hoseline from the rear of the truck and attack the fire. This leaves the front of the building clear for the ladder truck to set up as close to the building as possible. For this reason the first-in officer is almost always from an engine company. He owns it – it's his fire! This engine usually gets the bulk of the action. This is what we want to do. The second engine company, however, has to secure a water supply from a street hydrant to the first engine. This operation, though crucial, is not one of the glamour jobs. Therefore, if you are second-called and beat the first-called engine to the scene you can steal their fire and relegate them to water supply. You then have earned bragging rights, and if anyone can brag and razz the competition, it's firemen!

This sometimes results in what can only be described as NASCAR races through the city streets! In the time I've been on the department I can't recall a single accident caused by these races, although I have seen many near misses. When two large trucks approach an intersection with sirens blaring and lights flashing and neither one wants to back down, it can result in a daring game of 'chicken.' Those companies with the reputation of being aggressive often win these battles because the driver of the other truck knows that unless he's got a clear advantage over them, they won't back down. I've driven Engine 8 through a crowded area in our district called Olneyville Square on the left side of the median as Engine 14 was screaming down the right side. The traffic would usually dictate the winner. Whoever had to slow down for traffic would have to back down. Many times this would be Engine 14, probably because the traffic seeing them in their rear view mirror coming toward them had less incentive to move out of their way than the cars coming straight toward a large red truck barreling at them! I've been on trucks when you could reach out and touch the fireman on the side of the other engine. This was mostly before the switch to a more safety conscious approach to everything in the fire service, which began at the end of the eighties. Before that time we had no enclosed cabs on the trucks in the City of Providence. The firefighters 'riding the side' of the truck had a small jumpseat behind the driver and officer, facing the rear. Most of the time, however, we stood on a small 12" by 24" piece of diamondplate at the foot of the jumpseat, facing forward and looking over the cab. There were no guardrails to keep you from falling off the apparatus; you had to hold on to 'grab bars' on the side of the truck. After years of serious injuries and deaths to firefighters from falling off the side or being thrown from the truck in the event of an accident, the fire service began a transition to enclosed cabs, designed to protect the man riding the side. Those trucks which were unable to be refurbished with the enclosed cab right away were retrofitted with a safety bar that enclosed the standing area. Firemen have a long-standing tradition of being resistant to change, and this was the case in Providence with this transition. It only took a single cold winter to get us to embrace the shelter these cabs provided us. After that, it was an easy sell.

I stated earlier that firemen study the streets and know the quickest route to different streets in the city. This also applies to knowing the quickest route for other companies to get to the same location. This allows us to anticipate the location of another truck enroute to the fire. We know where it is that we'll most likely encounter them. These calculations are based on the company responding from their station. If a company is responding from a different starting point, the officer will transmit his location and direction of travel over the radio, to avoid 'surprising' other companies at an intersection. We had an incident in Providence, before I was on the department, in which two engine companies who were housed together in the downtown station collided at an intersection en route to a fire. One of the companies was responding from a different location in the district and surprised the driver of the truck responding from the firehouse. Neither could hear the other over the sound of their own siren. A few firemen were seriously injured, and one member was thrown from the truck at impact and died of his injuries.

I don't mean to give the impression that we're reckless out there – we're not. We realize that the possibility of killing someone on the street, firefighter or civilian, is not worth the risk, even when trying to rush to the scene to save a life. In recent years the emphasis is on safety throughout the job – both at the firehouse and responding to and working at the scene of an emergency. Firefighters are held accountable, by the department and by civil courts, for reckless behavior. This has cut down on some of the racing side-by-side incidents, but it won't stop the competition and the aggressiveness of firefighters. I believe we need this edge to be good at what we do. After all, an overly cautious person has no business being in this profession!

The third-called engine company can also steal the fire by getting their line to the seat of the fire first. Because the second-called engine has to secure the water supply, the third-called engine will actually have the second hoseline into the building. If they "get the wet stuff on the red stuff" quickest, they have successfully stolen the fire. This is the source for major company pride – or major company disgrace!

I remember working on Engine 8, one cold winter night years ago, when the call came in for a possible building fire on Greenwich Ave. "Attention Engines 10, 11, 8; Special Hazards; Ladders 5 & 2; Rescue 2; and Battalion 2, a Still Box...." When Engine 10 arrived on the scene, they found heavy fire coming from a second floor window in the front of a three-story occupied dwelling. The occupants reported that everyone was out of the building. They immediately stretched a hoseline to the front stairway to attack the fire. We were the third engine to arrive on the scene and we found Engine 10 and Ladder 5 already at work. Ladder 5 had already done a primary search of the second and third floor apartments and reported that no one was inside the building and that there was no fire extension to the third floor yet. Engine 10 was having a hard time advancing on the fire from the front stairway, as the heat was intense near the landing, and flames were beginning to lip out into the hallway. My Captain ordered me to stretch a hoseline to the rear stairway and try to advance on the fire from the back. When I got to the point on the stairs where my head was even with the landing, the heat and smoke wouldn't allow me to advance without my mask and a charged line. The Captain called for water, and before I put on my mask I could see that the main body of fire was in the front room, but that it was extending to the kitchen just inside the back door. The fire was rolling along the ceiling in the kitchen, but hadn't extended to the walls. It's always beneficial to get a quick idea of the location of the fire and the layout of the apartment before opening up the line. Things are surprisingly clear when the fire is in the free burning stage, and you can gain some valuable information in this brief survey. Once you put water on the fire, the smoke becomes much more intense and you lose sight of everything in the apartment with the exception of a small glow from the fire. When I was ready, I opened up the nozzle and started knocking down the fire along the ceiling. I was directing the stream through the doorway and working it in a circular motion to drive the heat away from us. As you spray a large volume of pressurized water in a circular motion into a confined area it creates a wind current that can push the heat and smoke in the opposite direction. I crawled on my hands and knees into the apartment as the Captain followed me, and helped feed me more line as I slowly advanced. I would crawl three or four feet and stop. I'd then direct the stream directly above and slightly in front of us to drive the water into the ceiling to completely extinguish the fire before moving past. One basic rule of engine company operations is to never advance past the fire as this can bite you in the ass by rolling over your head and banking down behind you, cutting off your escape route. Another cardinal rule is that the man backing up the nozzleman never be more than an arm's length behind him. In this smoky environment you can't see the man in front of you – you can't even see your own hand in front of your face. You *must* be able to reach out and touch him in order to know where he is. In this case, my Captain hadn't put his gloves on prior to entering the apartment. Every time I would advance a few feet, he would crawl up behind me and try to don his gloves while I was hitting the fire above us. This would create steam and hot water, which would fall down on us like an extremely hot shower, burning any exposed skin. Areas such as our ears and the back of our necks were susceptible to this, even though they were partly sheltered by the back flap of our helmets. This back flap is designed to help keep hot water and plaster, as well as glass, from sliding down our necks, and under our fire coats.

Each time he tried, I would begin to move forward again and he would have to abandon this effort in order to follow and feed me more line. His hands took a beating that night! When I reached the entrance to the front room, the heat was intense. I laid on the floor in an effort to stay under the worst of it. Heat and smoke rise, therefore the lower you are in a room involved in fire, the more tenable the atmosphere. We were taking a beating from the heat at this level, but we wouldn't have been able to survive in this room if we were standing. The temperature only a couple of feet above us was probably at least a hundred degrees higher than it was on the floor. It is not uncommon for the temperature at the ceiling of a room like this to be 1000 degrees Fahrenheit. I stretched the line in front of me and into the fire room. I didn't have to look while I was first darkening down the main body of fire. I had my face buried into the floor. I began to direct the stream upward and around the corner to the right side of the room in that circular motion. I could hear the hoseline knocking down the fire. The crackling of a free burning fire was beginning to diminish, and the hiss of the water being converted to steam began to overtake it. After dousing the room for a minute or so, I lifted my head and directed the stream in a more accurate manner toward the glow of the fire still burning, until it was knocked down. After a few more minutes we were able to get to our knees and begin to enter the room to more completely extinguish the remaining fire. We had stolen the fire!

All this had taken place in less than five minutes. Later, as we were mopping up, the pipeman from Engine 10 took a good-natured ball busting from our crew. We had worked our butts off to get this fire and we were going to enjoy the moment. There would be other moments when they would steal from us in the future – although I can't remember a single one!

I guess you only remember what you want to remember.

Chapter 12
Some Funny Little Thingies

Even in the fire business there are times when funny things happen in the middle of a serious situation. These things are not lost on us – even if we can't appreciate the levity at the moment. Fighting fires is a dangerous business, and if you assume that any fire is an easy job it could quickly change and bite you in the ass. A floor could collapse, sending you tumbling to the basement. The fire could reach an accelerant and suddenly flash through the apartment. *One* breath of superheated air from a flashover could sear your lungs, leaving you unable to breathe – killing you within minutes. Your equipment (ladder, hose, air pak, etc.) could fail, turning a routine incident into a situation where you're fighting for your life. Because of this, we don't really let our guard down too much during a fire. But we can appreciate the humor when we look back – after the fact.

One such fire for me happened when I was first assigned to the Branch Ave. Station. I had only been on the job for about two months when I was given my first permanent assignment to Engine 2. We were housed with Ladder 7, Rescue 3, and Battalion 3. I wasn't happy with this assignment at first. I had wanted to go to a busier engine company on the South Side of the city – Engine 10. When I first reported for duty here, I was the only new guy. Most of the other firefighters in the station had been on the job for fifteen years or more, so I felt like a loner – trying to find my own way, and eager to prove myself! I wouldn't have long to wait.

Our normal tour of duty (a cycle) consists of two consecutive day shifts followed by two consecutive night shifts. We then have four days off. By the time I came into work for my second night, I was beginning to feel a little more comfortable in the station. The guys had been good to me and made me feel welcome. I was still the junior man, but I was welcome. We had been fairly busy this cycle. We had a number of rescue runs, a couple of auto fires, a grass fire and an auto accident on the freeway – but no fires. I went to bed that night thinking that maybe next cycle will be the one that brings my first fire with these guys. During the night, the rescue went out a couple of times, but we never moved. At about 6:00 AM the doorbell began ringing – and ringing – and ringing! A couple of us slid the pole to see what this person was so excited about. When we opened the door the man, who was still ringing the bell, yelled, "There's a fire down the street!" We looked and saw smoke coming from an appliance store about a block away.

Someone pushed the emergency button at the watch desk and the rest of the guys responded to the floor. We jumped on the trucks and were in front of the store in about a minute. It was a small, single-story, cinderblock building with a basement. The smoke was coming from a grate on the sidewalk in front of the store, which led to the basement. There were no flames, and just slight smoke on the main sales floor. Ladder 7 pried open the grate to reveal stairs leading into the cellar. Heavy black smoke poured from the opening in the sidewalk into the bright morning sky.

I was riding the side of the truck, so I was the pipeman. I was going to be the first one going into that hole! I had quickly put on my boots, coat, and helmet before leaving the station, and now I was turning in my air pak, prior to pulling it from the jumpseat and strapping in on. As I was pulling the hose from the back of the truck I glanced over at the smoke, hoping I'd see someone going in before I got there! Instead, they were putting on their gear and waiting for me to bring the line to the entrance. When I got to the top of the grate I could feel the convected heat rising from below. It was like standing above a stove! As I donned my mask, I couldn't help but think that they've got to be kidding!! They couldn't possibly be going down these stairs – and they certainly weren't thinking that I'd be leading the way!!!!! I felt the water snaking through the hoseline toward the nozzle I held in my hands. When the water came, the hose suddenly felt like it weighed a ton. I was scared shitless!! My Lieutenant tapped me on the helmet. "All set, kid?" I just nodded and started down the stairs. It was like walking into a black cloud, I couldn't see an inch in front of me. I stepped slowly, leaning against the wall to keep my balance. I lost all sense of distance and direction. When I reached the bottom, I realized that the heat wasn't as intense at this level, and I crouched down to the floor instinctively. I thought I could see a slight flicker to my right. I opened up the nozzle in the direction of the glow and I could hear it sizzle as the water began to cool the boxes and crates that were burning. I kept that stream wide open and worked it over the whole side of the cellar where the fire was. This was my protection and I wasn't about to give it up. My Lieutenant had followed me down the stairs and was guiding me, "Straight up, kid, the ceiling's going a bit.

OK, go forward, to the right…" After a few minutes he said, "OK, I think we've got it knocked down. Stay right here, and if it flares up again, hit it with the line." He went ahead to check for any extension of fire that we couldn't see from here.

A minute or two later I could see the glow again from the same general area and it was getting larger! I was alone, and my Lieutenant was someplace in the cellar! I opened the nozzle again and hit the glow of the fire. I wasn't going to take any chances this time. I was going to keep pouring water on this fire until it was completely out. After what seemed to be a long time, I heard a muffled voice from somewhere in front of me, but I couldn't make out what it was saying. The fire was still glowing and I was still trying to knock it down with the hose stream. Finally I recognized my Lieutenant's voice, a little closer now, "Kid! Shut down the damn line!!!" I shut it down. "Let's go out and have a blow of fresh air," he said and led me back to the stairs. When we got outside and took off our facemasks, he started laughing hysterically. I didn't understand what was so funny. He began to tell me that when he went to the rear of the basement he could hear another company trying to force the rear door. He pulled back the deadbolt and opened the door for them. It was Engine 7. They had brought a second line to the rear entrance and began to move toward the fire area. The glow that I had seen was from the handlight that the Captain of Engine 7 carried. I had spent the last few minutes in the cellar wetting down the Captain and his crew!!! "The Captain's going to be awfully anxious to meet you, kid," he said. As he told other guys on the sidewalk, they began to laugh out loud.

I still didn't understand what was so funny. I was probably as scared about meeting this Captain as I was about entering the basement earlier!

At many fires, the first company on the scene is greeted by a person saying that "someone's still in there." This probably happens at about half the fires we have in occupied dwellings. We routinely search every floor of every building where people might be in danger. This is also true for vacant buildings, because you never know when a vagrant or a junkie might be using the house for shelter. In occupied houses we always assume there could be someone trapped inside.

One night we had a report of a building fire on Padelford Street. I was still on Engine 2 at the time, and we were first-in. When my Lieutenant, Joe, and I got off the truck a big black woman came running over to us and started screaming, "My baby's in there, hurry!" The house was a 3-decker and there was fire showing from the front window of the third floor. She told us that her baby was on the third floor.

With a 3-man company, this is one of the toughest decisions at the scene of a fire such as this one. One man has to stay with the truck to run the pump, providing the water needed to fight this fire. Do the two remaining men stretch a hoseline to the fire, or do we run into the building without a hoseline to search right away? It takes additional time to stretch the hoseline with two men, but if we are blocked by fire on our way to the third floor we can knock it down and move past. If we just run in without a line we can reach the third floor much faster, provided our way isn't blocked by fire. Each situation is different and the officer has to make a judgment call based on the specific circumstances – where the victim is reported, where the fire is located, and how quickly the next Engine Company will have their line in operation. In this case, Joe decided to rush right in – I followed.

We got up to the third floor doorway and stopped. We could see the room to our left, the front room, fully ablaze. The fire was free burning and had burst through the front windows, providing it with fresh oxygen to feed the flames. These windows were also drawing most of the smoke out into the fresh night air, so we could get a good look at the inside of the room. There was nobody in the front room. Joe crawled past the room toward the rear of the apartment and I was right behind. We worked as a team entering one room at a time and searching throughout – including under the bed and in the closet. Ladder 7 had joined us, having used the rear stairs, and we quickly completed the search of the apartment without finding anyone trapped. By this time, the fire had begun to spread throughout the apartment. We were about to be cut off from our exit, when Engine 7 brought a line to the third floor and started to attack the fire. When they knocked it down, we made our way to the rear stairs, and outside.

Joe looked for the woman in the street to ask her if she knew exactly where the baby was located, as I changed my air tank in order to go back inside. He had trouble locating her. She had moved to the sidewalk across the street – and was laughing! When Joe asked her about her baby, she said, "Oh, I'm sorry, he's alright! He's here!" She proceeded to hug her twenty-five year old son who was sitting on his neighbor's steps. He was obviously wasted. It turns out that he and his brother lived on the third floor, and his mother lived on the second floor. He had come home drunk and laid down on his sofa. He must have dropped a cigarette, got up, and went back out. When the couch started burning, his mother thought he was still up there. This was an honest mistake. I have searched many buildings in vain because someone *believed* their loved one was still inside. The problem that I have with this is that most of the time they find the person safely outside – and don't bother telling the firemen.

Meanwhile, we're still searching, with the belief that someone is inside.

The 'funny' part of this story happened the very next night at about the same time. We got a call for a stabbing at this same address. When we arrived on the scene, we found this woman's 'baby' lying in a pool of blood on the sidewalk, amid the rubble from the fire of the previous night. It seems the victim and his twenty-three year old brother had a fight. The brother grabbed a large kitchen knife and slashed 'baby's' throat. We tried to stop the bleeding and rush him to the hospital but he had lost too much blood. He had narrowly dodged fate one night, only to have his brother take his life about 24 hours later!

We have a building in the City of Providence, the Fleet Bank building, that looks just like the building used in the opening of the old Superman television series. It's about 27 stories high. It was always the dominant building in our city's skyline. Back in 1984 lights were installed to the exterior of the building to enhance its nighttime appearance. I was assigned to the Branch Ave Station at the time, which was about a mile from the building. You could plainly see the city's skyline from the second floor of the station. About a week or two later we were getting ready to eat our dinner during a night shift. It was about 7:00 PM and my Lieutenant, Joe, had prepared a hearty meal of Philly cheese steak sandwiches and French fries for the guys on duty that night. As one of the guys from Ladder 7, Dennis, was bringing his plate to the table he stopped at the window and said, "Shit, I forgot they put those lights on Fleet. I looked quick and thought the building was on fire!" We didn't pay much attention to this remark at the time.

About fifteen minutes later Engine 2 and Ladder 7 were barreling down the road, responding to a second Alarm of fire at the Fleet Bank building. We reached the building, parked our apparatus on the street, grabbed our gear and reported to the Chief at the Command Post inside the lobby. Typically at a high-rise fire, a firefighter on an engine company will carry two fifty-foot sections of 2 ½" hose, tools for connecting the hose to the building's standpipe[8], and an extra air cylinder. He'll carry them to the Forward Staging Area, which is usually located one or two floors below the fire floor. In this case the fire was on the 12th floor, so we had to carry our tools to the 10th floor. This equipment, along with our fire coat, boots, helmet, and air pak means that each firefighter was carrying over 200 lbs. of equipment up the stairs.

We began the long walk up ten flights of stairs in single file – the two Engine Companies and the Ladder Company from the second Alarm assignment. There's not much talking going on. We know that this is going to be a long haul, and that once we get there our real work is going to begin. So we march silently, trying to conserve our energy. We're also monitoring the radio transmissions to try to get an idea of the conditions above. Once we got to about the 7th or 8th floor the pace became noticeably slower. At this point we heard a feminine voice from below saying, "Boy, I thought firemen were supposed to be in good shape!" This stopped us all dead in our tracks! We looked below us and saw a woman TV reporter with her cameraman following us up the stairs. The cameraman was carrying his camera and a battery pack. He just rolled his eyes and shook his head at her comment. She was carrying a small notebook.

Joe was the one who took her to task. He said, "Hey sweetheart, do you know how much this stuff weighs that we're carrying? What are *you* carrying – a fucking notebook? How would you like that thing stuck up your ass? And who the hell told you that you could come up here anyway? This is a fire scene and you're not allowed in here! Now you take your pretty little ass down the stairs and park it outside the building or I'll get a cop up here to arrest you." She turned bright red – I don't know if it was from embarrassment or anger. Probably a little of both. It looked like she was about to say something else, but her cameraman grabbed her by the arm and began leading her down. As she was descending the stairs she could hear the echoes of the laughter and the high-fives of the other firefighters. We then began the trek up the last three floors – silently.

When we reached the Forward Staging Area we learned that it had been a small office fire that was quickly knocked down by the first Alarm companies and that we weren't needed. We then walked down ten flights of stairs – still carrying all that equipment.

Some of us would see that TV reporter on the street from time to time at other fires. We just couldn't resist the urge to bust her balls. "Can I carry that notebook for you, honey?"

And Dennis, from Ladder 7? He wasn't allowed a window seat during dinner any more.

On one occasion, years ago, I was detailed to Battalion 3, to drive the Chief. It was a night shift in October and the weather was absolutely gorgeous – a slight cool breeze and not a cloud in the sky. Battalion 3 was located in the same station as Engine 2, so I didn't even have to switch beds for the night. The Chief's Aide job was relatively easy. The duties were to drive the Chief around to the different stations in the Battalion to check on the firefighters under his command and pick up or deliver any departmental paperwork. This gives you a chance to see guys from other stations that you may not have seen in a while.

All in all, it's not that bad a job to have – once in a while. The down side of the job is that your main job at a fire is to terminate the utilities (shut off the gas and electric), and to stay near the Chief, on the outside of the fire building, in case he needs something done. The Chief's Aide doesn't really do much firefighting on the inside of the building.

On this night, around midnight, we were sent to a report of an old railroad bridge on fire. The bridge was over the Seekonk River, at the north end of Narragansett Bay. It connected Providence to the city of East Providence, and hadn't been used in about 25 years. It spanned about 300 yards, and the middle section was designed to bend to a 45-degree angle back toward the Providence side, to allow the boats to sail up or down the river. The tip of the track was lifted 100 feet above the water, and it was permanently left in this position. Railroad tracks are two rails of steel affixed to equally spaced pieces of lumber approximately 6" by 6" called railroad ties. These ties are treated with creosol to help them resist rot. When these ties soaked with creosol begin to burn, they are almost impossible to extinguish.

When I turned the car onto Gano Street we could see the top of the bridge clearly, and the top third of it was ablaze. This fire wasn't threatening to spread anywhere, as the raised portion, which was on fire, was about a hundred yards off the shoreline. Nevertheless, it was on fire, and we had to put it out. When we got to the gate leading to the bridge it became apparent that this wasn't going to be an easy job. It was going to take an awful lot of water to extinguish the railroad ties that were burning, and the nearest hydrant was about 1,500 feet away! That's a lot of hose to lay (and pick up later) for a nuisance fire such as this. The first two Engine companies on the scene tried to use their tank water to put out the fire. Each Engine carries 500 gallons of water in its tank. After both companies had used all the water in their tanks, and not affected the fire in the slightest, the Chief ordered that hose be laid from the hydrant to the scene. We were in for a long night!

After we had been there for a couple of hours, everyone was cold, wet, tired, and filthy! The Chief called me over and handed me two $20 bills and said, "Tom, go get 20 large coffees and 4 dozen doughnuts." I was still fairly new on the job and was shocked at this order. We were a couple of miles from the nearest all-night coffee shop, and we were still trying to put out his fire. And he was telling me to take the Chief's car and go get doughnuts!

I took the car and headed downtown toward the doughnut shop, with the lights and siren on all the way. I pulled up in front of the shop and turned off the siren. Imagine their surprise when a young firefighter got out of the car and casually walked into the store. It was about 2:00 AM! I was filthy and was still wearing my fire boots! I stood in line and patiently waited for my turn. When I got to the counter I told the girl taking my order, "Twenty large coffees and four-dozen doughnuts, please." She just looked at me for a moment, and then said, "You've got to be kidding!" I said, "Do I look like I'm kidding?" She looked at me again, then through the window to the car outside, still running and with the flashing lights on. She sighed and said, "This is going to take a few minutes." I told her that I wasn't going anywhere, and that I'd wait. When she finally finished, I told her to keep the change – I'm always a big tipper with someone else's money! It took me three trips to load everything into the car. When I came back in for the last tray of coffees I noticed that I had practically wiped her out of doughnuts. When I was walking to the door I said, loud enough for everyone in the shop to hear, "Time to make the doughnuts!" When I got to the car and sat behind the wheel, I noticed that she was looking at me through the window. I waved to her, put the siren back on, and headed back to the fire.

I now wear extended wear contact lenses. This means that I can wear them day *and* night for about a week straight. I switched to these types of lenses around 1985 so that I could get up in the middle of the night when I was working, and drive the fire truck without worrying about my glasses. I had a few occasions when I slid the pole only to realize that I had forgotten my glasses upstairs. In these cases I would just get on the truck and do the best I could. Let me start off by saying that I never got into an accident because of this. I'm not (or at least I wasn't at the time) that blind, although there are people who might argue that point.

On one occasion I was driving Engine 2 on a call to a reported building fire. It was about midnight and the roads were pretty deserted. While we were responding I heard Joe, my Lieutenant, yell from the officer's seat, "Holy shit! It's a good thing that bastard was quick on his feet!" I kept driving and said, "What bastard?" Apparently, as we were screaming down the street, a guy was leisurely trying to cross the street – doing his best ghetto strut. As we got closer he kept up his slow pace – that is, until he realized that we weren't going to slow down! As we got even closer, his eyes opened wide, and he ran like hell to get out of the way. We missed him by less than a foot…and never slowed down!! I'm relating this story as told to me by Joe. And by Pete, who was riding the side that night. I never even saw him!

Another night I was again driving Engine 2, and again Pete was riding the side. This night, however, another firefighter from Engine 2, George, was in charge. The bell tipped at about 2:00 AM for a report of smoke inside a church.

I slid the pole, got on the truck and reached for my glasses. I had forgotten them upstairs again! I managed to drive to the scene without any problems. Once we got there, however, I had to maneuver the truck between other apparatus and had a couple of tight squeezes. Again, no problem. After the fire was over and we had picked up and packed the hose we headed for our truck. I finally said, "George, guess what? I don't have my eyes in." He just looked at me and shook his head. "Pete," he said, "get up here! You're driving home!"

One night when I was a Lieutenant on Engine 15 I brought my camera and tripod into work. I've always been an amateur photography buff and I'm particularly fascinated with nighttime photographs – especially the effect of streaking lights. To get this effect you need to leave the lens open for a second or two. When you do this, you need to have the camera set up on a tripod to keep the camera perfectly steady. On this night, I wanted to get some dramatic pictures of the station, and the truck, in the dark.

In order to get the shots I wanted, I needed to set up my tripod in the middle of the intersection next to the station. I waited until around midnight so that the traffic wouldn't be too heavy, and set it up right in the middle of the intersection. I then had the guys shut off all the lights in the station with the exception of those on the apparatus floor. The chauffeur, Al, started the truck, turned on the emergency lights and pulled it halfway out of the overhead door. I took a number of pictures using different lenses to zoom in, and to widen the shot. All the while I had to dodge the traffic, which was still surprisingly busy for this hour. I'd take a couple of shots, pick up the tripod and move it to the corner until the traffic went through the intersection; then I'd set up again and take a couple more.

I then tried a moving shot, leaving the lens open until the truck was out of view of the lens. Al would pull the truck out of the station, take a right turn, and pass right in front of me. He'd then take the truck around the block, back it into the station, and do it again. He did this about four times – until I ran out of film. The neighbors, and the people in the traffic that passed by, had no idea what the hell was going on. The whole process took about 15 minutes, but I got some great shots. One in particular is of the truck moving. The truck isn't even visible in the photograph – only its lights! It looks like Engine 15 is responding - in Warp Speed!

We've often been accused of using too much speed on the streets, on the way to one of our runs – but not quite warp speed. Too much speed for whom? The person watching us go by on the street, or the person waiting for us because her husband has stopped breathing? In actuality, the speed we travel seems much faster than we're actually moving because of the lights and siren, and the size of the truck. We have the right of way when we're on an emergency call, but we still have to obey all the traffic laws, with the exception of the speed limit. For the amount of times and miles spent zipping around the busy city streets of Providence, fire apparatus actually have a very small number of accidents. That percentage has only gotten better since I've stopped driving!

Part of the reason we have so few accidents is that we know the streets so well. Firefighters take pride in knowing their districts inside and out - all the streets, all the break numbers, and most of the buildings. There are, however, always exceptions. I worked a callback one night on Engine 4 with the "dream team." This was a pair of firefighters who were notorious for being screw-ups. I don't know how they ever got assigned to the same crew. Whenever I worked with these guys, I prayed for a slow night. One of them would occasionally tell his officer, when they arrived on the scene of a run, that he forgot his turnout gear at the station. This guy was the absolute worst excuse for a firefighter (I even hate to call him a firefighter) I have ever had contact with. Anyway, on this night, the other half of the team was driving, so I felt a little better. Within fifteen minutes of my arriving at the station, we caught a run to a report of smoke in a home. We were called first – "Engines 4, 5, 2; Ladders 7 & 4; Battalion 3 respond to 545 Cole Ave…" As we shot out of the station and onto the street, I turned to see if Twiddle Dum had remembered his turnout gear. When I saw that he had, I thought we were home free. I was wrong. We made a right hand turn onto Cole Ave. and Twiddle Dee gunned the truck. I yelled to him that I thought the higher numbers were near here and, "slow down so I can check." He assured me that 545 was much further down the street. Hey, it was his district – I was from the other side of the city. I realized that I had been right when Engine 5 passed us going the opposite way, without even slowing down! Both trucks passing in opposite directions with lights and sirens on! "They must have passed it," he said. "Stop the fucking truck and turn it around!" I screamed. I shut off the siren. When he turned the truck around and we got to the house, Engine 5 had already beaten us in to our run – obviously. This is what we call a misrun. In my district, this is a very embarrassing thing. It didn't seem to faze either of these guys. Something told me that this wasn't their first misrun. Needless to say, I told him that under no circumstances was he to drive over 20 MPH for the rest of the night, and whenever we went out after that, I told him which way to go!

When I first became a fireman, some of the most annoying people we used to come in contact with were the insurance claims adjusters, who used to show up at fires and auto accidents at almost the same time we did. Ambulance chasers. They would cruise the city with scanners monitoring the fire and police channels. When they heard a report of a building fire they would respond as quickly as possible to "help" the homeowner. They would tell the owner that they would arrange to have the building boarded up, secured, repaired, and cleaned. They would also help the homeowner document the loss, and put in the claim with his insurance company. Most times the homeowner had no idea of how to go about doing these necessary jobs and was happy to have someone taking care of all the details. These claims adjusters would do much the same thing at an auto accident, many times trying to enter into a contract with the owner of the auto even as we were working on them and wheeling them into the Rescue. The city has passed ordinances preventing this type of harassment, so we no longer run into these guys on the street. If it still goes on, and I'm sure it does, it's done a little more discreetly.

What we've been encountering on the street in the past couple of years is an even sadder commentary on our modern 'civilized' society. Ice cream trucks have been following the fire trucks and rescues in search of a crowd. I've noticed, from time to time, that they've been working the crowds around many of our fire scenes. People seem to love to watch a fire, so the crowds seem to be natural targets for these venders. Lately, however, I've been seeing these trucks at the scene of shootings and stabbings – especially in the public housing projects around the city. I've even had an ice cream truck block my way when I've been driving the Engine to the hospital. As I've been trying to follow the Rescue, which is carrying a dying shooting victim to the hospital, they've been trying to rush to the scene of the crime before the crowd begins to disperse. I'm not sure who I think is a bigger piece of human garbage – these drivers or the parents who allow their kids to hang around the scene of a shooting or stabbing. We had a case in the city a few years ago of a drive-by shooting in the projects at around 10:00 one night. After we had transported the victim to the hospital, the police secured the scene. When they left, about an hour later, there was still quite a crowd in the area. Someone shot into the crowd and killed a 10-year-old little boy. What the hell was a child his age doing out of the house, at the scene of a previous shooting, in a dangerous housing project, at 11:00 PM??!! Where the fuck was his mother???!!!

That same housing project is notorious for stolen cars being dumped, stripped and burned. One day when I was working a day shift at Engine 2 we responded to an apartment complex because someone burnt their dinner and set off the smoke detectors. This is a very common occurrence, and there was nothing unusual about this run – until we returned to the station. The engine, the ladder, and the chief all responded to the box alarm, and we all returned together. I was driving Engine 2. As I was backing into the station, the Lieutenant of Ladder 7, which had already backed in, said, "Hey Tom, was your wife picking up your car today?" "No," I said, "why?" "Because someone just drove it up the ramp from the garage and is going down the street!" I looked quickly to my left, and sure enough, there went my car. Someone had stolen it from the garage beneath the firehouse. The other guys jumped back on the truck, as the Lieutenant of Ladder 7 called our dispatcher to have them notify the police, and we took off after them with lights flashing and siren blaring. We followed them for a few blocks – that is, until they hopped on the highway. The fire trucks in Providence were governored at 50 MPH at that time and we just couldn't keep up with the car. In the mean time, the police had dispatched a description of my car over their radio. One of their cars had spotted it and we got word from our dispatcher of its location. It was abandoned at a gas station just outside the projects. I had driven to work that day on fumes. When they stole it, they quickly realized that they needed fuel, and stopped at the gas station. After they put in $2.00 worth, they went to the liquor store across the street. When they left the liquor store, they saw a police cruiser behind the car and took off. I got it back with gas in the tank, but a busted ignition. I can only imagine that if we hadn't spotted it being driven off, we could have responded, an hour or so later, to a car fire in the projects. I guess a busted ignition wasn't that bad after all.

I remember when I first started seeing my fiancée and she began visiting me at the firehouse. She's always been curious about my job, and asked a million questions about fires, the truck, the equipment, and the station – she wanted to know about everything. She worked fairly close to the Mount Pleasant Avenue station, so she'd come and visit me after she left work if I was beginning a night shift. She'd bring me a coffee and we'd sit and talk until the alarm would call me away. It felt good to have someone who seemed to care about my profession. Nancy has a great personality and is a great listener, so she befriended my guys very easily. She'd always tease me that I wouldn't let her go upstairs. Only the Chief of Department can authorize non-departmental individuals to visit the living quarters upstairs in the station. "No women allowed upstairs," I'd say. She'd always tell me that I must have been hiding something up there. In this firehouse, our 'sitting room' (our living room) was located on the first floor – in most stations in Providence it's located on the second floor. This made it comfortable when she came to visit. We'd usually just sit on the sofa, talk, and watch TV.

She considered herself a real firefighter's flame and enjoyed going to the departmental functions and being around the action. It was exciting to her. One night she went out to a club with her sisters while I was working a night shift. Around midnight I answered the phone, and she asked me if I was in the mood for a coffee. Of course, I said yes. Whether I was or not, it meant that I'd get the chance to see her for a few minutes! When she came to the door I was pleasantly surprised to see that she was alone. After a few minutes I could see that she was 'feeling good', and I suddenly felt inspired. I walked out to the apparatus floor and she followed. After talking for a few minutes I reached over and kissed her. "I wish you weren't working tonight," she whispered. "Me, too," I said, "but I've got a great idea." I just looked up at the hose bed in the back of the truck, and smiled. "We've got a bed," I said. She smiled, and I grabbed her hand and helped her climb the steps to the hose bed. The lights were out and no one could see, so we proceeded to make love on the top of the hose bed, while the other guys were upstairs sleeping – just like in *Backdraft*. That was always my favorite part of the movie! Now I don't have to be jealous of Mr. Baldwin anymore.

Chapter 13
Nagging Little Injuries
(It Hurts So Good)

I told my fiancée a few years ago that she should apply for Social Security disability payments. She has MS, and the stress of her job had triggered an attack. MS is a progressive disease and is not going to go away. The only way for her to beat it is to take care of her health. I believed, and still believe, that the stress of a full time job would continue to trigger bouts with this terrible disease. The difference in the money she would take home is not worth risking her health.

Working on the fire department is a lot like that. Over the years the physical and emotional scars pile one on top of the other until you don't notice anymore. You just learn to live with the pain. You just notice that you don't have the strength you used to have. You notice that you don't have the flexibility you once had. You don't have the stamina you once had. I realize that everyone goes through this over the years – firemen just go through this at an earlier age. As I write this, I am 48 years old, and I feel like sixty. Firefighters have a much higher than average rate of heart disease, stress, and cancer. On average, a firefighter has a shorter life span than the average man by about ten years. These are part of the reasons many departments around the country have mandatory retirement ages. In the Providence Fire Department it is sixty. It is also the reason I hope this family business stops with this generation. I don't want this for my son!

With the development of many different chemicals and compounds over the last twenty-five years or so and the wide spread use of plastics, the toxins the modern day firefighter is exposed to on a regular basis is much more than our predecessors. The widespread storage and transport of Hazardous Materials is another health concern for firefighters, as is the changeover to diesel engines for fire apparatus that began in the 1970s. Up until the last few years, few departments realized the health risks associated with the inhalation of diesel fumes, or how long they lingered in the atmosphere in firehouses where firefighters were working. Over the last five to ten years, most fire departments, thankfully, have installed venting systems in the stations, which attach directly to the exhaust pipes of the apparatus. This, however, does nothing to take away the prolonged exposures that firefighters working in these stations over the last twenty years were subjected to.

Firefighters are generally not very highly paid city workers, despite the inherent dangers and long-term health risks. In Providence, for instance, the fire department dispatchers are civilian civil service jobs. They work fewer hours per week than firefighters, in heated and air-conditioned offices, but their weekly salary is higher than our firefighters. This, to me, makes no sense at all. Many firemen retire after twenty years, opting to take their pension – at half their salary. They do this to get away from the health risks that have already begun to take their toll on their bodies. Half salary is not enough to provide for a family, therefore, most firefighters will start a second career after leaving the fire department. It's a matter of survival.

I have no choice but to continue working as a firefighter at this point in my life. I must try to build my pension to 75% of my salary. To do this I have to work for 32 ½ years on the fire department. I'll be fifty-eight. At that age, if I'm still riding the trucks, I'll be at much greater risk of injury or heart attack on every single call to which I respond!

In addition to the inherent exposures and stresses of the job, I have had my share of injuries caused by accidents in or around the firehouse and fire scenes. Most of the sprains and strains, bumps and bruises go unreported and are long since forgotten. Firefighting is a physical job, after all, and a certain amount of wear and tear on the body is unavoidable. So is the continual exposure to smoke, chemicals, hazardous materials, and God knows what! It is part of our S.O.P.'s regarding hazardous material incidents and terrorist attacks, that the first fire company on the scene recognize the danger and communicate to all other incoming companies to stage at a safe distance until the agent is identified. In most cases this means that the first-arriving company is sacrificed! And this is part of our plan!

My first significant injury came when I had about a year on the job, and it still affects me today. Early in my career, I was riding the side of Engine 2 and we responded to a Master Box at a local hospital during a day shift. Back then we had a watch desk at each station. There was a firefighter at the desk from 0700 hours until 2100 hours (7:00 AM to 9:00 PM) every day. It was this firefighter's responsibility to keep track of any hydrants out of service, or streets closed in the district, as well as tip the bell if a company in the house was going out on a run. On this particular day I had the 'floor watch.' When the call came over the vocalarm for the hospital run, I tipped the bell, and walked over to the truck to put on my gear. I climbed on the side as the chauffeur started the diesel engine and began to move out the door. While I had been on floor watch there had been an announcement that Seventh Street was closed to traffic.

This was the street we normally took to the hospital. I leaned forward, sticking my head into the cab, to inform the chauffeur of this before he committed the truck to that route. Just as I was leaning my head into the cab, the truck rolled off the ramp and into the street…and into a small sinkhole around a sewer grate! As the truck crashed down into the sinkhole, my jaw came crashing down on the top of the air cylinder that was bracketed to my jumpseat. I went out cold and slumped, face down, onto the seat. Luckily, for me, we had four men that day, and the firefighter in the other jumpseat, George, saw me fall. He dove over the engine compartment and grabbed me by the shoulders to keep me from sliding off the truck and into the street – and possibly under the rear wheels! He slid to my side of the truck and held me in place until we got to the hospital. As we pulled up to the scene I was just coming around. I told my officer I was O.K. – I was too embarrassed, and too new on the job, to tell him the truth! Shortly after returning to the station, my jaw swelled up like a balloon, so my Lieutenant had the Rescue transport me to the same hospital we had just come from. I thought I had broken my jaw, but the X-rays were negative. I did do some damage to my neck, however, and although I didn't stay off injured, it's never been the same.

On another occasion during my early career, Engine 2 responded to a report of a dumpster fire. This was a very common type of fire which normally only required a single engine company to extinguish. These were usually relatively small metal containers (about 6'x 6' x 6') of trash that had been lit by kids or vandals… or by the building occupants, to reduce the amount of trash in order to fit more into the container. When we pulled up to the scene, we discovered smoke coming from a large dumpster that was attached to the side of a jewelry manufacturing company. The dumpster was approximately 10' high by 10' wide by 30' long. We called Ladder 7 on a Special Signal[9] to assist us in moving the dumpster from the building, and in extinguishing the fire within. Trash fires can be extremely difficult to extinguish, the fire is usually deeply seated within layers and layers of trash. You have to peel these layers off a little at a time, all the while wetting it down. This makes the trash extremely heavy, and difficult to maneuver.

The seat of this fire was deeply imbedded in the dumpster, and we had to pull out large amounts of trash to reach it. This meant climbing about 20' inside this enclosed dumpster. It took us about an hour to completely put this fire out. When we had finished, someone picked up a partially melted plastic gallon jug from the pile of trash and read the label. It was cyanide. We looked around at the trash and noticed several other jugs with the same label. Some still had what appeared to be a small amount of the product inside the bottles. We had been crawling around inside an enclosed, metal container that was burning plastic bottles of cyanide! Several of the guys, myself included, had severe headaches for the next few months. It's exposures like this one that make you wonder about the long term health risks associated with our job.

Freon is another type of gas that could cause a serious health problem in the event of an exposure. While on Engine 2, I had a call to an office building for a report of smoke in the basement. When we arrived on the scene, the building was being evacuated. We were met by the building manager. He told us that there seemed to be a "light haze" of smoke in the basement. My lieutenant, Joe, and I descended the stairs to the basement to check it out. I was pretty new on the job, and was trained to wear my air pak whenever entering a building for a possible fire. I didn't turn it in (turn on the air), or put on the facepiece, I just put on the harness and carried it on my back – just in case. Joe, on the other hand, was from the 'old school' – they don't put on air paks unless they absolutely need them. So – I had on my pak, and Joe didn't wear his.

When we got to the bottom of the stairs we could see what the manager had meant – there did seem to be a 'haze' in the air. There was no really visible smoke, however, nor any smell of anything unusual. Joe radioed that we were checking out a 'slight haze' in the basement, but that nothing was showing at this time. We proceeded further into the basement to see if we could discover the cause. As we were getting deeper into the cellar, we were both starting to feel strange – lightheaded and dizzy. Neither of us realized that the other was feeling this also, so we just ignored this feeling and continued on. After a few minutes more, Joe turned to me with a quizzical look on his face and asked, "Are you feeling fucked up, too?" I nodded. He said, "Let's get the hell outta here!" We began to trace our way back, following the same route as we used to enter. When he stumbled, I turned in my air bottle and took a quick breath. I then gave the mask to Joe so that he could get some fresh air. After he started getting his bearings back, he gave me back the mask and we started out again – sharing the air as we went along.

When we got outside, Joe reported what had happened to the Chief, and the Chief ordered that all other companies put on their paks before entering the building. Joe then went to the Rescue, and eventually to the hospital – where he spent the night. The oxygen levels in his blood were dangerously low. We found out later that there was a freon leak in the basement. Freon is a colorless, odorless gas used in air conditioning units. When inhaled, it displaces the oxygen in your blood, keeping your blood from carrying the life-giving oxygen to the rest of your body – and your brain. If we had collapsed in the basement, we surely would have been in deep trouble. Once your brain is without oxygen for four minutes, brain damage begins. After six minutes, you are brain dead! This explains a lot in my life – my brain must have been without oxygen for about five minutes! Only kidding!

My back problems can be traced to a number of incidents over the years. Falling down stairs, ceilings being pulled down on me, tripping over things I couldn't see in the smoke – all these are common firefighting injuries. Most of these are not reported unless they are serious enough to require medical attention at the time. All firefighters go through this, if you can shake it off you forget it – until you wake up stiff the next morning not able to move! One night we were called to a fire in a vacant house on Lydia Street. It was a 3-decker, and it was burning on all three floors as we pulled up. We were the second engine company into the building. The first line into the building was brought to the first floor so we began to take our line to the second floor. As we were going up the rear stairs, one of the steps gave way under my weight. I was about three-quarters of the way up the stairs and Pete was right behind me. We didn't realize at the time that the fire was burning in the basement below the staircase! I ended up waist deep in the hole. Pete and Joe grabbed hold of my arms and tried to pull me out. They had to be careful not to put too much weight near the part of the staircase that had collapsed. My legs were dangling in the air, so I didn't have much leverage to help them! I could see past them to the second floor landing and I saw an old refrigerator that was tilting our way. The floor beneath it had begun to sag. That was all we needed right now – a fridge falling on top of us, crashing through the stairs and sending us into the basement! They finally pulled me free, and we backed down the stairs and outside the building to safety. We told Engine 7 before we left that the fire was below us in the basement, and that the floors were weak – they backed out also. We told the Chief about the floors and he ordered everyone out of the building. Joe had gotten something in his eye and needed to have it flushed out, so Pete and I put a ground ladder to the third floor window and took our hoseline to the top, and attacked the fire from the window. Just as we began to climb the ladder we could hear the fridge crashing down on the stairway inside.

The next morning my back was killing me, but I was beginning my cycle of four days off, so I just went home figuring I just pulled a muscle and that it would be better by the time I returned to work. Although it bothered me for a few days, it seemed to be a little better by the time I started work again. Therefore, I never reported it. For myself, and for most firefighters, this is a common occurrence. Shake it off – it'll get better. It gets better, but it never goes away completely. The cumulative effect of many of these types of injuries over the years takes its toll. Believe me, I'm feeling it now!

Another time, a few years ago, I was fighting a fire in a two-story building where I had many previous fires. I was the Lieutenant on Engine 15 and I was very familiar with the building. On the first floor there was an open stairway to the cellar, in the back left corner. This particular night we had a smoky fire in the house, and we had our line to the first floor. I was leading my crew to the area where the fire was most intense. I was crouching low and feeling ahead of me with my haligan tool – trying to locate the edge of the hole in the floor. I still don't know what the hell happened, but the next thing I knew, I was heading face-first down the hole to the basement floor below. When firefighters travel through a pitch-black room we try to maintain physical contact with each other as much as possible – to avoid getting separated. The firefighter right behind me, Al, was a big kid. He felt me begin to fall forward and dove on my leg to keep hold of me. He kept me from falling to the basement on my face, but my knee felt like someone had ripped it right off the rest of my leg! My entire body weight, as well as that of my equipment was hanging over the edge, being supported by my bent leg. The next thing I knew I heard someone's radio echoing, "We have a firefighter down, we're bringing him out the side door. Have Rescue meet us on Side 4." They carried me out of the building and to the Rescue. I had strained ligaments in my knee and ended up with a month off.

Another injury of that type happened one icy night in winter. We had a fire in a 3-decker that was connected to a single-story commercial building. When we arrived on the scene with Engine 8, the entire first floor was engulfed in flames. We were told to take a line to the second floor, to check for extension of fire. My Captain that night, Joe, told us to put a ladder up to the roof of the store, as this was the easiest way to gain access to the second floor. We could walk across the roof and climb onto the fire escape of the fire building and make entry. After the other firefighter from Engine 8, Dave, and I raised the ladder, we began to climb to the roof. Dave and I were carrying the hoseline. It was extremely icy that night, so we enlisted the help of the Chief's Aide, Tony, to 'foot the ladder.' This meant he would stand on the bottom rung and hold the ladder so that it wouldn't slide out from under us on the icy sidewalk. The Captain went up the ladder first, followed by Dave, and then myself. Tony was one of those hyper guys who was always looking ahead to his next job. This can be a dangerous thing on the fireground. After the Captain and Dave finished climbing to the roof, Tony left to do something else. About ten seconds after he left, the ladder began to slide away from the building. I was about one rung away from the roof! As the ladder slipped away, I reached out and grabbed an old-fashioned light fixture that was attached to the front of the store. As the ladder crashed to the ground, I was dangling from the light fixture with one arm, as the other was still holding the hoseline. Dave and the Captain reached down from the roof, took the hose from my shoulder and then grabbed my left arm and pulled me up to the safety of the roof. My adrenaline was certainly pumping by this time, and we took the hoseline to the fire escape and into the second floor. My shoulder was a little sore that night but I didn't think it was that bad, so when we returned to the station, I went to bed as always. The next morning, when I woke up, I couldn't move my left arm at all! By the time I returned to work, four days later, it had loosened up a little, so I never had to take any injury time for this. My shoulder, however, has never been the same. It's still stiff and it still aches – and that happened about ten years ago.

Not all of these little injuries have left permanent reminders on my body. Some have been minor cuts and bruises that heal and go away, and some have been just near misses. These have only left funny memories. On one occasion years ago, while on Engine 2, we had a small fire on the first floor of a two-story house. Engine 12 had the first line into the building and was attacking the fire. We took our line to the second floor to check for any extension of fire above. As we were making our way into the front living room, which was directly above the fire, we had to go down a small corridor from the kitchen area. While I was walking down this corridor, my helmet was suddenly knocked off my head. I couldn't figure out what the hell had happened. I looked around but saw nothing. I went back, picked up my helmet, and started for the living room once again. It was then that I saw a plaster pole poke down through the ceiling directly from above, about two feet in front of me. A plaster pole is a six-foot long pole that resembles a spear. We use it to reach ceilings, poke through them, and pull the plaster down to search for hidden fire. The 'roofman' uses it to make sure the ventilation hole he put in the roof goes all

161

the way through to the apartment below. As I was walking below, the roofman had poked this plaster pole through the ceiling and it struck the back lip of my helmet, flipping it right off my head! The end of the pole is a metal point. If this had been six inches to the right or left, it would have impaled my shoulder. I learned a valuable lesson that day. Never take off your helmet in a fire building, because you never know when it's going to save your life. If I didn't have my helmet on that day, the plaster pole would have gone right into the middle of my back. This was the first of many times my helmet would save me from injury in my career.

Chapter 14
First-In

For my money, there's nothing like being the first-in engine company at a working building fire. This is the biggest rush I could possibly imagine.

I was a firefighter on an engine company for about eleven years, and I've been an officer on an engine company for about ten years now; so I've had my share of first-in fires in both capacities. I enjoyed being the pipeman and getting the first water on the fire. You take the line into the building and push forward as far as you can, for as long as you can. You don't have to be a rocket scientist to do the job, but you do have to have strength and stamina. You have to carry 200' of hoseline up three flights of stairs under tough conditions. Once you've reached the fire floor and your line is charged,[10] you have to be able to control the hose. There's a surprising amount of resistance to an operating fire hose. You also have to move the charged hoseline throughout the building as needed. A charged hoseline is very heavy and very difficult to maneuver, especially when it gets caught up on something in the apartment, or in the stairway. You have to be able to do all this in the heat, and the smoke, and the dark – with an air pak on! You're the one leading the charge; there's no one in front of you. If you lose physical contact with your backup man, you feel completely alone. Even so, you continue to push forward until it's physically impossible to go any further, or your officer grabs you by the coat and yells to you to "back out."

I remember the first fire I had as the pipeman after I transferred to Engine 8. It was a two-story occupied house on Hammond Street. When we pulled up to the scene, we were told that everyone was out of the building. There was heavy fire showing from one window in the front corner room of the first floor. It was going good, but it didn't look like it had spread to the whole apartment yet. We needed to get water on this fire quickly. I quickly made note of the location of the fire, and headed to the back of the truck.

I grabbed 200' of hoseline from the hosebed and started to the back door. There was heavy black smoke coming from the apartment. I knelt down in front of the door and donned my facemask. My Lieutenant was right behind me. We flaked out the hose and called for water. "OK. Let's go," he said from behind his mask. As we entered the apartment the heat was intense. The smoke made it impossible for me to see my hand in front of me. I was crawling along the wall toward the front of the house. When I came to a doorway and started to crawl through, the heat became even more intense and I could hear the crackling of the fire not far away. When I made my way into this room, I could see the glow of the fire in the far corner. Apparently there was another room off this one. I was crawling on my belly now because the heat was forcing us to keep low. When I got close to this last doorway I could see the flames beginning to lap around the doorframe trying to consume this room also. I laid on the floor with my arms stretched out in front of me and opened up the nozzle. *Hissssssssssss.* I could here the water turn to steam as it reached the fire above our heads. Hot water rained down on us, burning the exposed skin of our ears and necks. I quickly stuck the nozzle into the bottom corner of the doorway and directed the stream blindly into the fire room. More hissing and more pops. I stayed that way for a couple of minutes, swirling the nozzle in a circular motion to push back the heat. After a short while, I was able to crawl to the door and take a look inside the room. Most of the fire had been knocked down, and I could make out the glow of the areas that were still burning. I directed the hose to these spots and darkened down the rest of the fire. We had kept the fire from spreading to the rest of the house. We backed out and took a break.

When the smoke had cleared and we went back in to wet down any hot spots, we walked through the master bedroom. This was the room adjacent to the fire room. The room we crawled through to get to the fire. We saw a large disc-like piece of plastic on the bed in the middle of the room. We couldn't figure out what it was. We looked on the top of the bureau and saw another disc-like piece of plastic, with pieces of metal scattered throughout. We still couldn't figure out what these things were. The fire investigator saw us looking at this and said, "Do you want to buy a slightly used stereo?" That's when I realized that this pile of plastic on the bureau *had been* a stereo. The plastic casing had completely melted, and was beginning to re-harden as the air in the room cooled. I looked again at the plastic on the bed and glanced up at the ceiling. This had been a ceiling fan mounted above the bed. That's how hot the air on the upper half of this room had been! "Holy shit," I muttered to no one in particular. That's why we stay as low as possible when advancing a hoseline toward the fire; the air is cooler close to the floor. If we could tell just how hot the air in the top of the room was, we'd probably never try to make entry.

When you're responding to a call and you're not the first-in company, you have a good idea of what you're going to find as you're rolling in. The first-in company has already arrived on the scene and given a report of the conditions they've encountered, via the radio. You get a moment or two to prepare yourself, to visualize the scene, and go over your plan in your head. When you are the first-called engine company you have no idea what you're going to find until you actually pull up to the scene. Sometimes you've been given a clue by Fire Alarm – "numerous calls," "people trapped," or "smoke from a boiler." These are all descriptions given by the dispatcher that can help you visualize the scenario, help you prepare your plan of attack. Sometimes, however, a situation can take you completely by surprise.

Such was the case one night when I was riding the side step of Engine 8 – the nozzleman. We were having a relatively good night – a couple of minor runs early in the shift but nothing after 9:00 PM. I turned in around midnight, hoping to take advantage of a quiet night by getting some sleep. At about 3:00 AM the bell tipped. Everyone was going out – Engine 8, Ladder 2, and Battalion 2. We were being dispatched to a familiar place – Huntington Tower. This was a high-rise building in our first-in district. It was primarily housing for the elderly and the disabled. This was a problem building. We've had numerous nuisance runs to this address in the past, and we used to call this building, and the tower that was adjacent to it: 'the nut house.' We all assumed it was another nuisance run, so I wasn't about to wake up any more than I needed to. This way it would be easier to get back to sleep when we returned to the station.

I slid the pole, slipped into my boots and bunker pants, grabbed my fire coat and climbed into the jumpseat on the side of the apparatus. We rolled toward the building as I was sitting with my back toward the front of the truck. I tried to keep my eyes shut to keep from waking up too much. When we reached the side of the building and took the corner toward the front entrance, I heard the Captain say, "Oh shit!" from his seat in the cab. This woke me up! I turned to look and saw heavy flames blowing from a couple of windows on the 5th floor. Any remnants of sleep immediately disappeared. I grabbed my air pak and hopped off the truck. I grabbed the high-rise pack from the rear compartment and followed the Captain into the building, and toward the stairs. We carry 150' of folded hose, with a nozzle already attached, especially for high-rise fires – our 'high-rise pack.' When we reached the 4th floor landing I broke down the hose and connected it to the standpipe, which supplies firefighters with water in these types of buildings. We put on our masks and headed for the 5th floor.

When we entered from the stairway we could see heavy smoke in the hallway, layering down from the ceiling. We could see the smoke was coming from under the door of the second apartment on the left. One of the guys from Ladder 2 joined us with a master key he had taken from the Fire Alarm Box in the lobby.

As the Captain opened the door with the key, we all crouched down low, and to the side of the doorway. Smoke and heat poured from the apartment and the hallway quickly became like a hot, dark tunnel. We crawled through the doorway and spotted the fire along the outside wall. We opened up the nozzle and began to darken down the fire. We slowly advanced through the room, searching for victims as we went. There were three rooms in the apartment. This building was of fire resistive construction – the walls, ceilings, and floors are made of concrete and steel. In most cases, this helps contain a fire to a single apartment. There are, however, plenty of combustibles to burn – carpeting, furniture, cabinets, linen and clothing, etc. This fire had been burning for a while; the flames had spread to the bedroom. If we didn't stop it soon, it could burn through the door and spread deadly smoke throughout the entire building.

The same construction that keeps the fire from spreading also keeps the heat trapped in the apartment. This makes fighting a fire in a high-rise apartment feel like crawling into an oven! When we entered the apartment door, all of the heat and smoke that had been building up in the apartment rushed past us toward the hallway. We had to crawl on our hands and knees to keep beneath the superheated gases, which were banking down from the ceiling. We took a beating reaching this fire, especially the fire in the bedroom. We spent the next couple of hours wetting down the apartment, hauling out the debris, and ventilating the smoke from the building. So much for trying to get a good night's sleep.

Pulling up to a fire as the officer on the first-in engine company is a completely different experience. The immediate rush is just as intense – maybe even a little more intense. When I pull up to a fire as the first-in officer, I own the fire! It's mine. I give the initial report. I do the initial size-up. I decide the initial tactics. And I do all the follow-up paperwork.

Every fire is a different incident. Every fire has its own specific set of circumstances that make it unique. The most important jobs of the first-in officer are to do a complete size-up of the situation, relay any significant information to the in-coming units, and to select the most favorable tactics to mitigate the situation. He has to do all this within the first 30 seconds on the scene, however, because by this time his crew is ready to enter the building and begin the fight.

We have a set of pre-fire SOP's in place for fighting a fire in a 3-decker. The chauffeur pulls just past the house, so as not to block the ladder company's access to the front of the building. The pipeman grabs the 1 ¾" pre-connect hoseline from the back of the truck and carries it into the building, via the back stairway. He attacks the fire at the lowest level of the structure that is involved. This is our set plan for a residential building fire. This plan is implemented with only slight variation in 70 – 80% of dwelling fires. It serves us well – it works.

Therefore, when the first-in officer arrives on the scene, he knows what his men are planning to do. He has only seconds to stop them and change plans, if he so chooses. Depending on several factors gathered in his size-up, he might want to attack this fire in a different way. For instance, if there is heavy fire threatening a neighboring home, he may tell his men to take the larger (2 ½") hose off the truck to protect the exposure. If there are people trapped on the third floor, he may tell his men to go directly to the third floor even if they have to pass fire on the first two floors, or he may tell his men to put up a ground ladder to the third floor. If he pulls up to a vacant building that has burned before and has heavy fire showing, he may tell them not to enter the building, and implement an exterior attack. There are a thousand variations, but the officer must size up the situation, and decide the best tactics, in a matter of seconds.

Actually, his size-up begins when the bell tips. He gathers as many factors as he can from the information given. Time of day – is it nighttime with people asleep? Is it in the *middle* of the night? Fires often get a good start at that time, because no one notices them right away. Location – are there mostly vacant buildings in the area? Are the buildings close together? Initial report – did Fire Alarm report smoke in the basement? It could be a boiler malfunction. Past history – have we been there before? If so, what did we have? Again, there are an infinite number of things an officer can ascertain from the dispatch that might help him begin to get an idea of what he may find upon arrival. He uses every bit of information at his disposal.

An officer can't hesitate in implementing his decisions – right or wrong. There is no time for discussion among the company. A fire company is not a democracy – it's a dictatorship and the officer is the dictator. Now, this doesn't mean that he shouldn't change tactics if he realizes they're not working. You have to be flexible enough to adjust your tactics to an ever-changing fire scene. It also doesn't mean that he can't take input from his firefighters. I give my guys the opportunity to suggest any ideas they may have at the scene of a fire.

If it's a good idea, I'll give them the OK. If I don't like it, I say no – end of discussion. If you have good firefighters on your team, why wouldn't you want them to use their heads? I don't want robots on my crew – I want good firemen. I respect them, and I want them to respect me.

A good example of this came on a day we were working during a pretty severe thunderstorm. As the thunderstorm rolled through the city, the entire fire department was swamped with calls. This often happens during thunderstorms – the lightning strikes can cause fires, and set off fire alarms in the high-rises. The wind knocks down trees, which bring down power lines. The rain causes flooding and motor vehicle accidents. All these things add up to a busy time for the fire department.

On this day we had responded to a commercial building whose alarm was caused by a lightning strike close enough to send a power surge through their system. This was about the fourth run we'd had since the storm began – back to back to back… When we were clearing the scene, Fire Alarm sent us to a reported building fire on Harold Street. We arrived on the scene to find the street in front of the house flooded, up past our ankles. The building had been struck by lightning and you could see the blackened wood on the outside of the building, near the roof. The electrical service line had been connected to the house in that area, and now was arcing in the driveway next to the house. I immediately went to the third floor to check for fire on the inside of the building. I told the pipeman to stand by outside the building in case we needed a hoseline. I didn't want to bring it in if we didn't need it, but I also didn't want to waste any time, by having him have to go back out to get it if we did need it. Meanwhile, my pump operator was standing in ankle deep water in the middle of a thunderstorm and about ten feet from a live wire! When I checked the interior of the building I could see that the lightning had knocked out the power to the building, but there was no extension of fire on the interior. I told the other companies responding to slow down, as I checked floor by floor. When I was sure there was no fire, I cut the other companies loose and went back out to the truck. The occupants were very lucky. If the attic area had caught fire it could have traveled through the entire house. I got on the radio and told Fire Alarm that the building owner was going to have an electrician check the wiring in the house before restoring power. "Engine 15 in service," I said.

"Roger, Engine 15. Respond to Unit Street for a reported lightning strike," was their reply. As we headed for Unit Street, Fire Alarm began to dispatch other companies to the incident. When we arrived on the scene, there were people outside a three-story building pointing to the flashing just below the roof.

I looked up and saw flames coming from the front of the building. I asked if everyone was out – they assured me they were. I also asked if the front stairs went all the way to the third floor – they said yes. I told the pipeman, Joe, that we were going up the front stairs instead of the back. I wanted to reach the fire as quickly as possible and it had started on the exterior of the front wall. He said, "OK Loo, do you want me to hit it from the outside first?" Normally this is a no-no for us. Hitting the fire from the outside usually tends to push the fire further into the building. I looked up toward the roof again and said, "Yeah. Knock it down quick and then bring the line to the third floor." I thought that since the lightning had struck the exterior of the building, most of the heat was on the exterior also. This was a case of a firefighter making a suggestion on the fire scene that proved to be a good call. If I had said no, he would have taken the line directly to the third floor without any argument. He may have asked me about my decision after the fire was out, but he wouldn't have questioned me at the time.

When I reached the third floor apartment there was a slight smoke condition evident. I called for a ladderman with a plaster pole to come to the third floor right away. When he got to the apartment I had him pull the ceiling in the area of the lightning strike. There was some burning on the inside of the front wall, but it hadn't advanced any further. After the ceiling was pulled, Joe had a clear shot to open up the nozzle and knock down the flames. When we were packing the hose after the fire, I patted Joe on the shoulder. "Good call," I said, "it worked out perfectly." I no sooner got the words out of my mouth, when Fire Alarm called us on the radio, "Engine 15." "Go ahead," I answered. "Are you clearing the scene there?" "Momentarily." "Respond to…" We were heading to another run. But not before we finished packing the rest of the hose.

In Providence we respond to a reported building fire by having the engine company go before the ladder company. There are times, however, when a ladder company may be the first company to arrive at a working house fire. I can tell you from first hand experience that this can be a helpless feeling. No matter how good the firefighters on the ladder truck are, 'you can't put out a fire with an axe.' If the building is heavily involved in fire, you can't even begin to extinguish it without water. Ladder companies carry ladders and tools, but not water. It's a very helpless feeling pulling up to someone's home and not being able to put out the fire!

The firefighters on the first-in ladder company raise the aerial ladder to the roof and ventilate by cutting a hole at the peak. The quicker this is done, the smoother operations below, on the interior of the building, will proceed.

Releasing the superheated gases and smoke allow the engine company to push further into the building, and allow any victims trapped inside a few extra minutes to be rescued. Similar to being the pipeman, I always enjoyed 'getting the roof.' I have to admit, though, that I wasn't as good at this as a seasoned ladderman, but I enjoyed the rush of being on top of a burning building and chopping away with an axe. I wasn't as good at handling an axe as I was at handling a hoseline. In firefighting, there may be many jobs that you know how to do, but the more experience you have in specific areas, the more proficient you become at these tasks. Experience under pressure is the best learning method available – experience *and* failure. I believe that you learn more from your failures and mistakes than you do by your successes.

I've had a couple of failures on roofs that come to mind.

When I was assigned to Engine 8, I was often detailed to Ladder 2 for a shift. This was always a good thing because they were in the same firehouse. I could work with my regular crew. For a while there was a running joke in the station that every time I was on Ladder 2, I would draw blood. It seemed to be true. This is where the experience comes into play. I was on Ladder 2 one night and we were the first-in ladder company to a building fire on Westminster Street. As we pulled up to the building, another firefighter, Bob, and I climbed into the bucket and headed for the roof. Being an engine man most of the time, it was a strange sight for me to look down the street from above and see the other companies hurrying to our location. Bob set the bucket just over the edge of the flat roof, we each grabbed an axe, and headed toward the center of the roof. We first opened up a scuttle[11] above the stairway and smoke rose in a column, straight up into the clear sky. If there is a scuttle on the roof, it's best to open that first, because you can open this quickly to begin the ventilation process. The problems with these openings are that they are too small, and not necessarily in the right location. You always try to put the ventilation hole as close to directly above the fire as you can estimate. You would rather have the superheated gases travel straight up and out, as opposed to traveling across the entire building before escaping.

We then picked the best location to ventilate, and began to chop. As we began to put a hole in the roof, I reached down and tried to peel the roofing materials from the plywood. I sliced my finger on a piece of metal sheeting that was below the asphalt shingles. It was a pretty nasty little cut, but nothing serious. I finished helping Bob with the rest of the cutting and started back to the bucket to get a plaster pole. As I began walking away, Bob said, "Tommy, look at your axe!" I looked down and saw that the yellow fiberglass handle of the axe was covered in blood. I hadn't realized it was bleeding that much. I took the axe back to the bucket to rinse off later, grabbed a plaster pole, and headed back to the scuttle. Bob and I were going to climb down through the scuttle to assist the companies working on the interior of the building. Before I entered the scuttle, I put on my gloves. I should have done this when I first left the bucket. A lesson learned!

On another occasion I had a night callback on Ladder 3. I had just returned to fire duty after having been off injured for over a year after a motor vehicle accident with Engine 8. It was my first day back. I was working for a Lieutenant, Russ, who had been assigned to Ladder 3 for over a year. I had worked with him as a firefighter on Engine 8 before he took the promotional exam that earned him his "Lieutenant's bar." I told him at dinnertime that I was looking forward to an easy night. I said I was hoping to ease my way back into the flow of things. He said, "Don't worry about it, I haven't had a fire here yet, and I've been here since last May." There's an old adage in the fire service that says, "never talk about how long it's been since you've had a fire, unless you want one." When he said it had been unusually slow, I cringed.

Sure enough, around 1:00 AM we were awakened by the bell, and dispatched to a reported house fire about a block from the station. Even as we were pulling out of the door, we heard Engine 12 report, "Code Red, three-story occupied dwelling." The chauffeur pulled the tiller truck into a parking lot next to the fire building. As soon as the aerial ladder was extended, I climbed to the roof and made my way to the peak. I estimated the location of the fire and began to make a hole. As soon as I poked the axe through the plywood, heavy smoke poured through the opening. The wind carried it right into my face. I was taught, a long time before this incident, that you always make the cut in the roof from upwind, to avoid the smoke. I quickly climbed over the hole and began opening it up from the upwind side. This was much better. When I finished the hole, there was a large volume of flames shooting from the opening along with the smoke – all being pushed away from me by the wind. I was glad I had changed positions.

It was now my job to descend the aerial, and join Engine 12 inside the building to assist them by opening up the ceilings and the walls. I began to head for the aerial when another lesson from long ago popped into my head – about ten minutes too late. Never put the vent hole between you and your escape ladder! This hole, which was now shooting flames high into the night sky, was directly between me and my means of escape. I no longer could crawl over this hole as I had earlier. The roof had a steep pitch and the shingles were wet and icy, so I couldn't safely just walk around the hole. I had used the peak of the roof to maneuver thus far. There was no one on the turntable to reposition the aerial, so I placed the blade of the axe into the vent hole, and used it to hold me up as I held onto the handle and circled the hole from the opposite side of the peak.

I had made a mistake and learned another valuable lesson, *and* I never did it again.

Chapter 15
Cow Snots

I had only been on the job for about three weeks when I learned first hand of the firefighter phenomenon called 'cow snots.' This happens when every bit of fluid from your sinus cavity runs out of your nose - in an avalanche of moisture. The sinuses are usually joined by the tear ducts – opening up like Niagara Falls. This occurs when smoke is inhaled, as you are struggling to breathe through your nose because of extreme exertion. Usually the firefighter will find an open window to stick out his head, to try to get a breath of fresh air. It seems inevitable that a news photographer will snap a picture of this firefighter. He looks like a cow salivating while chewing his cud.

I knew nothing of this phenomenon when I first joined the fire department after my six months in the Fire Academy. I learned of it the same way most firefighters do – through personal experience. It didn't take long.

I was only on the job for two weeks and didn't have a permanent assignment yet. I was in what is called the Manpower Pool. This meant that every morning I had to call the Deputy Assistant Chief's office to find out where I was being assigned for the day. This particular Saturday I was told by the Chief to go to Engine 14. When I arrived at the station I was happy to see that one of my classmates from the Academy, Pete, was also assigned to Engine 14 for the day. I would later work with Pete for six years on Engine 2, but for today it was nice to see a familiar and friendly face. We were meeting many of the firefighters and officers on the job for the first time during our first few months on duty, so it was a plus to have another 'rookie' with me. We checked out the truck and the equipment; then went upstairs to meet the other guys. Our Lieutenant that day, Bob, was a fairly young guy, but was definitely from the old school of firefighting. He was a great firefighter and fire officer, and was also very cognizant of the traditions of firefighting. He was very intelligent, however, and was right on top of the modern changes in the fire service. He was an innovative fire officer on our department for many years. Pete and I would be in good hands today. We also met the chauffeur of the truck, Skippy. He had been stationed here for quite a while, so he knew the streets and the truck. He also knew me. Skippy had been my father's chauffeur when my dad was the Lieutenant on this company, before he had retired. That was about four years prior to my being appointed to the department. So he had seen me around the station before.

We drilled with the company later that morning. Pete and I were eager to learn, and the Lieutenant was happy to teach us the fundamentals that may have been overlooked during the Training Academy. There's no substitute for on-the-job training experience. When we were Trainees, we were only allowed to handle the hoselines and ladders in the drillyard. Being on an actual fire company was the best training we could receive. We trained with the foam pipe that morning. That was something we never did at the Training Academy.

As lunchtime rolled around, Pete and I took our plates down to the watch desk. Pete had drawn first floor watch and I had drawn the second spot, so we decided to both stay downstairs and study the street directory. While we were finishing lunch and quizzing each other on the streets, the vocalarm squawked out, "Attention Engines 8, 10, 11; Ladders 2 & 5; Rescue 1; and Car 22 a stillbox." Car 22 (Battalion Chief 2) was stationed here, so Pete tipped the bell. They were being sent to a reported building fire on Bridgham Street. Already our pulses were rising, anxious to get a taste of a real fire! The Chief rolled out the door with lights flashing and siren blaring, as we looked up the location of the fire in the street directory. It wasn't that far from here. "Maybe if it's a big enough fire and they need more help, we'll be called," I told Pete. I needn't have worried. Before this day was over, every fire company in the city would be put to work at this fire.

"Engine 8 to Fire Alarm, Code Red, 3-story, occupied, fully involved and extending to another 3-decker. Give me a second Alarm!" I was getting my wish. Engine 14 was among the second Alarm companies, so we were quickly mounting the truck to respond to our first real fire. As we began to head up the hill on Atwells Ave. we were still about a mile from the fire, but we could plainly see a large column of heavy black smoke to the south. Skippy quickly maneuvered the truck through the side streets heading towards the fire. Pete and I were riding the sides of the truck and checking our gear as we anxiously listened to the radio chatter from the fire. The Lieutenant opened the small sliding window separating the cab from the jump seat area and yelled over the whine of the siren to us, "When we get there, you guys stick with me. Don't do anything until I tell you to!"

We exited a side street to a main artery and we could now get a view of the flames leaping through the roof of the original fire building. We were almost on the scene! At just about this time we heard the Chief call for a third Alarm. Holy shit! This was a little more than I had bargained for. When we turned the corner onto Brigham Street I almost shit my pants. There were flames blowing out of the front of the house into the middle of the street. I'd never seen anything like this before. I saw a crew with a hoseline wetting down Ladder 2 because the flames were melting the lights and beginning to burn the paint on the cab – and now I could see that 3 buildings were on fire!

When we turned onto a side street off Bridgham, I was confused. It seemed like we were moving away from the fire. We pulled to a stop right next to a hydrant around the corner from the fire scene. As we got off the truck, the Lieutenant said to Pete and I, "You guys grab the 2 ½" (the large diameter handline) and stretch it to the rear of the building." We grabbed the line from the hose bed and dragged it through a couple of back yards, to position ourselves directly behind the middle fire building. We were about thirty feet from the building, but the heat was still so intense that we had to shield our faces. We crouched down and readied ourselves for the water. While we were doing this, the chauffeur and the Lieutenant were connecting feeders to the hydrant so that we'd have an adequate water supply. When the Lieutenant yelled to ask us if we were ready for water, we waved OK. As the water snaked through the hoseline we could hear it hiss and pop, as it stretched the canvas jacket and snapped the folds straight on its way to the nozzle. Pete opened the nozzle while I backed him up. Until you handle a charged 2 ½" fire hose, you can't imagine the amount of resistance you encounter trying to control it. As this was our first time, we weren't fully prepared, and the pressure shot us backwards, right into a wooden fence, about two feet behind us! That fence was the only thing that saved us from losing control of the line.

We repositioned ourselves and used all our strength to keep control of the hose. We worked together like this for about ten minutes before the Lieutenant came to join us. When he saw us struggling he told us to shut down the line. "I'm going to show you guys a trick," he said. He told us to circle the hose away from the fire and then bring the nozzle back toward the direction we wanted to shoot the stream. He said, "Now slip the nozzle under the loop." When we had done this he told us to sit on the line and open up the nozzle. With our weight and the weight of the loop of the hose holding it in place, the line was much easier to handle! Pete and I had learned a trick that we'd never forget, one that we'd employ many times in the next few years.

We stayed in this position, moving only a few yards one way or another, for the next forty-five minutes or so. While we were pouring water on these buildings from the rear yard, we could hear over the portable radios that the fire was escalating. It had gone to a 4th, then a 5th Alarm. The roof of a large church across the street began to burn as embers from the triple-deckers landed on them. A few minutes later a warehouse down the street caught fire! This was becoming bigger than I could comprehend with my limited experience. I learned another valuable lesson that day which, as an officer, I now try to pass on to firefighters who work with me – no matter how big the fire, we (as a company) can only do one job at a time. Realizing this fact makes it easier to decide what to do when you first pull up to a fire and the sheer size of it overwhelms you. You remember that you can only do one job, you prioritize what needs to be done, and then go about tackling the first job on the list. You let other companies tackle the rest of the tasks as they arrive on the scene. On this day, at this time, our job was directing this 2 ½" from the rear of the building.

After knocking down a large amount of fire in one of the exposure buildings, the Lieutenant decided to reduce down to a 1 ½" and take it to the inside of the building. To do this we shut down the 2 ½" nozzle and attached a fitting that allowed us to connect 200' of 1 ½" hose with a smaller nozzle. This gave us a charged handline that we could maneuver inside the building. The Lieutenant led Pete and I into the building and up the stairs. Pete and I had taken off our air paks when we were outside. We were too new on the job to say anything to the Lieutenant when we realized how smoky it was on the inside of the building. We just sucked it up and followed him up to the third floor. We tried to breath through our noses but quickly realized that we couldn't get enough air in our lungs while we were exerting ourselves by humping this hose up three flights.

When we got to the top floor, and the fire, we couldn't get the hose close enough to the doorway to attack it head on. This meant that I had to go back down the stairs to pull more line from the outside. I had to go up and down those damn stairs five times! Each time I went down, I stuck my head out of the second floor window to quickly get some fresh air. This is when I realized I had 'cow snots' hanging from my face. I could feel it in my mustache and feel the cool air on the moisture on my face. I just wiped it off with my glove and continued down the stairs. When we finally knocked down all the fire that we could, the Lieutenant led us outside for a break. As we sat outside in the back yard the Lieutenant said to us, "You guys really look like shit." I looked at Pete and saw that he had soot stains over his whole face, red eyes that looked like he'd been crying all day, and snots that would make a Saint Bernard proud dripping from his nose. When I told him what he looked like, he told me that I looked just as bad.

We went back to work after a short rest. It was a long day, but we were still pumped up because this was our first real fire. After work we went to the Firefighter's Club to have a few beers and talk about the fire. The place was crowded. I guess we weren't the only ones thinking a cold beer would hit the spot. Pete and I raised a glass to each other in honor of breaking our cherries at such a good fire – and together.

We learned a number of valuable lessons that day – the most important of which was to always wear your air pak when going into a fire building!

Chapter 16
911/Ground Zero

I was working a day shift on September 11th, 2001. It started out like any other day. I had arrived for work around 7:00 AM and had coffee with the off-going platoon. There's always a fresh pot of coffee on at the firehouse. This is the normal morning ritual for any change of shift – morning or night. We spend the first few minutes discussing fire department issues – the apparatus, equipment or station. Any official departmental notifications are passed on to the on-coming group at this time also. Once this important business is out of the way, we get down to an old-fashioned jaw session.

There's always something to catch up on. Someone's wife is having twins – someone's kid is on the honor roll at school – someone's going on vacation. These are guys that we not only work with, but we live with. We share a common home. Many of us spend more time with each other than with our own families. These guys *are* part of our family. We spend a lot of time together off the job also – golf trips, canoe trips, parties and family picnics. We know most of each other's families and are involved in each other's lives on *and* off the job. I work on 'A' Group, and the off-going platoon was 'C' Group. Our groups work opposite each other – when we work our 2-day and 2-night tour of duty, 'C' Group is enjoying their 4 days off duty. This means that we only see this particular group of guys once a week at the firehouse. There's a lot of catching up to do!

In the case of the FDNY firefighters that fateful morning, I'm sure that the same thing was going on in their firehouses as well. Friends ('brothers') were sharing a cup of coffee while catching up on each other's lives. Guys from the off-going shift were still hanging around the firehouse, chewing the fat. They were already off duty and free to go home when the first plane hit the north tower. They could have climbed into their cars and gone home to their families. Many of them, however, grabbed their gear and climbed onto the trucks instead. They knew that their brothers were going to need all the help they could get. They didn't worry about whether they were getting paid for this, they didn't worry about where they were supposed to be going that day, and they didn't even worry about their families (they knew that they were safe at home and away from this horrible scene). What they were worried about at that moment were the people in that tower; and their fellow firefighters responding to the alarm. That's what a firefighter does (paid or not – on duty or off duty): help people during an emergency. If ever they were needed – it was now. These guys weren't going to let down their brothers or the citizens of NYC – not today.

The fact that so many off-duty firemen responded on the trucks that were dispatched to the World Trade Center, is one of the main reasons that the FDNY had such a difficult time calculating an accurate list of those firefighters *murdered* that day. These guys weren't on the riding list for their company, because they weren't supposed to be there. They were supposed to be on their way home. A lot has been written about the firefighters of FDNY "just doing their jobs" that day. I'm sure that they'd agree. Let's not make any mistake about it, however, I'm sure these guys were scared shitless responding to that scene, but they were "doing their jobs" because they wanted to be there. They wanted to be there for those innocent people trapped in the tower, and they wanted to be there for their brothers! God bless them all!

On this particular morning, after the guys from 'C' Group had left, we went about our daily routine. Rick and Al checked over the truck and equipment, as I went upstairs to my office to do the morning paperwork. I was in my office when one of them yelled up the pole hole, "Loo, turn on the *Today Show*, there's a fuckin' fire in the World Trade Center!" Like most Americans that day, I was shocked by the image of so much black smoke coming from one of the towers. Unlike most Americans watching that day, I had a pretty good idea of how serious a fire it was by the color and the amount of smoke visible. My very first thought was – shit, they're [FDNY firefighters] going to have a terrible time reaching this fire. We have a couple of thirty story buildings in Providence and many about fifteen stories. I know, from personal experience, that any climb beyond six or seven floors takes a good deal of time, and takes a tremendous toll on the stamina of a firefighter carrying the hundred-plus pounds of equipment needed to fight a high-rise fire effectively. I struggle climbing anything over three stories at this point in my career. The news media reported that the fire was in the north tower, on the 90th floor! These guys were in for one hell of a long day! I wish that had been the worst of it.

I immediately called my fiancée, Nancy, at home to let her know what was going on, and tell her to put on the TV. This was a scene repeating itself all over the country. People seemed to need to share this moment with loved ones. I needed to share this with her, but I also needed to share it with my guys, so I went downstairs as I kept her on the phone. She immediately thought of the people working in the building above the fire floor – she asked me how they were going to get down. At the time, no one on TV knew how the fire started although there were reports that a plane had crashed into the tower. I, along with millions watching, assumed that it was a smaller plane, not a 767. I told her that the people above the 90th floor would find a stairway that was clear of smoke and use the stairs to evacuate. I said that I was worried about the firemen who would have to use these same stairs to climb ninety floors to get to the fire! She gasped on the other end of the phone at the thought of them having to climb the stairs that far. She was silent for a minute, as we both continued to take in the horrific scene playing out live in front of us. She finally said, "No, there's got to be another way to get to the fire. What about the elevators?" I told her that, depending on how many of the elevators were still functioning, some of the firefighters might be able to use them. Most, however, would have to use the stairs to reach the fire – and the victims.

As we both watched the same scene from different locations, we were horrified by the sight of another plane, this time recognizable as a commercial jetliner, crashing into the second tower – the south tower. We could see first hand the size of the plane, and the size of the explosion and fireball. We both instantly knew, along with the rest of America, that we were witnessing a terrorist attack. What a terrifying and helpless feeling! This plane struck the second tower on a lower floor than the first plane had. Nancy's thoughts, again, went immediately to the victims trapped above the fire floor – and mine went to the firefighters. They were now facing two major disasters, in the middle of a war zone! No one knew what was coming next. She saw the coverage of the firefighters rushing to the buildings and said, "Are they crazy? I wouldn't go into those buildings!" I told her that they had no choice: "that's their job." I also told her, as we watched debris (and people) fall from the buildings, that the most dangerous spot for the firefighters right now is in front of the buildings. I mistakenly thought that they'd be safer inside the buildings.

When we saw pictures of the intensity of the fire raging from the second tower I told Nancy that it was only a matter of time before that tower collapsed. There was no way to get water to the fire floor, and as the flames continued, the intense heat would weaken the steel framework of the building. With the enormous weight above the fire floor there was no way that this building wasn't going to fail. I believed, however, that the upper floors would tip and fall, leaving the part of the building below the fire intact. The building's own design, unfortunately, prevented this from happening. Once the weight from the upper part of the building fell on the fire floor, it collapsed straight down like a giant house of cards. These floors could not support this additional weight.

When the tower collapsed, Nancy cried on the other end of the phone line. I quietly said to her, "We've just lost a couple of hundred men." I was now openly crying in the middle of the firehouse sitting room. I couldn't believe my senses. This was beyond my comprehension. We both watched as the video showed, over and over, the collapse of the tower, and the people, including firemen, running as fast as their legs would carry them to escape the debris. She was completely at a loss when she also saw the firefighters running back to the scene when the dust had begun to settle. I told her that a couple of hundred of their brothers were trapped in that debris and that they wouldn't rest until they could rescue every last one of them. At the time, no one really understood the totality of the devastation. How could we? This type of collapse was unprecedented.

We immediately contacted our Union office to inquire about volunteering for rescue operations at "Ground Zero." We felt so helpless (and useless) here in Providence. We're only about 150 miles away from NYC – we could have been there in three hours! They told us we had to wait until our 4-day tour of duty was over. By that time, the FDNY was requesting that all firefighters wishing to volunteer with the rescue operations, remain in a stand-by mode until they called for extra help. They never made that call. They preferred to rescue (and recover) their own. They later put out a request for firefighters from outside their department to come to NYC to attend some of the many funeral and memorial services which were being conducted on a daily basis – sometimes three or four a day! There weren't enough FDNY members to adequately represent the department at each and every service.

For the next few weeks, every moment I wasn't on duty was spent in front of the TV, watching the cable news networks. Hoping, at first, for news of rescues. Hoping next for successful recovery of remains. All the while listening, as the estimates of the total number of casualties rose, hour after hour. Thankfully, after a few days, the numbers began to fall. Unfortunately, as the total numbers of estimated victims fell, the number of firefighters confirmed dead continued to rise. It rose to 343 men!! I found it nearly impossible to come to terms with that number.

Just about a month after the attacks, I went to NYC for the first time to attend a couple of funerals being held at St. Patrick's Cathedral. I was overtaken with emotion as I stood in the middle of Fifth Ave., at attention, as the FDNY Fife and Drum Corps marched by. It was even tougher when the family's limousine drove slowly past. Seeing the wife and kids of this fallen firefighter sitting in the back of this limo really brought the human side of this tragedy home. They sat there with shocked, blank expressions on their faces. They seemed to be afraid of looking into the faces of the firefighters lined up to honor their husband and father. I understood. I don't know if I could have kept from breaking down if they had looked at me directly! I think this was probably the toughest emotional moment of my life. As I stood on Fifth Ave., saluting the passing cars, it brought all of the terrible moments of the previous month to my mind – of this national tragedy. It made me realize that, for the enormity of this cowardly act of terrorism, the real victims of this tragedy were real people, with real families who loved them – and missed them terribly. These families' lives had been forever changed in a single instant. It's always more difficult to deal with the human side of tragedies. I guess that up until this moment, I had been able to keep the thought of the personal human suffering at bay.

When the family and friends of this hero had made their way into the cathedral, they were followed by the firefighters who had been lining the street. I followed into St. Patrick's and sat somewhere in the middle of the church. As the mass turned to the memorial, it began with words from Mayor Guiliani and other FDNY members. These were moving eulogies, but when the victim's best friend began to speak, it put a truly personal feel to the memorial. Talking about how this man lived, and how he loved, brought smiles and even some chuckles – but also brought the entire church to tears. It was a tough service to sit through – emotionally. When it ended, we filed back onto the street. We stood silently at attention as the family exited the church.

The following morning I went to another memorial at St. Patrick's Cathedral. It was much the same as the previous day. The bagpipes and the muffled drums seemed to reach deep into my chest and wring my heart like a sponge, until the tears were flowing again! This time, however, I couldn't put myself through another service. After the family made its way into the church, and the firefighters started filing in, I left. I went, with a group of other firefighters, to a pub a couple of blocks away. We stayed until it was time to line up again at the end of the service. We toasted the hero of the day – we toasted all of the fallen heroes of the FDNY. Then we solemnly made our way back to Fifth Ave., and stood in tribute for the end of the service.

After the memorial the first day, I took the subway to Ground Zero with a group of other Providence firefighters. After the emotional experience of the service, I thought I was completely drained. I felt numb as I sat in the subway car in full dress uniform. That is, until we arrived at Ground Zero. Seeing first hand many of these sights we'd all seen on TV for the past month, snapped me back. When visiting this area in person, the first thing that strikes you is the sheer size of the area that was devastated. It's much larger in real life than you could ever imagine by watching television! The next thing that hits your eyes is the incredible devastation to the whole area. There were 50-story buildings with substantial damage all around the perimeter of the area. Some had heavy mesh curtains draped over the entire front of the building to keep debris from falling and injuring the workers on the site. One large building had a piece of one of the towers sticking right out of one of its upper floors! The pile of debris on the spot where the towers once stood was still very high, and it was still smoking! This was about a month after the attack! When we were told that this pile continued below ground for another seven stories, it was just impossible to imagine.

The thing that struck me the most, however, was the feeling that this entire area was somehow sacred ground. I felt it for myself as soon as we were allowed to enter the area that was closed to the public. I also sensed it from everyone who was working there – the FDNY members, the NYPD members, and the steel workers. For all of the work that was going on, the site was very quiet. I can honestly say that not one person I saw there that day – workers or visitors – acted in any way inappropriately. As a NYPD Lieutenant showed us around the area, it strangely seemed like we were being given a tour of the Vatican.

We visited the "Tenhouse", the firehouse that was directly across from the World Trade Center. It was closed off and had sustained considerable damage, but there were cards, banners and memorials from all over the world adorning the building. There was also a memorial journal, for visitors to sign and jot a note or prayer, in front of the station. As we stood there quietly, understanding that this was the final resting place of so many innocent people and so many heroes, we were struck by the importance that we, as a country, never forget the horror of that historic day. When we left Ground Zero, we were all strangely quiet as we piled into a cab and headed for another firehouse and the FDNY store – somewhere near Chinatown. This firehouse had lost seven of its members at the WTC – their names still on the riding lists on the wall of the firehouse. The guys on duty this day were very friendly and thanked us for coming to NYC for the services. It was a strange feeling to be in this firehouse and see these guys eating lunch and carrying on with a somewhat normal firehouse routine after what they'd been through just a short month ago. The outside of the firehouse was adorned with pictures, cards, and flowers in a makeshift memorial. It seemed surreal.

The FDNY and NYPD members I met on this trip – at Ground Zero, on the streets, and in the pubs – couldn't have been more gracious or appreciative of our support. Even the ordinary people on the streets would smile and thank us. Some would even stop us and tell us how much they appreciated and respected firefighters. This was very strange to me. I've been to NYC many times before, and people on the streets of NYC just don't do that! Because we were in uniform, we rode the subway for free. Amtrak also let firefighters in uniform ride the trains free of charge to and from NYC, to attend any of the numerous memorial services for our fallen FDNY brothers. The terrorists may have toppled two of our tallest buildings. They may have destroyed countless human lives. And they may have wounded a great city, and great nation, very deeply. It seems, however, that they've also rejuvenated this city and nation. Isolation and indifference have been transformed into togetherness and patriotic pride. I sincerely hope that this part of the 911 legacy lives on.

Before my group of firefighters returned to Providence, we stopped at a bar that, we were told, was owned by a NYC firefighter – Turtle Bay. It turned out to be a great place. We never found out if it was actually owned by an FDNY member, but there were plenty of FDNY firefighters, as well as many firefighters from other parts of the U.S. and Canada. It was the perfect place to conduct an impromptu Irish wake! Swapping stories with other firefighters, and celebrating the heroism of the fallen seemed to put everyone in a better frame of mind. People would pass the bar, see all the firefighters, and come in to personally thank a few of us for doing our jobs.

When they finally held the memorial for all 343 firemen who gave their lives at the WTC disaster, it was October of 2002. It was held at Madison Square Garden, and over 56,000 firefighters from all over the world marched the streets of NYC. I felt compelled to attend this memorial. I also felt compelled to share this moment with Nancy. From the time we met, she seemed to have an understanding and respect for my profession. She's also witnessed first hand (and understood) what this "brotherhood" means to me. I felt I needed to show her how universal this feeling was among firefighters. She was hesitant about making the trip at first. She was afraid that the memorial would be too emotional for her to handle. She finally agreed, however, and we booked a room for the weekend. It turned out to be the best weekend we ever spent in NYC! The memorial service itself was limited to the capacity of Madison Square Garden. Preference, rightfully, was given to families and FDNY members, so we didn't get to attend the service. I did get a chance to honor the fallen by marching, along with a number of other Providence firefighters, in the largest gathering of firefighters ever assembled in a single place. This march felt more like a celebration than a day of mourning. This was in stark contrast to the memorials I'd attended the previous year. I also had a chance to revisit Ground Zero, now open to the public, with Nancy. It was now a huge hole in the ground with all traces of debris having been removed. There were even signs of fresh construction at the site.

We saw firefighters from all over the world that weekend – Canada, Italy, Great Britain, Poland, Paris, Luxemburg, Australia, New Zealand, and from all over the U.S. It was an experience I'll never forget. I took Nancy to Turtle Bay and it was filled with firefighters – mostly FDNY. Again, these guys were great to me and to Nancy. We talked for hours with one particular NYC firefighter and a bunch of his buddies. They were great guys and seemed to be having a great time, but you could tell by looking into their eyes that they were still numb. These guys had lost five firefighters from their house, and only three of them had been recovered thus far. It's hard to put it behind you when it's an ongoing ordeal.

Finally, on September 8th 2003, the funeral for Michael Ragusa was held. This was the 343rd, and final, funeral or memorial for the FDNY firefighters who were killed on September 11th 2001. Again I felt compelled to be there. I think I needed closure for this terrible tragedy, as I know the entire fire department from NYC did. It was held in Brooklyn, in Michael's old parish, and was attended by about 2,000 (mostly FDNY) firefighters. Just three days prior to the second anniversary of the attack, and they were finally having the final service.

As I drove into Brooklyn that morning and saw Manhattan's skyline out of the passenger's window, I thought to myself that it was another clear, bright September morning that had begun this horrible nightmare. How fitting it was to be having the final service today. Life goes on, and those of us who lost someone that day, or as in my case, felt like they lost someone, have to continue with the process of living. The time for grieving must end. In a case such as this, I believe that closure comes in a sense of peace with ourselves. Knowing that we did all we could to help, and knowing that we honored the memories of the victims and the heroes of that day. I think this was part of the reason it was so important for me to be there.

There is one danger, however, in coming to peace with September 11th. The danger is in forgetting. We must never forget! We must never let ourselves, or our children, forget about, or minimize, the horror, or the evilness, of that day. I'm afraid that people trying to keep from offending the viewers, will censor some of the more graphic images. I believe that when children are being told about this tragedy, they should be as offended as possible. War is offensive. Murder is offensive. Let's not dehumanize this horrible act. The real tragedy of that day was the loss of so many innocent human beings – not the loss of two buildings. What sense of understanding would we have of the Holocaust if what we saw and heard had been cleaned up so as to not offend us? Seeing the horrible pictures of skeletal prisoners, and the piles of bodies being buried in mass graves by bulldozers, gives us at least a partial understanding of the atrocities those people went through. I believe the telling of the story of what happened on September 11th 2001 should be handled in the same way. We need to insure that this will never happen again. We need to insure that the memories of the innocent victims of this horrible act of terrorism are not relegated to a footnote in our history books. They were living, breathing human beings whose only crime was living in a free society.

The emergency workers that day – PAPD, NYPD & FDNY – were true American heroes! It was the greatest display of peacetime heroism in our country's history! I salute them all!!!!

Chapter 17
The Worcester Six

On the night of December 3rd, 1999 I was working a callback on Engine 3 – the busiest fire truck in New England. It was a pretty cold night for early December and I was hoping for an easy night. As it turned out, we had a few runs soon after I put my gear on the truck. Nothing major – a couple of EMS calls and a trash fire in a dumpster. Still, the shift was barely two hours old and it had the potential of being one of those nights. Engine 3 is quartered in the downtown firehouse, and is normally very busy at night with what many of us consider nuisance runs – drunks, brawls and trash fires.

I was doing the paperwork for the earlier runs when I heard the call over the intercom: "All hot!" It was about 8:30 PM and dinner was ready. I left the rest of the reports for later and headed for the sitting room to enjoy a nice hot meal. One thing about this station is that they always have great meals. One of the guys on this group, Dan, would go on to win a national cooking contest the following year, and travel to Los Angeles to appear on the *Tonight Show*.

As I brought my plate to the dinner table, the news was on the TV in the corner of the room. There was a live picture of a fire in a warehouse, so naturally it caught my attention right away. I also noticed that the firefighters around the table seemed to be especially quiet and attentive to the picture on the screen. I asked where the fire was and was told, "It's in Worcester, and there's a couple of firemen missing." This put a whole new importance to the story playing out on the news for us. Many of us have been at fires where a firefighter or two have been considered missing only to be located safely outside the fire building. In those cases there was never any mention of anyone unaccounted for to the media. We all realized immediately that the fact that their department had let the media know that some of their firefighters were missing was not a good sign. We also hoped that this situation would turn out as men who were simply separated from their companies and not trapped inside the building. Thus began a long night for all of us in the fire service – and an even longer night for our brothers in Worcester.

In between runs that night, I would park myself down in front of the TV as the scene continued to play out. The news wasn't good. I was hoping to hear that the firefighters had been found or rescued. Instead, the number of firefighters missing rose from two to four – and then to six. It's a strange feeling to be riding a fire truck while you are watching fellow firefighters fight a life and death battle on television – realizing that some of them are paying the ultimate cost. Most firefighters are aware of the dangers that may be faced on our next call, but we don't like to dwell on our own mortality. That makes a person scared, and a scared firefighter is prone to making deadly mistakes. I thought about my own mortality that night. I couldn't help it. I had been on the job for twenty years at that point and I had experienced the sense of loss all firefighters feel when another firefighter is killed in the line of duty – no matter where he's from. But watching it live on TV as you're working is a strange feeling.

The fact that it was in Worcester, Massachusetts was another reason this hit home with me. The city of Worcester is only about an hour from Providence. The Providence Fire Department and the Worcester Fire Department have a lot in common. We are both about the same size departments, working in similar cities, under the same type of circumstances. Our two departments are often compared when researching the number of apparatus, manpower, and pay scales. In this respect, many of us on the Providence Fire Department considered the Worcester Fire Department as a sister department – even before this fateful night. This made the news even more personal. Most of us stayed up until early in the morning awaiting some official word as to the condition of the missing firefighters. When it became evident that there was no official word coming any time soon, I went to bed – and tried to sleep. Not before saying a silent prayer and asking God to watch over them and deliver them to their brothers safely, however.

When the official word finally came that there were six firefighters missing and presumed dead we were devastated. How could that be? we wondered. Weren't we invincible? Didn't I pray hard enough? The scene continued to play out on TV and in the newspapers for the next couple of weeks as they struggled to retrieve the remains of these brave men. The fact that it took so long to find them in the rubble of the building just added to the tragedy – dragging out the pain and sorrow for the families. Even the memorial service for these guys, held about a week later, was held before they all had been recovered. It was incredibly difficult for the families and for the members of the Worcester Fire Department to find any closure. The loss of these men was also a huge blow to the City of Worcester. I don't know how this tragedy played out in other parts of the country, but I know that it profoundly touched the people of New England. People on the street would come up to us while we were on duty and tell us how horrible they felt about it, and how much they respected firefighters.

These six were heroes who died trying to do their jobs, protecting the public – and each other. There were many other heroes there in Worcester that night. Most of us will never hear their stories, or know what they did. They don't think of themselves as heroes. Without ever having talked to them personally, I know that they all feel that they failed that night. They lost six of their own – how could they feel anything different? The fact is, they all acted heroically that night. It has always been my belief that the heroes we recognize publicly are born of circumstance and opportunity – losing their life or saving someone else's life. I believe these individuals are heroes, but I also believe that the men who do the same job, in the same building, without such dramatic results, are equally heroic. The real honor and the real heroism is in the attempt – overcoming your personal fears and trying to locate and save a life. I know there were more than six firefighters in Worcester that night who did just that.

The memorial service for these men was held while some of them still hadn't been removed from the rubble of the warehouse. While the service was being held, Worcester firefighters continued to dig at the site to find their brothers and bring them home. Over 22,000 firefighters from all over the world marched in this memorial to honor them. Until the service for the WTC firefighters, three years later, this was the largest gathering of firefighters anywhere in the world. A large group of guys, including myself, from the Providence Fire Department attended the service. I felt I needed to be there. President Clinton attended and spoke at the service, which was held at the Worcester Centrum. The procession was enormous, and marched a couple of miles through the streets of Worcester. There were people lined up on both sides of the street along the entire route. Just about the entire city was closed down; schools were closed so that children could attend, and most businesses were shut down for the day. Many people, especially the kids, held signs of support for the six members who were being honored – or just firefighters in general. Everyone along the route seemed to clap and cheer as we paraded past.

It was quite evident how deeply this tragedy had affected the people of this city. It was a very emotional and deeply moving experience to be part of this memorial. I found myself wiping away tears more than a couple of times along the way. One of the toughest moments was passing in front of the Fire Headquarters where the families were sitting. We marched past the reviewing stand while saluting the families, and then marched under the huge American flag which was draped between two aerial ladders. Thank God this was at the very end of the parade route. The Centrum was right around the corner. There were too many of us to allow us all to get into the memorial, so most of us stayed outside. They had set up a jumbo-tron to allow us to see the service. It was also being televised live on most television stations in the New England area.

We decided to go to a bar in the area and watch it on TV as we toasted them farewell. This seemed to be the best way to honor these men. We were sure that this is how they would have wanted it. So we found a nice little bar around the corner from the Centrum and went in for a sandwich and a beer…or two…or… It seemed that quite a few of the firefighters who had marched also thought that this was the most appropriate way to see them off. The bar had a big screen TV that was broadcasting the ceremony. Every time one of the guys was mentioned, the entire bar would cheer and raise a glass. When I called my fiancée, she was shocked because she could tell that I was feeling good. She thought this was very disrespectful, just as I'm sure many people reading this are thinking. All of the firefighters understood that we were really giving them a fitting tribute – in our own way. We also really did believe that Tim, Jay, Joe, Jeremiah, Paul and Tom would approve!

Chapter 18
Odd Jobs

When a person signs up for the fire department, it's hard for him to imagine the types of "emergencies" he will be called upon to help mitigate. Most people think of fighting fires when they think of firemen. While this is our main function – the one area in which we are the exclusive agency to handle the situation, firefighters are called to an infinite number of different situations. Some we are equipped and trained to handle, and some we are not. For the people calling for assistance, however, it is comforting when we arrive on the scene. They expect us to be able to help them through the emergency, either by handling it ourselves or by contacting someone who can. Countless times I've arrived at a call only to have the person who meets me say, "I just didn't know who else to call." No matter how long I stay on this job, I'm sure there will always be calls to which I'll think to myself as we respond – well, this is a first! This is part of what makes this job so exciting, you never know what to expect on your next run.

Firefighters are routinely expected to be plumbers, electricians, policemen, judges, counselors, exterminators, locksmiths, taxis…and the list goes on!

Emergency medical care is also one of our primary duties. Most people associate us with this type of response. Some people, however, are genuinely surprised when we pull up to their house in a fire truck, after they've called for a rescue because they're having difficulty breathing. "We didn't call the fire department," they'll tell us, "we called for a rescue." We have to explain to them that the rescues are part of the fire department, and that we respond with them in order to begin treatment prior to their arrival. Most people are grateful to have qualified personnel caring for them as soon as possible. Some people, on the other hand, are quite pissed off. "Jesus Christ! I don't need a fire truck – I need a God-damned rescue. If I needed a fucking fire truck, I would have asked for one. What a waste of my tax money!" It's tough to help these people. They're more upset that we're there, unnecessarily in their view, than they are about their illness or problem. Still, all in all, most people understand that EMS calls are part of our jobs.

The most common of our odd jobs is that of plumber. Water emergencies are a common response for the fire department. They can range from leaky faucets to entire neighborhoods being flooded. I've responded to water emergencies for *running* toilets. All we had to do was jiggle the handle a little bit, and then show the tenant how to do this on her own next time. I've also responded to the flooding of entire basements of large commercial buildings. On one occasion, a large vacant department store was flooded when a large diameter water main in the downtown area burst. By the time the Water Supply Board shut down the main, there was well over 100,000 gallons of water flooding the basement of this old, abandoned building. My company, Engine 2, spent over two days pumping out this store.

One night I responded, with Engine 15, to a report of a basement of a single-family home that was flooded. When we arrived at the house, it was obvious what the cause of the flooding was. The entire neighborhood was under two to three feet of water. We had just experienced a torrential rainstorm and the ground was too saturated to handle this massive amount of water. There was nothing we could do for this homeowner until the water in the area receded. We got off the truck and waded through water in the street, which was up to our waists in some areas. We located the storm drain covers in the middle of the street and removed them. It looked like a giant whirlpool as the water rushed down the hole. We had neighbors watch the area to keep people from walking on the street while these covers were open. We didn't want anyone falling through the holes! Before we left the scene, I called the Water Supply Board to notify them of the situation, and requested they send a crew out to replace the covers as soon as possible.

Dealing with most water emergencies is a five-part process. Identify any serious peripheral problems – water intruding on electrical equipment or heating units. Identify the source of the water problem – burst or leaking pipes or water leaking through the foundation from outside. Stopping the flow of water – a remote shut-off if possible, so as not to leave the entire property without water. Getting rid of the water – pumping the standing water from the property. Clean up – drying out the property and removing the last few inches of water. When we respond to the scene of a water emergency, we are usually able to take care of the first 4 tasks for the homeowner. The clean up is his responsibility. We tell him he can do it himself or contact a professional salvage company to restore the property. If the water is contaminated with raw sewage or petroleum products, we can't pump the water. A licensed clean-up company must be called to clean up and dispose of this. We contact DEM to oversee the removal of this contaminated water.

I can't count how many hours I've spent pumping water from people's basements. This is a cold and tedious task. These situations usually occur during the cold weather, as the water in the pipes freeze and crack the pipe. When the water eventually thaws, it flows through the cracks and into the building. It takes quite a while to remove hundreds of gallons of water with our pumps. We constantly have to pull out the hose to clean the strainer as debris clogs the opening. We then have to set up the operation from the beginning. This makes for a long process.

Most people can remember where they were when the Challenger space shuttle exploded shortly after take-off. I was pumping a cellar in an old run-down house of a poor, single mom with five kids. It was cold out and she had no heat – and no place else to go. The boiler serviceman wouldn't respond to fix the furnace until all the water was removed from the basement. We spent the entire morning pumping this cellar so that she could try to get the boiler repaired to heat the house. What I remember about that morning was coming up from the cellar and finding her and her kids gathered around an old black and white television watching the news coverage of the explosion. As our pumps were running, we sat in chairs in the kitchen with the family and watched along with them. I remember her crying as she watched. I thought to myself that this woman had enough serious problems of her own today, yet she was still touched by the suffering of these astronauts and their families. She offered us coffee, eggs and toast. We accepted her offer of coffee but declined the toast – this family was obviously dirt poor and we didn't want to take any food away from her kids. She taught me a lesson in sharing that day, and in compassion. Just because things are difficult in your own life doesn't give you the right to turn your back on the misfortunes of others. She was a good woman!

Whenever there's an emergency with no easy solution – we're called. Such was the case one day when a local hospital lost power. They immediately called the Electric Company, only to find that there was a major power outage in the entire area and it could be hours before the power was restored. The hospital's emergency generator failed to start, and their engineers were unable to provide any power to the building. In the mean time, there were people on life support ventilators in the hospital. There were patients in the middle of surgery in darkened operating rooms, and there were supplies of blood and bone marrow that needed to be kept refrigerated to keep from being ruined.

All these things required power – immediate, continuous power. The hospital administrators called the fire department. When we responded, the Chief conferred with hospital personnel and determined the priorities for supplying emergency power. He assigned companies separate tasks. I was on a callback to Ladder 4 that morning, and the Chief assigned us the responsibility of restoring power to the operating rooms. We stretched hundreds of feet of electrical cord from the portable generator we carried on Ladder 4 into the hospital, and up the two flights of stairs to the operating rooms. There were three surgeries in progress. We set up power to the three operating rooms, and continued to monitor the rooms to insure that the power supply was not interrupted.

As I was standing in the foyer outside the Operating Rooms, I was approached by a nurse. She told me that the bone marrow storage container was in danger of heating up and spoiling all the specimens stored in the cryogenic atmosphere. These specimens, I was told, were irreplaceable. The container was located on the same floor as the operating rooms, so I went with her to check on the situation. I found that the container's temperature was rising quickly and was close to the critical point. I relayed this information to the Chief via radio, and told him that our power supply was maxed out by the Operating Rooms. I asked him for another company to stretch power cords to the second floor via another stairway. He sent Ladder 8 to bring us power from their generator. When the cord reached our position, we provided power to the freezer unit. There wasn't a moment to spare, as the temperature was within five degrees of the critical point. We also provided power to the blood bank's refrigeration unit from this supply.

We spent about six hours at the hospital before power was restored. We waited for a little while before we began to break down our power lines – just in case there were additional problems while trying to restore the power. We had successfully provided electricity to the critical areas of this area of the hospital. At the same time, many other fire companies were hard at work doing the same thing in other areas of the hospital. Special Hazards was busy during that time extricating people from the many elevators in the building. It was a long day for all of us – the fire department, the hospital personnel, and the patients and their families. No patient was lost during this power outage. This made it all worthwhile.

Another job that we're frequently asked to perform is that of locksmith – or cat burglar. Lockouts and lock-ins are common calls for the fire department. People frequently lock themselves out of their homes. Many times these are second or third floor apartments, and they call us to 'break in.' Of course, they don't actually want us to 'break' anything. On some occasions, people will send a bill to the fire department for a window or door that was damaged during the process of gaining entry. We are careful not to damage their property, but sometimes it's unavoidable.

It's very important to get as much information as possible before helping someone gain entry to a home. Beginning with, verifying the fact that this person actually lives here. This might sound ridiculous, but there have been cases where the person allowed into the home was actually a burglar. More common than this, however, is a divorced spouse trying to gain entry while their ex is out. We always call for the police to take a report and verify the person's address. We always ask if there are any dogs in the house. If so, we allow the occupant to climb in the window first, to take care of the dog. Even normally friendly dogs seem to have a mean streak when strangers are climbing in their windows!

We try to be as thorough as possible with our questions, but sometimes we don't think to ask the obvious question – is there anyone else at home? One night I was working on Engine 2 and my buddy Pete was in charge, because the Lieutenant was on vacation. A woman pulled a Fire Alarm Box at around midnight. When we pulled up to the box, she was standing there with bags of groceries in her arms. She told us that she lived across the street, on the second floor, and that she had locked herself out of the apartment when she went to the super market. She said her kids were home, but they were small and sound asleep. She pointed to an unlocked window and said we could go in through the living room. Pete asked her if she had any dogs, as we took a ladder from the truck and raised it to the window. "No," she said.

Pete climbed the ladder, pried open the window, and climbed in. As he headed toward the door, to unlock it from the inside, he passed the sofa. There was a man sleeping on the sofa and snoring up a storm. He looked to be about six feet tall and well over two hundred pounds. Pete quietly opened the door to the apartment and quickly went down the stairs to the outside door! When he asked the woman who was on her couch, she said, "Oh, that's my husband, but I didn't want to wake him up. He gets mean if someone wakes him up from a sound sleep." We just shook our heads in disbelief. What if this guy had awakened while Pete was trying to force open the window? He probably would have pushed him off the ladder. What if this guy woke up when Pete was in the darkened house? God only knows what would have happened then. When we told her that she should have never called us in the first place, since her husband was home, she looked confused. She just didn't understand. We got back on the truck and Pete radioed Fire Alarm, "Engine 2 in service. Lockout – needless."

We also get many calls for lock-ins. Most of the time a parent has locked his small child in the house or the car. Sometimes, however, the person locked in is an elderly or disabled person unable to make it to the door. We treat these calls as a little more serious than a lockout. If a child is locked in an apartment or an auto, they are usually upset and panicking. We try to open up the door as quickly as possible so that the parent can comfort the child. In the case of an elderly occupant, many times the person is unconscious or has passed away. These runs are usually dispatched as a "check on the well-being" call. In these cases, it's important to gain entry as quickly as possible because if the person is unconscious, but alive, we need to transport that patient to the hospital right away. Many times these calls come from a son or daughter, sometimes from another state, who has been unsuccessfully trying to reach their mother or father for an extended period of time, and fears the worst.

Rescues are frequently called to people's homes to transport them to a doctor's appointment. We have to explain that the Rescue is an emergency vehicle – a Mobile Intensive Care Unit – not a taxi. There are only five Rescue trucks in the City of Providence and on numerous occasions, all five of them are on calls. If we allowed people with non-emergency medical conditions to use the Rescues for transport to doctor's appointments, a life-threatening call such as a shooting victim or a heart attack patient, might have to wait an extra five to ten minutes for a Rescue to respond from another city or town. This happens frequently as it is. An Engine Company will respond to these cases quickly, but we don't have the equipment the Rescues have, and we don't have the ability to transport the patient to the hospital – and the awaiting doctors.

This is not to say that we're heartless, or that we're not sympathetic to these patients' needs. One of our fire companies will often respond to a person's home to carry a person in a wheelchair down two or three flights of stairs, just so that they can leave their apartment for a little while. We'll then return later to carry them back upstairs to their apartment. We'll do whatever we can to help our neighbors, just as we would in our own personal neighborhood. We frequently assist our elderly neighbors by carrying their groceries in from their car. We sometimes go to their homes to pick up letters that need to be mailed, so that they don't have to walk on the icy sidewalks. All these things are just part of being good neighbors, and firefighters never turn their back on those who are less fortunate and in need of assistance.

We're often called to "investigate a foreign odor." This is one of my least favorite types of run. It's similar to when your spouse or kid says, "Ughh! Taste this and tell me if it's gone bad." These calls range from not finding any discernable odor at all to walking in on a body that has been in the summer's heat for a week or more. The first thing that we smell for on these calls is natural gas. This is a dangerous condition, and natural gas has a distinctive odor. The same holds true for gasoline or other petroleum products. We try to eliminate the hazardous conditions first. Most other harmful gases or vapors, including carbon monoxide, are colorless and odorless – therefore, if the problem is an odor, you can pretty much eliminate these as a cause.

Other common odors for which we're called are backed up sewers, must and mildew, electrical shorts, and decomposing bodies. Decomposing bodies is, by far, my least favorite smell. It is an overpowering smell. It stays with you, in the hairs of your nose, for days. One hot summer afternoon, when I was on Engine 2, we were sent to a high-rise apartment building to "investigate a foreign odor." While responding, we were told by Fire Alarm that the elderly occupant of the apartment hadn't been seen for a week. This run is just getting worse by the minute, we thought. When we reached the building and took the elevator to the 5th floor, we were immediately overwhelmed by the unmistakable smell of a decomposing body. My Lieutenant sent Pete down to the truck for an air pak. One of us was going to have to enter the apartment and verify the obvious – that the occupant was deceased. We tried to open the door with the passkey we received from the apartment manager. The door unlocked, but would not open. We tried several of our tools, but the heavy metal door wouldn't budge.

When it became obvious that we weren't going to gain access this way, we called for a ladder company, so that we could gain access through the 5th floor window, via the aerial. When Ladder 7 raised their aerial to the apartment's window, Pete and I climbed to the top. Pete went before me, pried open, and climbed in the window, as I backed him up. He had his air pak on, so he couldn't smell anything. I didn't have a pak on, so I could smell the odor from the room, even on the aerial outside the window. The window was located directly over the victim's bed, and as Pete climbed in the window, he climbed right over this guy. Pete could see, through the mask, that the man was black, and that he must have weighed 300 pounds. He checked for a pulse – none. The victim had advanced rigor mortis – a definitive sign of death. As Pete made his way to the door, he could see why we were unable to open the door. There was a large pipe across the back of the door. The pipe was slid into two heavy metal brackets that were welded to the inside doorframe. This guy was serious about not letting anyone into his room.

When he left the room he told us about the pipe, and he verified that the man was dead. As he was describing the large black man, one of the neighbors overheard and said, "No. That's not him. This guy is a skinny old Polish man." We had to go back to the apartment to find out who the victim was. When we opened the door and looked into the room we could see the man lying on the bed. Without our masks on we could now see that this man was bloated and dark skinned due to the decomposition process. When we saw the condition of the body, and were hit by the aroma coming from the room, we quickly shut the door. Pete was almost sick right there in the hallway. We called for the Medical Examiner to respond to the scene to verify the patient's identification and remove the body. Now there's a job you couldn't pay me enough to do!

Exterminator. Fireman. I can't see the connection. As far as I can tell, these two occupations have nothing in common. In spite of this, I've responded to numerous calls, over the years, to find that the occupant has spotted a mouse, or a spider. They want us to go into their house and get rid of the pest before they'll go back in. I have to explain to them that they need to call an exterminator. "We don't do that," I've had to tell them, "that's not our job." I do remember two different times that we did assist homeowners get rid of unwanted pests, however. Both times involved bats. In one case, a woman called us because there was a bat flying around her daughter's bedroom. We went into the room and closed the door. The bat was hanging on the curtain. One of the guys reached out and grabbed it in his gloved hand. We took it outside and set it free. The other time was a case of a bat that was hanging from the outside of a person's house. In this case we sprayed the bat with our hoseline and washed him away. Although we helped these two homeowners, I've never understood why people would think of calling the fire department for these types of problems.

Another job that we're sometimes called upon to do is to assist the police. Many times the police will call us to break down a door for a raid on a suspected drug house or gambling operation. We don't get involved with this kind of job anymore. We'll just give them a battering ram and an axe, and let them break down the door themselves. Other times the police will chase a subject and corner him on a roof or in an upper floor of a building. They'll call on us to put our aerial ladder to the roof. Again, we'll set up the ladder and give them whatever they may need, but they will have to climb to the roof to search for the criminal.

As you can see from the assorted jobs we're called upon to perform, there's no easy way to describe what a firefighter's job is. *I* don't even know every type of job that might be considered our responsibility. I only know that when something *isn't* in the realm of our responsibilities, I recognize it. Capturing armed criminals is definitely *not* our job.

Chapter 19
My Driving Adventures
(Get Ready 'Cause Here I Come)

Let me begin this chapter by stating that I'm not really a bad driver. OK, that having been said, there are a number of people that know me who would chuckle at that statement. OK, maybe they'd fall down in hysterics and roll on the floor laughing. I still stand by my first statement; I'm really not a bad driver. I've just had some bad luck. Make that some downright terrible luck. I was involved in 5 motor vehicle accidents while driving fire apparatus in my first eight years on the department. I'm not at all proud to say that I've been told that I hold the dollar record for the most damage done to fire apparatus in department history. There are some guys on the department who insist that I was given the answers to the Lieutenant's exam so that the department could promote me, and get me out of the driver's seat. That part I know is not true. I wish it had been. I would have been promoted a few years earlier, and I'd be a Captain by now.

My first accident driving a fire truck was not much of a story. It was just a small fender bender on the way to a box alarm. As I was trying to make a left-hand turn I clipped the front left fender of a car that had stopped to let me go. There was no visible damage to Engine 2, and only slight damage to her car. It was really no big deal, but I had only been on the department for about two months. I felt terrible – and embarrassed. Little did I know at the time, that this was the beginning of a lousy stretch of luck behind the wheel of fire department apparatus.

About a year or so later I was driving Chief 3's car on a cold and raw winter day. I always hated driving the Chief. I had only been on the job a short time, so I didn't feel comfortable around the chiefs. When I had to drive a chief, I'd keep my mouth shut and speak only when spoken to. I'd also do my best not to get lost! There were only three chiefs on duty in the city at one time, so their cars could be dispatched anywhere in the city. It wasn't like driving the engine, only having to worry about the streets in a small area. I had to know my way around the entire city. So I was already nervous. The morning went OK. We had a couple of runs, and luckily, I knew where the streets were. Sandwiched in between the runs, we visited the five firehouses in the Battalion. The chief I was driving on this day was a great guy. He was an easy person to work for and was always good to the new guys. He had been a Captain in my training academy, so he knew me pretty well. Also, the fact that we had been stationed in the same firehouse for the past year made it a little easier on me. We returned to our firehouse just before lunch, and the chief said, "Tommy, I don't have any plans for this afternoon, so after lunch just relax. If I need you, I'll come and get you."

The day was half over and everything had gone fine. I was feeling a little less nervous now. After lunch Pete and I began playing cards at the table in the sitting room. As we looked out the windows we could see snow beginning to fall. Around 3:00 it began to come down a little heavier. You could see the streets beginning to get covered, as the snow began to stick. The bell tipped. Fire Alarm was sending out companies to a Master Box on the other side of the city, and at the end of the list of companies the dispatcher called, "Chief 3." I slid the pole and hopped into the car, waiting for the chief. When he got in, he could see that I didn't know where this building was located so he told me, "Just go straight down North Main Street into the city and I'll direct you from there." That seemed easy enough. I started down the street and was trying to be careful. The snow had piled up more than I had realized. As we began descending a hill heading toward the city I pumped the brakes to try to slow down, but the car just seemed to pick up speed! At the bottom of the hill the street took a hard right hand turn. As we moved closer to the bottom, it was obvious that we were going too fast to make the turn. I heard the chief yell, "Oooo deee" as I was desperately trying to maneuver the car around the bend. The left front wheel struck the curb as the car skidded to the left, and the car momentarily lifted onto two wheels – then came to a stop. I timidly looked at the chief. He just asked if I was OK. I nodded. "Can we still move?" he asked. I tried driving forward and it seemed all right. "I think it's OK," I said, and continued on toward the Master Box. "That was close," he said.

Everything seemed to be OK until we began driving under a bridge about a mile away. The pavement was dry under the bridge, and when the car was able to get traction it pulled drastically to the right. As we went through the underpass and the car pulled to the right, we almost clipped a park car – another "Oooo deee." It had taken me by surprise! I struggled to keep control of the car, and we finally made it to the address. When we got out of the car and looked for damage, we saw that the left front wheel was bent inward at a forty-five degree angle! I have to say that this chief was really good about it. He never screamed at me, or made me feel bad about it. "Hey, accidents happen," he said. He also never had me drive him again.

A couple of years later I was detailed into Rescue 3 for the night. Another firefighter, George, was in charge of the Rescue. We had worked together on Engine 2, and he was a friend of mine, so I thought we'd have an easy night working together. Things started out just fine, we didn't have a single run for the first few hours. We just hung around the station and watched a little TV. We even stayed in long enough to eat supper with the rest of the guys. That was unusual for Rescue. We finally had a call around 8:30 for a report of an elderly woman having difficulty breathing. When we arrived on the scene, the engine company had already put her on oxygen and taken her vitals. The vitals seemed fine, but she had a slight build up of fluids in her lungs. We suggested she come with us to the hospital to be checked out. We wheeled her to the truck, and George monitored her in the back as I climbed into the driver's seat.

As we were transporting her to the ER I had the lights and siren of the Rescue on. The cars pulled over as we approached them, heading for the hospital. When we were about two blocks from the hospital we came to a traffic light. I had the red light, so I began slowing down. As I approached the intersection, the traffic heading in both directions of the crossing street came to a stop to let me pass. I took my foot off the brake to proceed through the light when I saw the flash of a car pass in front of me, from left to right. I immediately tried to reapply the brake, but it was too late. CRASSSSSHHHH! My right front bumper crashed into her right rear fender and spun her around. "Fuck! Not again!" I yelled. George yelled up front to see if I was OK, and checked on the old woman we were transporting. She was fine. I got out of the truck to check on the woman driving the other car. She was fine – just shaken up. She had a green light and passed the stopped traffic on the right hand side. The view of the intersection was partially blocked, so she never even saw me coming – and I never saw her. George called for another fire company to respond to the incident, to stay with the woman as she waited for the police. We waited for the engine company to arrive and then finished transporting our patient to the hospital. When we returned to the scene, the Chief was there. He just smiled at me and shook his head. I was already getting a reputation as a bad (I say unlucky) driver – and the worst was still ahead!

A couple of years later I was the chauffeur of Engine 2, when we were called to a report of a fire in a McDonald's Restaurant down the street from the station. The restaurant was located in a shopping plaza, which was built up above the road. Two sides of the plaza had entrances that were on hills. The front had a ten foot wall that ran the entire length of the plaza, along the sidewalk of the street below. While we were responding, Fire Alarm advised us that they had a report of smoke in the building. When we pulled up along side of McDonald's, I engaged the air brake and the pump before getting out of the cab. My Lieutenant, Joe, and Pete went straight into the store to see what was going on. My job was to wait at the truck, and supply them water if they needed to bring in a hoseline. The chauffeur of the first-in engine company is always the pump operator at a fire.

As I waited to hear from the Lieutenant, a worker told me that there was a fire in the air conditioning unit on the roof. He was pointing toward the back of the building. As I went toward the area to look, I heard someone yell, "The fire truck is moving!!!" I looked back toward the truck, and sure enough it was rolling toward the wall. I ran along side it and jumped into the cab just as it struck a parked car. By the time I applied the foot brake, the truck had pushed the car over the wall and the front wheels of the truck followed. The car was standing upright on its trunk, wedged between the truck above, and the sidewalk below! I was in the cab, which was hanging over the wall, and looking into the traffic below. The Chief was on the road below, responding to this alarm. I could clearly see into his car, and I could read his lips – "Ooooo deeeee!!!"

A few years later, this same McDonalds would construct a drive-through window in this same area of the parking lot. The running joke on the fire department after that was, "Tommy Kenney was the inspiration for that drive-through window."

It seemed I wasn't having very much luck driving fire department vehicles from the Branch Ave. station. I transferred. I went to the Messer Street station to join Engine 8. I had better luck driving at this station – for a couple of years, anyway. There were three firefighters assigned to Engine 8 under the command of a Captain, Bob. He was a good officer and I had known him before I got on the job, so it was an easy transition for me. The other two firefighters were Russ and Mike. I had worked with Mike's brother, Pete, at Engine 2 for the first seven years I was on the department. It was a good crew and we were a very busy company, so it was fun to be there, and I learned quite a bit during my time at Messer St. The firefighters alternated the driving duties, a month at a time. After I had been there a while, Russ and Mike both passed the Lieutenant's exam and were transferred to other companies as Acting Lieutenants. This left only me to drive Engine 8 on our group. I didn't mind this because we had a new truck and I enjoyed driving it.

One night in December, about a month after Mike and Russ had left, we had a callback Captain, Steve, in charge, and a new firefighter riding the side. We had a terrible night. We must have gone out about six times before midnight and six times after midnight! It had been drizzling all night, and the roads were wet. Every time we went out, I'd try to be conscious of this and keep my speed to a minimum. Around 5:00 AM we were dispatched to a brewery on Elmwood Ave., along with several other fire companies for an alarm sounding, inside the building. As I headed for the brewery, I traveled straight down Potters Ave. to Elmwood. There was no evidence on this run of any problems along Potters; this would all change later on. The first-in company determined that it was an accidental alarm and released the remainder of us. We returned to the station and tried to salvage a little sleep before the night was over.

About an hour later we were sent to a Master Box Alarm, to a high-rise on Potters Ave. We had just driven past this building an hour before. As I headed up the street toward the building, I tried to tap the brakes to slow down before I got too close to the turn-off to the driveway. When I tapped the brakes, they locked up on me! We began to skid on black ice, which had formed on the road. I tried to pump the brakes – nothing! I tried to steer the truck – nothing! We were just sliding toward the left side of the street and I couldn't do anything to slow us down! It seemed as though we were picking up speed, instead of slowing down! In my memory, it seems like we were floating on this street. I don't remember the siren - it just seems eerily quiet. It also seems to happen in slow motion. I saw a telephone pole in our path and I said to the Captain, "We're going to hit!" I never even saw the huge tree behind the pole. We crashed into the pole and then immediately into the tree. The tree had to be forty feet high and three feet thick! We knocked it right over! The Captain hit the windshield and bounced back into his seat. I was thrown against the steering wheel and the dashboard, and then into the Captain's lap. Billy, the firefighter riding the side was thrown against the side of the truck, striking his shoulder. The Captain and I were unconscious in the cab. When I came to, I saw firemen standing on the front of the truck, trying to get us out of the cab. They had already put cervical collars on us and were putting us on backboards. They had to remove us through the windshield area.

When I saw the truck at the Repair Shop a couple of months later, it seemed amazing that either of us lived. If we had struck the tree in front of one of us, we would have been crushed in our seats. The only thing that saved us was that the tree had struck exactly in the middle of the cab, between both of us.

The indentation of the tree was so deep that a good-sized man could stand in the dent and not be seen from the side!

Both the Captain and Billy came back to duty from their injuries, but were never the same. They have both since retired from the department because of these injuries. I was out of work for over a year with knee, back, and neck problems. I've put in 14 years since the accident and I'm not ready to leave yet!

When I returned to duty on Engine 8 it was difficult to get behind the wheel again, but I knew I had no choice if I planned to remain on the department. After an investigation into the accident the police Accident Reconstruction Team determined that there wasn't any excessive speed involved. The black ice on the road surface and the weight of the truck, which includes 500 gallons of water, were the major factors. Even so, I was one of the slower drivers on the department when I returned. Even now, when we're going to a run on icy streets or snow, I always tell my chauffeur, "Take it slow, we don't have to beat anyone. I don't care if we get there last, as long as we get there!"

Chapter 20
Meals on Wheels

When I was first appointed to the Providence Fire Department, back in 1980, the Trainees were being certified as Emergency Medical Technicians (EMT's), as part our training in the Fire Academy. This was around the time that the fire service, at least in this area of the country, was beginning to see a heavier load of emergency medical runs. The Fire Academy prior to mine was the first to receive this training by the department. Prior to that, the firemen on the job were only required to be trained in basic first aid. A few members of the department had taken the EMT course on their own and been licensed, but their number was probably less than ten in a department of over 500. At around this same time, the State of Rhode Island passed a law requiring all personnel assigned to Rescue Units be at least a licensed EMT. This was now the minimum standard for riding these units. There were three Rescues in the city at that time. Prior to our classes being appointed, the firefighters on the job were probably only required to work a tour of duty on one of these rescues once or twice a year. Once we were appointed to the department, and the higher standards for riding the rescues were passed, it seemed that guys from our classes were being 'detailed' into these units once or twice a month. (A 'detail' is a temporary assignment – usually for a single day or night.)

Let me give you a little background on the rescue units of the Providence Fire Department. Our rescues are similar to ambulances or EMS (Emergency Medical Service) units in some other cities. They are part of the fire department, and are manned by two firemen, usually one firefighter and one rescue officer. Around the time I started on the department, our busiest engine company was doing about 3,000 runs per year. With the majority of engines doing about 2,000 each. The three rescues were each doing between 4,000 and 5,000 runs per year. They respond to any and all EMS calls made to our dispatch office – anything from a cold or a small laceration to heart attacks or shootings.

At that time, most applicants to the fire department were men who were interested in fighting fires. To most of us, the rescue runs were a necessary evil that we simply put up with because we had no choice. In our eyes, the more interesting of the rescue runs were the trauma calls (shootings, stabbings & auto accidents), and an engine company would be dispatched on these runs, along with the rescue. Engine companies would also be dispatched whenever there was a report of chest pains, difficulty breathing or a drug overdose. Because of this, many of us believed that most firemen permanently assigned to rescue were only there because they had no taste for fire duty. Things have come a long way in this area over the last twenty-five years. Now people are applying to the fire department with the express purpose of making a career of EMS. The fact that engine companies were responding to the 'better' EMS calls anyway, we would be pissed off whenever we were sent to fill in on these units. The worst part of being detailed to the rescue for a tour of duty, however, was that we had no chance of fighting a fire while there. We couldn't join our comrades if there was a fire; rather, we had to stand by at the scene, in the event that someone was injured.

I never took to riding the rescue, although I did do my share the first five or six years I was on the department. I also have to admit that many of the more memorable moments I've had over my career have been on rescue calls – both funny and tragic.

I titled this chapter Meals on Wheels because when I think back over the years and try to recall some of the rescue runs with which I've been involved, I remember that I used to hate hearing that phrase. Any time we were dispatched to a run that was reported by Meals on Wheels, it always seemed to be bad news. They would call us when the meals the volunteers delivered had piled up for two or three days. Since they didn't deliver on weekends, this often meant that the resident hadn't been heard from in almost a week. This is not a pleasant task – especially in the middle of summer when the heat is oppressive and many elderly people keep their windows shut for security reasons. This would often make their apartments feel like ovens. Sometimes the reason the meals piled up would simply be because the elderly resident was out of town, or in the hospital. They had just neglected to contact the organization. Many times, however, it was not. Most times these calls ended with us crawling through a window, or forcing a door, searching for a body. Too many times, that's exactly what we discovered.

One day we were called to a high rise for the elderly by Meals on Wheels to "check on the well-being of an elderly woman and investigate a strange odor coming from the apartment." We were in the middle of a spaghetti and meatball dinner when this call echoed over the vocalarm, and it didn't sound like it was going to be a run with a happy ending. I was assigned to Engine 2 that day, and we were dispatched along with Rescue 3 who was also from our station. There was also a ladder company quartered with us – Ladder 7. I remember that they laughed at us and said, "Don't worry boys, we'll keep your meals nice and warm for you so you can enjoy them when you get back. That is, unless you lose your appetites."

Guys on ladder trucks are like that. They don't respond too often to rescue calls. They refer to them as nuisance runs. Ladder men want *no part* of nuisance runs. When the bell tips, and the house lights go on in the middle of the night, for the frequent rescue calls or trash fires or auto fires to which the engine men have to respond, the ladder men simply pull the covers over their heads and roll over. We call that the "Ladder-Man Roll."

On this day, we were met in the lobby by the building manager and the volunteer from Meals on Wheels. As we rode the elevator to the 7th floor, they reported to us that the volunteer was concerned when she found two meals already stacked outside the apartment door, when she came to deliver today's meal. When she knocked on the door and got no response, she sought out the building manager. They both returned to the apartment and the manager opened the door with the master key. They both said that the smell coming from the open door was so horrendous it drove them both back into the hallway. That's when they called us.

The building manager handed me the key as we departed the elevator and told me, "Apartment 714." He and the woman delivering the meals stayed at the elevator. As unpleasant as it may be, even to us, the smell of a decaying human body is something to which we've become accustomed. I had only been on the job for a few years at this time, but I had already had my share of similar situations. As I began to open the door, we felt prepared for what we thought we would encounter. When I pushed the door open we were overtaken by an overwhelming odor that was totally foreign to all of us. That is, with the exception of my Lieutenant, Joe. He was a twenty-year veteran of the fire department, and he immediately recognized this smell. Strangely enough, we did too.

When we were in the Academy and the Training Officers would tell us stories about the job, we would sit and listen intently. We'd then proceed to bombard them with a thousand questions about all aspects of the job. Inevitably *the* question would come: "What does burnt flesh smell like?" Most would answer in a similar fashion, "I can't really describe it to you, but I *can* tell you that you'll know it when you smell it." That wasn't the answer that a bunch of Trainees thirsty for information about our new careers were looking for, but they were absolutely right.

We stopped at the doorway for a moment to reassess the situation. If someone was burnt in here, maybe this was a fire also, not just a rescue run. We looked into the apartment, but saw no sign of smoke. There was neither heat rushing toward us, nor any sound of fire crackling in the room. We also saw no sign of the woman who lived here. As we all entered to search, we split up into two groups. Some of the guys headed for the bedroom, as the Rescue Officer (George) and I started to the kitchen. As we rounded a corner to enter the kitchen, we were startled at what lie before us. The old woman was sitting on the floor, propped up against the kitchen cabinets, with an electric stove in her lap. She was obviously dead, and had been for at least a couple of days. Her left arm was stretched across the burners, holding the back of the stove. One of the burners, which her arm was covering, was still on, and glowing red. All the flesh and muscle on this arm had burnt off, down to her bones, from her wrist to just above her elbow. Her face and upper body were bloated, charred, and split from the heat. The pungent, sweet aroma, and this horrible sight, was too disturbing for us to want to linger too long in this area. There was nothing any of us could do to help this poor woman now, so we headed back out to the hallway. Joe radioed our dispatcher to send a police sergeant. It's the police department's job to begin the investigation into the cause of death, and to contact the Medical Examiner and the victim's family.

We explained the situation to the building manager and began to wait for the police to arrive. As we described the awful scene, we remembered that the stove was still on – and that we needed to shut it down before our job was done. George and I took a couple of deep breaths and re-entered the apartment. When we returned to the kitchen, we saw that part of the flesh from her arm had melded onto the burner's control knob. We wouldn't be able to simply shut it off. We decided the best way to shut the stove down was to unplug it from the wall socket. Unfortunately for us, this was located on the wall behind the stove, almost at floor level. George had to drape himself over the top of the stove, as I held his belt to keep him from sliding onto the woman. When he finally accomplished this task we retreated to the hallway as quickly as possible.

While we were waiting for the police we tried to figure out what exactly had happened to her. We came to the conclusion that she must have gone to the stove to heat something and turned on the burner. She then had a sudden heart attack and grabbed the back of the stove to keep herself from falling. When she did fall, she pulled the stove down on top of her with her arm across the burner. This had probably happened three days prior to our arrival, based on the number of meals stacked in the hallway. This scenario seemed to explain the unusual circumstances. It also gave us some solace in thinking that she was gone before suffering from that awful fate.

When we returned to the firehouse, the guys from Ladder 7 asked us what we had. I told them, "Oh nothing, some woman went on vacation and didn't tell anyone. Now, who the hell touched my plate of spaghetti?"

Chapter 21
Odds and Ends
(The Pros, The Cons, & The Routine)

THE PROS

There are a lot of things I enjoy about being a firefighter. For one, it's the job that almost all little boys dreamed of doing when they were kids. I know I did. In that respect, it almost doesn't seem like a job at all. It almost seems like being at a fantasy camp of some sort, similar to the baseball fantasy camps that aging yuppies pay so much money to attend. Just coincidentally, this is the other profession most little boys dream about growing up to become – Major League Baseball players.

As I've stated before, most firemen are adrenaline junkies to a certain degree. The excitement of responding to emergency situations and working in a chaotic atmosphere is an adrenaline junkie's dream job. This, however, is certainly not the only reason people are drawn into this profession. Restoring order to these situations and helping to alleviate the suffering of innocent victims is a rewarding undertaking. Most firemen I know have an overwhelming desire to be part of the solution, rather than part of the problem. We take pride in the fact that most people in the general public understand that we are there to help. They respect us for that, and we work hard at maintaining that respect and trust. Most firefighters make no distinction between the rich and powerful and the down and out. Respect is a mutual thing. If you respect us, we'll respect you. If you don't, we can treat you like the scumbag that you are (being a scumbag is not a socio-economic condition; it is a condition of the mind – of attitude – of the spirit. If you treat others as if they are not worthwhile human beings, you're a scumbag. Definition according to Tom). Firefighters, as a whole, are smack dab in the middle of both extreme ends of the economic ladder. We will never get rich doing what we do, but we will never go hungry, either.

Security was once another reason people were drawn to fire department jobs. Job security, and thus economic security, for their families. Civil service jobs, in general, and fire department jobs, in particular, were jobs that were felt to be free from the threat of layoffs and cutbacks. They were jobs that had good fringe benefits that weren't in danger of being stripped away in an instant by over-eager politicians. In the wake of the recent economic woes affecting many cities and towns, this is no longer the case. Union givebacks and layoffs seem to be the new solutions to the financial problems facing many cities and towns.

The new face of the fire department, over the last twenty years or so, is that of a college graduate. Although he is certainly capable of earning a much higher wage in the private sector, he is drawn to the fire service for his own personal reasons – possibly the excitement of the job, or the desire to help others. The trade off for the cut in pay he must endure is the security of a municipal job, and the benefits, and security it provides for his family. Firefighting has become more of a thinking man's profession. Hazardous Materials incidents, terrorist threats, high-rise fires, and EMS emergencies are not the type of incidents that you just jump into without first evaluating the problem, and the possible solutions.

When a person joins the fire service, he immediately joins one of the largest brotherhoods in the world. He immediately has a connection to millions of men and women around the globe. The fire service is an extremely close, extended community. We share a common bond that no outsider can fully understand or appreciate. No matter where he may find himself, a friendly face and assistance is only as far away as the nearest firehouse. This brotherhood extends, to a certain degree, to police officers. Their job is very different from ours, but we face many of the same situations. We both face the dangers of the streets. When we, as firefighters, find ourselves in trouble on the street, we call the police for assistance. They respond to our calls for help in much the same way they respond to the call of a fellow officer. We are different, yet we are linked.

Belonging to this 'brotherhood' breeds pride – pride in your occupation, pride in your department, and pride in your company. The strongest of these, is pride in your company. This is because *these* are the guys you risk your life alongside. These are the guys who you'd die trying to save. These are the guys who would die trying to save you. If the fire service is like a family, and it is, *these* guys are your siblings.

One of the best 'fringe benefits' of firefighting is that kids look up to us as heroes and as role models. We take this responsibility seriously. In this day and age there are very few people a parent can tell their children to trust – to turn to for help. Firefighters and Police Officers are the two groups of people I've always taught my kids to turn to for assistance. We have many encounters with children. We visit schools and day cares. We attend block parties and social gatherings involving the community. We sponsor children's sports teams and take part in their parades, etc. I've been fortunate enough to lead my son's Little League parade, riding the fire truck, on a couple of different occasions. On one of these occasions, he rode in the cab of the truck with me and operated the siren and air horn. That was a memory that will last a lifetime – for both of us!

My oldest daughter, Joy, can say she drove the tiller of a ladder truck. My second daughter, Caitlin, has accompanied me to the Fireman's Ball. My son, Teddy, is still embarrassed by the time I dropped him off in front of his school with the fire truck when he was in the 7th grade. His friends thought it was great! My stepson, Bobby, has ridden the truck and slid the pole at the station on numerous occasions. These are things they'll always remember.

THE CONS

The dangers of the job, both immediate and long term, are by far, the greatest negative aspect of a career in the fire service. Almost every year, firefighting has the largest on-the-job fatality rate of any occupation in the U.S. Firefighters go into this profession knowing this fact. There is no completely safe way to fight fires effectively. There has been a large-scale effort toward safety measures for firefighters instituted by fire departments around the country in the last twenty years or so. From my point of view, these changes are largely superficial. They are, sadly, primarily motivated by financial considerations. Liability is the name of the game. Departments are afraid that members of their own department, or the member's family, will sue the department (and the city or town) if the member is seriously injured or killed in the line of duty.

Departments often set policies that are impossible to adhere to, in order to protect their own liability. For instance, in our department we have an SOP that states that in no circumstance shall a firefighter enter a burning building alone. It further states that when two firefighters are in a burning building, there must be *at least* two firefighters outside the building, in full turnout gear, ready to rescue the firefighters on the inside if the need arises. This is referred to as the two-in two-out rule. This, on the surface, seems like a commendable policy designed to protect firefighters. Unfortunately it becomes a farce when half of the companies in the city are manned with only three firefighters. My present company, Engine 15, has only three men per shift. We are often dispatched alone to areas in the city where the response time of the next due fire company would be five minutes. This means that if we responded to such an area and found a building fire, per SOP, we would not be allowed to enter the building for a full 5 minutes after reaching the scene. Try explaining this to the homeowners.

In reality, this is not what happens. I would take one of my firefighters into the building to search for victims and to begin extinguishments of the fire. Leaving one firefighter on the outside of the building to run our pump, and supply water to our handline. I, as the officer in command of my company, would be (and have been on numerous occasions) in clear violation of this written two-in two-out policy. The Chiefs on the department are well aware that this is the way things work on the fire ground, but they have *never* reprimanded any officer for this reason. If, however, I took the firefighter into the building and the building had collapsed, killing both of us, the department would be able to state that Lt. Kenney was in violation of departmental policy. Therefore, the department was not at fault. Many of the new so-called safety policies to protect firefighters are similar to this; if it's dangerous – don't do it. I'm not over-anxious to needlessly put myself, or my men, in danger, but I think the public has a right to be protected by their firefighters, even if the situation is dangerous. That's part of our job. We knowingly accepted this risk when we took this job.

There are some safety features that do help minimize firefighter injuries and deaths that have been implemented over the last twenty years. These, however, are mostly changes that have been forced on departments by federal safety regulations or by the firefighter's unions. Enclosed cabs for all members riding on a fire apparatus, is one example. Diesel fumes exhaust systems in stations is another. Mandatory fire resistant bunker pants for all firefighters, is yet another. These, and many other changes, are steps in the right direction toward firefighter health and safety. I think it is naïve for anyone to think, however, that these changes would have been made by any department on their own accord. All these changes cost money, and the cost is *always* the bottom line.

The proof of this fact is that the best-known way to cut down on firefighter injuries and deaths is to have sufficient manpower on each piece of apparatus; and yet the cities and towns across the country continue to cut manpower for budgetary reasons. They point out the savings to the taxpayer and try to sell them the fact that the safety of the general public is not being jeopardized. This is an out-and-out lie. They point to Mutual Aid agreements with neighboring communities. If there is a fire in the city or town, they say, that demands extra apparatus or extra manpower, the neighboring community will send help. This may sound great on paper, but when you consider the fact that in most fires firefighters are not going to pull anyone out of a burning building alive after the first five minutes of the fire, these companies from neighboring towns are not going to do anything to contribute to the safety of the public.

The politicians deliberately lie to the public to save money. They don't want to be responsible for having to raise taxes. If the politicians were honest with the public, and the citizens decided to cut back and take the gamble with their safety, this would be an entirely different issue. I have yet to see this happen. I see cities and towns with paid fire departments that regularly man their apparatus with only two firefighters (or worse – one). I can tell you that it is, without exception, impossible to effectively operate an engine company or a ladder company with two men. In these cases, the public safety is in jeopardy. Worse yet, the general public rides by the firehouse and sees an engine truck, a ladder truck, and a couple of firefighters, and they think that if there were a fire in their home that they would be adequately protected. This is a common scam by the local politicians of this country. Unfortunately for the firefighters manning these trucks, in the event of a fire they are more likely to be injured or killed in the line of duty if they try to overextend themselves due to a lack of manpower.

Fire department staffing is not the only fire-related issue on which politicians and fire departments have differing views. The politicians consistently bow to the demands of the almighty dollar, while accusing us of using scare tactics to misinform the public. One such issue has always been the requirements of sprinklers in places of public assembly. Fire departments have long been the biggest advocates of sprinklers. Local and state politicians have consistently resisted this requirement. Business and property owners have lobbied city and state officials and threatened to close up their businesses due to the economic hardship such requirements would put on them. When the lawmakers have agreed to pass grandfather clauses to exempt pre-existing businesses from these requirements, they have often been the recipients of campaign contributions from these same businessmen. Unfortunately it has taken a tremendous tragedy, The Station Night Club fire, to prove that the firefighters were correct in saying that it was only a matter of time before something like this would happen. Most people who witnessed the horrible video of the inside of the club that night, were amazed at how quickly the flames and deadly smoke traveled throughout the building. Firefighters were not surprised at all. We've seen many buildings consumed this quickly. The only difference is that usually we're the only people inside the building when this happens.

It's been interesting to watch these same politicians who are responsible for the grandfather clauses and building code variances that have allowed this unsafe condition to continue, *demand* tougher fire codes. It's been even more interesting to watch the process of passing these *new(?)* regulations into law. For all of the rhetoric, mostly with good intentions, generated by these politicians after the public outcry immediately following this tragedy, the final versions of most of these codes seldom have the same sweeping changes that were so publicly promised. Compromise (the politician's specialty) has usually watered down the requirements by the time they are passed into law.

This tragedy was also a local tragedy to me. West Warwick, Rhode Island is just one town away from my home. I have talked to firefighters who were on the scene that fateful night. One aspect of this tragedy that has yet to be discussed by the media is the initial response of the fire department to the scene. The initial firefighters who responded to this incident acted bravely and heroically. The unfortunate fact is that they could have done much more, and possibly saved more of the victims, had their trucks been adequately manned. The first fire department responders to the scene were an Engine and a Ladder from a nearby fire station. The Engine Company was manned by only two men! The Ladder Truck (I can't even refer to it as a company) had *only 1 man* on board!! What could these men possibly do at such a large incident with so many victims trapped? I believe they did *much more* than humanly possible that night – unfortunately it wasn't nearly enough. I guess the city officials believed these trucks were adequately manned. Apparently none of these officials have any idea what a firefighter's job consists of.

Another negative aspect of the modern fire department is the lack of better equipment. It seems strange to me that we have the technology to send men into space but we're unable to develop a portable, and affordable, air pak for firefighting that allows a firefighter to spend longer than fifteen minutes in a hazardous atmosphere. Most new breakthroughs in firefighting equipment are very expensive. This just about precludes some cities from purchasing them. I understand, from a friend in the field, that Scott (the company that manufactures Providence's air paks) is introducing a new *and improved* version of their product. When it is introduced they will no longer sell the old version. Naturally, the newer model is more expensive than the present models. Most cities and towns have put in orders for the older model before they become obsolete. This would make no sense if the primary concern were the protection of firefighters, and through them, the protection of the public. It does make perfect sense, however, if the primary concern is money.

Stress is also an occupational hazard for firefighters. I understand that stress in the workplace is a major factor in many of today's fast-paced jobs, but how many of the workers in these jobs deal with life and death situations on a daily, or weekly, basis? How many of these workers can be diagnosed with Post Traumatic Stress Disorder because of the horrible scenes that replay in their heads each and every night? Severe stress is a way of life for the firefighter.

The inconvenience and hardship placed on a firefighter's family due to having to work on nights, weekends, and holidays are often cause for marital troubles. Firefighters have a high incidence of divorce. Spouses often grow tired of going to family functions alone and frequently having to watch over the kids themselves. Having to spend Christmas, Thanksgiving, or Easter without dad around the house isn't the easiest situation for any family. Holidays are just like any other work day in the schedule of a firefighter. There *always* has to be someone on duty. These never-ending work shifts away from home, coupled with the day-to-day stress of the job, often lead to firefighter burnout.

THE ROUTINE

The routine of the job is much like the routine at your home: cooking, cleaning, eating, sleeping and watching TV. We live at the station; therefore all the normal things associated with maintaining a home are normal activities at the firehouse. Cutting the grass, shoveling the snow, washing the windows and floors, and food shopping. Even buying appliances and furniture as they wear out. Sharing the bathroom and showers, making our beds, washing our clothes and linens, washing the family vehicle – in our case the fire truck. These are the things we do in the station as we await the next alarm.

In addition to these normal household things, we also spend time training each day. We train with the equipment. We train with the truck. We study the streets in the district. We inspect the existing buildings in the area. We check on the construction features of the new buildings going up. We also inspect the schools and apartment buildings in our district.

The most competent chef on the group usually does the cooking. I've been lucky since I've made Lieutenant as I've always had a couple of good chefs on my truck. Engine 15 is stationed in a single house – that is, we're the only truck at the station. We usually only have to cook for three, but that doesn't keep us from having some great meals. Al's specialty is swordfish or tuna or shark steaks on the grill. He catches the fish on deep sea fishing expeditions on his father's boat. Rick's specialty is shepherd's pie with the ground beef drained of every speck of fat! Doug's specialty is whatever is on sale at the market. He'll cook anything and make it taste good. Me? I can't cook. Every time I've tried to prepare a meal at the station I've burnt it. One day we had to hook up the smoke ejector in the kitchen to clear out all the smoke. And that was just for BLTs!

Many of the stations used to have mascots – almost always dogs. This, unfortunately, is a dying tradition. At the present time, the only mascot left on our department is Penny – a Dalmatian who lives with the guys from Engine 12 and Ladder 3 at the Admiral Street Station. When she passes, there'll be none left. That will be a sad day. **[ED. NOTE: KIND OF A PERSONAL NOTE, BUT WHY IS THIS? COULDN'T YOU GUYS GET ANOTHER DOG FOR THE STATION, OR ARE THERE REGULATIONS AGAINST THIS?]**

Chapter 22
My Heroes – My Teachers
(Past and Present)

As is probably apparent to the reader by this point, I have an admiration for firefighters. Good firefighters. I always have. I guess this is not all that surprising, since my dad was a fireman. I, like most little boys, idolized my dad. I thought he was the biggest, strongest, and toughest man in the whole world. As I grew to be a teenager, I realized he wasn't big at all – in stature. He was only about 5'8" and 150 pounds. It wasn't until I became a firefighter myself, and gained an understanding of what he had been through, and the things he had done, that I realized how big…and tough… and strong he really was. Not because of the size of his frame, but because of the size of his heart. I have also come to appreciate the difference between a firefighter and a good firefighter. My father was a good firefighter. I never got the chance to work with him, but I have worked with guys who have. They all tell me the same thing – your dad was a fireman's fireman. This is the ultimate praise from a firefighter. Somehow, those words always bring me back to when I was a little boy…and dad was larger than life.

I remember one brilliantly sunny afternoon when I was about 8 years old. It's funny how some memories are so vivid in your mind, even after forty years, while others from a week ago are nothing more than a shadowy blur. Such is the case with this day. It was a summer day and my father had taken my brother and me to the store with him. We were riding in a brand new car – a white Chevrolet Impala with crimson red interior. This was the first new car my father had ever bought. Naturally, it was our first new car also, so my brother and I were still begging to go with him every time he left the house. Just so we could ride in the sharp new car! It was 1963. My father let me play with the channels on the radio as he drove. My brother would yell, "stop," when he heard a song he wanted to hear, and I would continue to turn the dial. Usually just to make him mad, showing off because I was the oldest and I got to sit in the front seat with dad. As he approached the corner of Plainfield St. and

Alverson Ave., my father pulled to the side of the road and parked the car. He crossed the street and entered Harry's Variety Store.

When he came out of the store, he ran across the street. I saw him pass the car, run to a fire alarm box mounted on a pole, and yank the hook down. He ran back to the car, reached inside, turned off the ignition, and told us, "Don't move from this car, no matter what"! He ran back past the store, to a 3-decker around the corner. I could now see heavy black smoke coming from the third floor apartment, and people in front of the building screaming. My father ran over to them and grabbed a woman by the shoulders and yelled at her, "Is there anyone still in the house"? Just then I heard the distant sound of a siren approaching, I turned to look for the fire engine I knew was coming, Engine 19, but it was too far away to see as yet. When I looked back at the house I just caught a glimpse of my father's white shirt disappearing into the front doorway. I remember being scared that my daddy was gone. I didn't really have an understanding of what a house fire was, but I knew that it wasn't good. As he disappeared inside the building, the smoke began to drift across the street, turning this sunny afternoon suddenly dark. Even in the darkness, I began to see flickers of light from the windows on the side of the house, as the flames became more intense.

The siren was almost deafening by now, I'm sure the truck was in sight. I didn't see it, however, because I couldn't take my eyes off that house! The one that had swallowed my dad! Out of the corner of my eye I saw a red blur as the fire truck passed right next to our car, and pulled up in front of the house. The fireman got off the truck and moved faster than I ever saw anyone move before – at least it seemed that way to a scared little 8 year old boy. I remember the sirens of other trucks coming from the distance. I remember the smell of smoke – I remember the sound of breaking glass and screams – I remember seeing an aerial ladder going to the roof and the silhouetted figures of firemen swinging axes, as the smoke rose all around them – I remember the salty taste of my own tears. The tears stopped when I saw my dad coming back toward the car, his shirt was black with soot, but he was OK. You can imagine what kind of hero I thought my dad was after watching that fire. He seemed to stand ten feet tall to that scared 8 year old kid at that moment. From that time on, I knew I wanted to be just like him. Although I may have lost sight of that image from time to time, it was always in the back of my mind. When I became a firefighter, my respect for him only grew.

I really don't know what I can say about my first Lieutenant, Joe, without sounding corny. As my father was my teacher in the art of life, Joe was my teacher in the art of firefighting. He was my first permanent superior on the job, but he never treated me like a subordinate. He was more like a guider, a fine-tuner, a teacher. He was the first person to be a father figure *and* a friend – both at the same time. I think the biggest lesson he taught me was that in this business you have to laugh. Firefighters deal with a lot of sadness on a daily basis and laughter helps us heal our souls and move on – to be ready for the next call. Laughter also brings the crew closer together as a unit. Joe, Pete, and I laughed through almost our entire seven years working together. The other great lesson he taught me was that it was important to put together a crew that you had complete confidence in. Confidence in their ability, confidence in their loyalty, and confidence in their integrity. Once you put together a crew like that, if you have patience, everything else just falls into place. Patience is something Joe had in spades – at least with us. It's funny, but he had a reputation of being a screamer when Pete and I were first assigned to his truck. I can honestly say that he never screamed, or lost his patience, with either of us. He must have had confidence in us – I know, we had confidence in him. It was an honor to work for him. I was proud of that company "Engine 2 – Second to None." Thanks Joe, I love you.

Joe was hurt at a fire in 1987 and never returned to full duty. This was the beginning of the end of the first phase of my firefighting career. Once he left, the Branch Ave. station never felt the same to me. I had been on the job for seven years and I was itching to go to a busier company. I found a home at the Messer Street station, on both Engine 8 and Ladder 2, but I never forgot what Joe had taught me. I look back at those years at Branch Ave. as the good old days.

Pete, my partner in crime in those early years, was the best firefighter I've ever known. He was, and still is, very quiet and unassuming by nature. When it was called for, however, he was as aggressive as anyone I've ever worked with. We went through the Academy together, and spent the next seven years working side by side. We learned the job together, making many mistakes along the way, but always learning from them, and becoming better firemen. I grew quite a bit while working with Pete. The biggest thing I learned from Pete was that you don't have to blow your own horn in order for people to know how good you are. He taught me that it's not important that anyone else knows, as long as *you* know. The rest will follow.

With Pete, there was no gray area in any situation – only black and white, right or wrong. If ever I had a best friend, Pete is it. He's like a brother to me. I don't see him as often as I'd like; he's retired now. He hurt his shoulder, tore his rotator cuff at a fire and it was never the same, even after two surgeries and over a year of physical therapy. I know that convincing himself that he'd no longer be a firefighter must have been the hardest thing he's ever done. He loved this job and never wanted to leave, especially after just ten short years. As far as I'm concerned, he'll always be a firefighter. You don't judge a firefighter by his longevity, you judge him by his heart. Peter has heart. He's a firefighter's firefighter! I love you, Pete, may God watch over you.

Two guys who worked with me when I was a firefighter, and later when I was a Lieutenant, are Joe and Al. They reminded me quite a bit of Pete and I. They went through the Academy together, and worked along side each other for the better part of ten years. They were best friends also, and Joe retired early after being injured on duty. They are both great firefighters. They've often been responsible for making me look good as their officer. They have great instincts at the fire scene, and they both have heart. I respect these guys because they have always been guys I could count on when the going got tough. They're also very loyal to me. I know that they respect me, although you'd never know it by watching us together – they'd bust my balls relentlessly sometimes. They never let me off the hook because of my rank – I was just one of the guys around the firehouse. Another thing about these guys that reminded me of the good old days was the amount of laughter around the firehouse when the three of us were on duty.

I miss this crew; we shared some great times – and some tough fires.

My present crew is another great company. I seem to have been blessed with good men surrounding me throughout my career. As an officer, I'd like to think that these guys wanted to work for me, but I know better. I'm only a part of the reason good firefighters are drawn to my company. The other reasons are the guys who are already there. Good firefighters are drawn to companies with good firefighters. Al is still with me at Engine 15. I've worked with Al longer than anyone else – about twelve years now. I guess we enjoy working together. Doug and Rick are also on the company; and these guys, too, are great firefighters. Rick didn't get on the fire department until he was about 40 years old. Most guys who join the department at that age are looking for a slow company to work on – but not Rick. Engine 15 is a busy company, but he enjoys working here. He's about my age, but a Firefighter and a Lieutenant have different responsibilities. A Firefighter's job is usually more physical than an officer's – I don't know if I could do his job at this age. Doug is the newest addition to the company, even though he's senior to Rick, and I couldn't have handpicked a better firefighter to come aboard. He's like a bull at a fire scene, and has a heart the size of a lion. Recently he took a promotional exam and I was secretly rooting against him. He's a smart kid and I know he'll make Lieutenant soon enough. I'm selfishly looking out for myself, however. Being the 'old man' on the truck, I want Doug around to watch my back at fires. If I go down, I know he'll get me out.

I love all these guys I've mentioned. I'm proud to have known each and every one of them – they are good men. I'm not exaggerating when I say that I'd die for them – and I'm sure they feel the same. We've been fighting a war out on the streets, and there's no one I'd rather have had by my side than these guys. I've learned an incredible amount from them.

There's one more person I'd like to include in this list of my heroes. His name is John McKenna. He was a Lieutenant on the Providence Fire Department before he was severely injured at a fire, and was forced to retire. He was put to the test, and responded in a manner that all firefighters hope they would – if ever called upon to do so. He was with his company at a basement fire when the stairs collapsed beneath them, dropping them to the cement below. One of his crew separated his shoulder, but stayed with the crew as long as he could stand the pain. Lt. McKenna and the other member of the company eventually lifted this injured firefighter to a company above, and then went back to work attacking the fire. When their air paks were running low, they were forced to retreat. As the conditions grew steadily worse in that basement, they followed their hoseline back to the burnt-out stairs. John helped lift the other firefighter to the outstretched arms of the rescue crew above, but was unable to get himself out of the basement before running out of air, and collapsing to the floor. He was finally rescued successfully, but not until he had spent another fifteen minutes in that basement – unconscious. We believe that it was his instincts that saved him – he put his face next to the flowing fog nozzle on the floor before losing consciousness. This produced just enough oxygen to keep him alive until he was rescued.

He put his men's welfare first, ahead of his own, and almost paid the ultimate price. His bravery made me proud to be a firefighter. It made me proud to be his friend. God bless you, buddy.

End Notes

[1] 200' of hose filled with water weighs approximately 150 lbs.

[2] Two pieces of canvas connected in the middle, with wooden poles on the outer edges. Used to carry patients in areas the stretcher will not fit.

[3] A six-foot piece of finished wood with holes on the sides for straps. Used to stabilize a patient's spine prior to being moved.

[4] Attach the gated adapters each Engine Co. carries to the ports of the hydrant.

[5] Each Engine Co. has two 'beds' of 3" feeder hose. Each bed holds 600' of hoseline in 12 individual 50' sections. 'Couplings' on the hose connect these sections to each other. Each 50' section has a male end and a female end. You can 'break down', or disconnect these sections at any of the 50' intervals to utilize only as much hose as is needed.

[6] Hoselines attached from the hydrant to the pump of the engine company, to supply water.

[7] All of the lights in the firehouse come on automatically when the bell tips for an alarm. —

[8] A hose connection inside a building to which firefighters hook their hoselines.

[9] When a company calls for extra help at an incident.

[10] Charged – full of pressurized water. Ready for use.

[11] Scuttle – A small covered opening to a roof from the attic area. Usually accessed via a ladder inside attic.

Printed in the United Kingdom by
Lightning Source UK Ltd., Milton Keynes
139081UK00001B/121/A